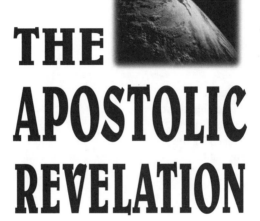

THE
APOSTOLIC
REVELATION

The Reformation of the Church

John Kingsley Alley

PEACE
PUBLISHING

The Apostolic Revelation.
Copyright© 2002 by John Kingsley Alley.

Published in Australia by:
Peace Publishing
Rockhampton, Queensland, Australia.
Email: books@peace.org.au
Web: www.peace.org.au

Published in the United States by:
Selah Publishing Group, LLC
Surprise AZ
Web: www.selahbooks.com
Book Orders: orders@selahbooks.com

Distributed in North America by:
Selah Publsihing Group, LLC
Surprise, AZ
Phone: 877-616-6451
Fax: 866-777-8909

Unless otherwise indicated, all Scripture quotations are taken from the *HOLY BIBLE, NEW INTERNATIONAL VERSION*. Copyright 1973, 1978, 1984 by International Bible Society. Used by permission of Zondervan Publishing House. All rights reserved.

Scripture quotations marked KJV are taken from the *King James Version* of the Bible.

Cover and Interior Design by Christine Smith.

First Edition
    First Printing - October 2002 - Printed in Australia.

Second Edition
    First Printing - February 2003 - Printed in The Philippines
    Second Printing - March 2003 - Printed in India.
    Third Printing - June 2003 - Printed in Canada

ISBN: 1-58930-094-7
Library of Congress Control Number: 2003094001

To JESUS
who leads us to the City of God

*"In your unfailing love you will lead
the people you have redeemed.
In your strength you will guide them
to your holy dwelling.
You will bring them in and plant them on the
mountain of your inheritance-
the place, O LORD, you made for your dwelling,
the sanctuary, O Lord, your hands established.
The LORD will reign for ever and ever."*

The Song of Moses
(Exodus 15:13-18)

*"In that day will I raise up
the tabernacle of David that is fallen,
and close up the breaches thereof;
and I will raise up his ruins,
and I will build it as in the days of old"*

The Prophecy of Amos
(Amos 9:11 KJV)

The Prophecies of Isaiah

"This is what the LORD says-
your Redeemer, who formed you in the womb:
I am the LORD, who has made all things,
who alone stretched out the heavens,
who spread out the earth by myself,
who foils the signs of false prophets
and makes fools of diviners,
who overthrows the learning of the wise
and turns it into nonsense,
who carries out the words of his servants
and fulfills the predictions of his messengers,
who says of Jerusalem, 'It shall be inhabited,'
of the towns of Judah, 'They shall be built,'
and of their ruins, 'I will restore them,'

...he will say of Jerusalem, 'Let it be rebuilt,'
and of the temple, 'Let its foundations be laid.'"
(Isaiah 44:24-26,28b)

"Your people will rebuild the ancient ruins
and will raise up the age old foundations;
you will be called Repairer of Broken Walls,
Restorer of Streets with Dwellings."
(Isaiah 58: 12)

"They will rebuild the ancient ruins
and restore the places long devastated;
they will renew the ruined cities
that have been devastated for generations."
(Isaiah 61: 4)

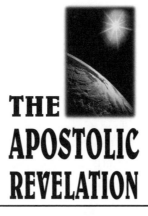

THE APOSTOLIC REVELATION

CONTENTS

Chapter Outlines

Chapter 4	**The Nature of an Apostle**	**61**

Chapter 5	**The Authority of an Apostle**	**85**

| Chapter 6 | **Women in Apostolic Ministry** | **113** |

| Chapter 8 | **Apostles and Elders, with the Church as One Body** | **163** |

| Chapter 9 | **Fathering and Sonship in the Ministry** | **195** |

Chapter 10	**The Humanity of Apostles**	**215**

Chapter 11	**An Apostolic People**	**231**

Personal References

concerning the life and ministry of the author:

The following references are for the purpose of affirming the validity of the call and anointed ministry, as well as godly character, of the author. They are not intended as recommendations of everything published in this book, since most of these writers have not had the opportunity of reading the manuscript before publishing. The reader must assess the contents of the book personally, by being sensitive to the inner witness of the Spirit of Grace.

In 1999, we held a Convention in Brisbane to which we invited five well-known speakers from within and outside Australia. Brother John Alley was one of our speakers.

Pastors came from Singapore, Malaysia, India, The United States, New Zealand and from other parts of Australia. After the Conference, all of us (Pastors, Leaders and saints from different churches) felt as one, a deep respect for brother John Alley as a servant and statesman of God.

He truly carried on him an evident display of the life and nature of Christ. His life was his message in Christ. His understanding and teaching of apostleship is always on the cutting edge. Each time I hear brother John speak on Apostleship, I know that he does not just impart revelational knowledge, but he imparts the Lord's apostleship and the authority associated with it, to many lives.

We thank God that our fellowship has been richly blessed through brother John Alley's life and impartation as an Apostle. We thank God for this heavenly connection and friendship with Apostle John Alley.

Dr Sim Choo Jek
Resurrection Life Ministries
Brisbane, Australia

I have known John Alley since 1997. I attended one of his talks on Apostleship in Northern Ireland U.K. that year. I invited him to my country Zimbabwe in Africa while in the U.K. He eventually made it in 1999. He held a few seminars on the same subject and others. Way back in 1988 God had audibly spoken to me telling me that he would send an Apostle to baptise me by immersion, and when this happens he would tell me what to do then. Since this was said in 1988, and almost ten years had passed when I had not seen the apostle God had promised, I had forgotten about it. Then when John Alley visited me, early one morning I went where John Alley was meditating and the Lord told me that he was the Apostle he had sent to fulfil his promise. God in a vision showed me the place where I was to be baptised, in the Zambezi river, at Victoria Falls, some 878 kilometres away. That was done.

It is not human thinking and imagination to say that God is setting aside some people to be Apostles. I found in John, especially after fulfilling God's promise of 1988 when I had no idea of Apostles, that God surely is setting up this office in churches. As a new thing that is being revived as a second reformation to the church, it is bound to meet with resistance and scepticism. But I am totally convinced that John Alley is one of those already chosen by God to spearhead this office of Apostleship. I recommend him to all the Christians and churches that are keen to learn of what God is doing, and also to those with doubts on Apostleship to invite him and listen to him. Please accept John Alley as one of the Apostles sent by God to carry out the second reformation of the church of God on earth.

Rev. Claudius Murau Matsikiti
Zimbabwe, Africa

The world is divided into several different groups when it comes to the idea of apostles and the apostolic ministry for today. There are the vast majority who are totally unaware of apostles and spend no time whatsoever considering it. Then there is the vocal group that is well aware of the apostolic due to the fact that they have been schooled by their religious traditions with the idea that apostles are not for today and therefore anyone who suggests that they still exist is heretical. Then, there are those who can accept the idea that apostles may still exist, at least in a conceptual way, but they have little or no idea of what that means in present day life.

Finally, there is a group of believers who not only accepts, but embraces, the notion that God is still calling men and women into the five-fold ministry, including the office of the apostle. Apostle John Alley is of this last group who has spent many years seeking God through study, prayer, fasting, and a constant quest to understand what the Lord is doing in these last days. His words come from a long season of such seeking and living out the apostolic experience in the places of the world where God has sent him. His words are worthy of your consideration. May God inspire you to such seeking of the truth.

Bob Hauselman, Senior Pastor
Restoration Christian Church
Sellersburg, Indiana, U.S.A.

When we first visited John Alley's church in Rockhampton, in 1994, they were engaged in a 40 day fast. It was an awesome experience to walk in there to minister, and to be ministered to by John in such an atmosphere of God's great glory. It is John's great gifting from the Holy Spirit to establish, very human, lasting and deepening personal friendships. This has been a major source of strengthening in my ministry.

We had the privilege of staying with John, his wife Hazel and their lovely children during our visit to Australia in 1997. Truly we felt that the beautiful presence of Christ was in that home. My wife and I could clearly see that this was a very special 'Levite' family.

When John visited us during our period of ministry on the Shankill Road, Belfast in 1999 we believe our area of the city of Belfast was greatly touched as he led us in intercession at the interfaces of some of the most impoverished sections. John is one of God's specials, always involved as a vital part of God's vanguard, pushing out the frontiers of what God plans for His Church before His longed for second coming.

Rev. Clifford Taylor, M.A.,
Superintendent of the Mutare Circuit of the
Methodist Church in Zimbabwe.

I first met John a few years ago when I was the incumbent General Secretary of the Quezon City Pastoral Movement. He was the guest speaker of the anniversary of the Movement. He truly proved to be a blessing. He gave a powerful prophetic word that motivated and set in motion the beginnings of our thrust for city taking. I had several other opportunities to fellowship with him after that which proved to be a personal blessing.

The Body of Christ needs more ministers like him, who have a heart both for the Lord and His Body. He possesses a sensitivity to the Holy Spirit that is refreshing. May you be blessed by his ministry as I have been and continue to be.

Rev. Joey Zabarte
Senior Minister
Words of Life Christian Ministries
Manila, Philippines

I have known John for the past 3 and 1/2 years. He is one of the most sincere servants of the Lord. John has a special gift of imparting the blessings of the Holy Spirit. He is also a very good teacher and has opened the eyes of many Pastors in Chennai. He has been a great blessing to me and my ministry.

This book 'The Apostolic Revelation' by John will be a real blessing to the readers. God has anointed him with knowledge of apostolic ministry, and he is very good in sharing this knowledge with others. Hence this book will be a boon to whoever reads this.

Pr. Vincent Samuel,
Senior Minister
Calvary Community Church
Chennai, India

It was John Alley's 'Tower of Intercession' that first grabbed my attention. Here is a minister who is making a priority of prayer and respects the role of intercessors. Then he was willing to come and pour himself for days into Logan Intercessors as passionately as he does from large pulpits around the world. I appreciate this man's heart and his accessibility.

My heart resonates with his messages. John is articulating what so many of us have been feeling for years - God is moving on. The old ways are becoming obsolete. The church as we know it has little relevance. We have failed as the representation of Christ in the earth, His Body, God revealed among men. Non Christians are saying, "Jesus yes, but the church no".

John is talking about a new era where old things are passed away and all things are become new. It is exciting and full of hope and the glory of the Lord. Not personality cults and powerful leaders, but humble servants showing hungry wherever he is with whomever God's people are. We are in transition. What *was* is passing, and what *will* *be* does not yet quite appear. John's prophetic eye is seeing a little more clearly than the rest of us. John is an apostle raised up by God to help us make the transition, a forerunner preparing the way of the Lord, making His paths straight.

I am sure what he has written, out of the wealth of what God is revealing to him, will help you make a smoother transition through the turmoil of the death of the old and birth of the new. This book will help you cope with the change.

Joye Alit
Global Intercessor
Jubilate Ministries
Maleny, Queensland, Australia

I believe that in John we have a true apostle. He has been through refining fires and not stumbled, nor has he said "Too hard, God".

I have been sitting under his teaching as much as possible for five years, and know him to be a man of humility, integrity, obedience, and deep faith — a man God has ordained for this time, who has the apostolic heart to nurture apostolic sons. Therefore it is my honour to recommend John, and I believe God will use him to equip apostles for the future.

Olive Gates
Team Leader
Logan Intercessors
Logan City, Queensland, Australia

It has been my pleasure to get to know John Alley from Australia as a result of a number of visits to Northern Ireland in recent years. He is a man who has a heart after God, and a deep desire to see unity in the Body of Christ.

He has a God-given passion to see the Church function in the way God planned it to be, and to see churches, leaders, and individuals flow together in the five fold ministries irrespective of denominational affiliation.

God has raised this leader to focus our thoughts on Apostleship, and bring together across many different nations people of like mind. He is a man of vision, who has a heart for prayer. I personally look forward to his early return to Northern Ireland.

Rev. Leslie Spence
Superintendent Minister
Glenavy and Moira Circuit of the
Methodist Church in Ireland

As the pastor of a church that has reaped the benefit of John's apostolic covering and friendship for the past 12 years, I count it an honour to recommend both the man and the book.

This is a very timely work marked by wisdom and grace, and born out of the experience of a man who has a hunger to see the church come into its true calling and destiny. The pursuit of that vision, however, has not always been without misunderstanding, trials and disappointments. And yet, true to his calling, John has consistently maintained a spirit of warmth, grace, integrity, and intimacy with the Father. I appreciate his example and recommend the book."

Phillip Walters, Senior Pastor
Keppel Coast Christian Church
Central Queensland, Australia

John Alley represents a rising breed of men within the Church world wide who have been ordained by God and raised up to exercise apostolic ministry. My experience of John within the context of seminars, workshops, one on one and in his home setting has convinced me of his call to this ministry, and his gifting to exercise apostolic ministry.

John's ministry has had a profound effect on my calling as an ordained minister within the Uniting Church tradition. Through his teaching, mentoring, spiritual fathering and apostolic covering I have had the unique experience of being released into the apostolic philosophy and anointing of ministry; as a result I have experienced an empowerment for equipping and releasing other leaders and small struggling congregations into the mission God calls them to.

John's teaching on the Apostolic Reformation brings into a clear spiritual focus the changes in the world and the Church which have mainly been expressed in sociological terms. John's teaching presents an insightful revelation of Biblical teaching which defines these social and spiritual transformations that we are witnessing around our globe; he is able to articulate these current trends through Biblical exegesis and reveal God's plan for action, through inspired and a careful exposition of the Scriptures.

I believe that as you engage with the pages of this book you will also encounter the transformational thinking which is the Apostolic Reformation.

Rev. Craig Mischewski
Uniting Church, Tingalpa

Rev Craig Mischewski is an ordained minister within the Uniting Church. He is pastor to a small congregation in suburban Brisbane in Queensland; Craig's other role is a regional ministry which is focused on developing a pioneering ministry model which identifies, equips and releases small congregations into mission and ministry within their local context.

I praise God for answering my prayers. He has allowed me to personally meet my Brother John Alley who has this gift of Apostleship from God. I heard him preach with biblical clarity and conviction. He hit the nail of the need of the times right on its head.

Many are guilty of the sin of idolatry. Dependence and faith are anchored no longer in the power of God the Almighty, but on the institutionalized instruments of God such as the established & organized denominations and movements.

God's power will pour and fill His servants not through institutions but through relationships. God, Alley says, wants this kind of a covering to bless and protect his workers.

The christian with the gift of apostleship is God's instrument to mentor, encourage and care for his workers transcending all denominational barriers.

Let's therefore welcome this ministry as from the Lord with open minds, hearts and hands.

John Joseph Leo B. Castillo
Senior Pastor
Fairview Fundamental Baptist Church
Fairview Park, Quezon City, Philippines.

John Alley is a man appointed by the Father to bring winds of change to the stagnant waters of religious practice. His understanding of the apostolic call upon today's church comes from much study and revelation of the purposes of God.

John's ministry has been of great blessing to my church, especially during this time of transition. I count his friendship of utmost value and always welcome his advice and input into my own ministry.

David Trigg, Senior Minister
Oakey Church Unlimited
Oakey, Queensland, Australia

We have been greatly blessed by the ministry of John Alley. We always look forward to his visits to us here in the Philippines and his teachings on "listening prayer" and on "grace" have greatly impacted our lives.

His fatherly advice to us pastors is always greatly appreciated.

Pastor Hector C. de Leon
Senior Pastor
Covenant Renewal Church
Quezon City, PHILIPPINES

John Alley is a man of total sincerity and steadfast Christian faith. The Word of God is the foundation of his life and ministry, and he teaches in the power of the Holy Spirit. His commitment and his prayer life give an impressive example of what it means to be a man of God.

He has a forceful personality. He would not require a sacrifice from others that he would not be willing to make himself. He is a strong leader with a generous and kindly heart. Opinions may differ as to the precise definition of an apostle today, but John Alley is a man who's ministry has been described by others as apostolic.

Rev. Norman Moss
Towards Revival Ministries
Wimbledon, England, U.K.

FOREWORD

by the Author

The Apostolic Revelation

I have been reluctant to write about the apostolic reformation of the church and the place of Apostles, for two reasons.

One is that the 'revelation' is still unfolding and our understanding still growing; anything published may soon become inadequate. Yet I now feel compelled by the Spirit to write, because the time is short, and the power anointing for apostles and prophets is about to be poured out.

The other is, there are some subjects that by their nature are living when in thought or preaching, or in deeds and relationships, but when committed to writing in some systematic way can sound narrow, binding or legalistic. Subjects like church government and relational authority are amongst those that can easily become, unintentionally, the dead letter of the law. Yet this subject is at the forefront of what the Spirit is doing in the church and the world today.

Perhaps this is one reason Jesus presented most of the truths of the Kingdom of God as parables. I noticed that Philip Yancey took this precaution in his approach to the writing of his wonderful book *"What's So Amazing About Grace?"* *(Zondervan, 1997)*. He felt grace could not be best communicated except through stories about grace. Theory and definition seem to remove the life of some things in the process of the examination, reducing the subject to a corpse.

I feel inadequate for the task, and yet find I am carrying a burden of the Spirit about some things which, after having been sent on many occasions to preach them in various parts of the world, they must be written. I hope that the message will bear fruit to the honour of Christ.

This book is written without legalism being intended, and the exercise of authority is to be liberating, never controlling. I would ask for the best possible interpretation to be applied in the light of this intention.

I feel another inadequacy, and that is in my inability to deal with some of the related aspects of this subject more extensively. Like mentoring as part of spiritual fathering, for example. I know the importance of the principles, but cannot claim special expertise to teach the detail. There are others who do this and I greatly respect them.

But here is rather, I trust, a big picture. Like a compass bearing, it is meant to point in the right direction, and also keep us from the wrong direction. It doesn't tell us about every hill and valley on the journey, but does tell us, I believe, the direction in which we will find the City of God.

John Alley.

A Personal Word

From my Spiritual Father

In the years that I have known John Alley, he has been an inspiration to me and to those that he has had an opportunity to minister to. He has been a man of integrity with great humility. The book that he has written will, I am sure, challenge those who are open to hear what is coming from John's heart.

In hearing his heart over the years, and observing the work of his hands, he has demonstrated the apostolic heart of a true father.

I am encouraged by the topics that have been addressed. This book is a must for every Christian leader who wants to lead their people into present truth. Priorities must be set in proper spiritual order for the new breed of leaders that God is raising up at this hour in the Church. I am looking forward with anticipation to receiving a new copy myself. I believe this book will bring a real, practical and balanced foundation to the apostolic office.

Apostle Chuck Clayton
Apostolic Resource Ministries
Versailles, Indiana, U.S.A.

From a Spiritual Son

Apostle John Alley's life has been a great blessing to many pastors and churches in the Philippines. I am privileged to be one of them. I consider him as my spiritual father and mentor. I praise God for the opportunity of working with him as partner in the apostolic ministry God has called us to.

It's almost a decade now since I first met him, and truly he is such a gift not only to me but to the Body of Christ in the Philippines. He has a father's heart and carries with him a great anointing from God. His life is characterized by love, prayer, faith and grace.

His teachings are on the cutting edge as he shares revelatory messages from the heart of God. His tape on Listening Prayer has blessed many pastors, as it reached many places, being endorsed by the Intercessors of the Philippines. His teachings on the apostolic reformation have blessed the Quezon City Pastoral Movement.

I'm sure, as I have been encouraged by the life and ministry of Apostle John Alley, many others would say the same. That's why when he said he is writing a book on the Apostolic Revelation, my heart says "Hallelujah!"
All glory to God!

Rev. Felix de Ramos, Apostle
Senior Minister
Peace International Ministries, Inc.
Manila, Philippines

Introduction
The Apostolic Revelation

All around the world an apostolic message is being brought to the church. God is raising apostles everywhere. It took me many years to come to the place where I could say that I was an apostle, not a pastor. As I became established confidently in this truth, I discovered the Biblical pattern that apostles identified themselves. I also discovered that it takes humility and obedience and faith to take a stand in your calling as an apostle. Of course false apostles claim to be apostles too, but the New Testament church tested apostles and proved those who were false *to be* false. Nevertheless the New Testament pattern is that apostles declare their call, and the church is able to recognise and accept true apostles.

In this book I seek to lay out what I understand of the apostolic revelation for the church. Many others have made and will continue to make great contributions, and greater insight will yet come as Christ continues to instruct us and bring about the restoration of all things (Acts 3:21).

The Work to be done

With respect to the apostolic reformation, we have work to do. We can't simply hear about these things and be passive. The work begins with each of us personally.

We have to gain understanding of what God is saying and thinking, and what is in Scripture with respect to this. As we begin to hear God and come into a better understanding of things, it is necessary to set our values in order. Many of our values will have to change. A lot of the values we hold are of a denominational worldview, and not really biblical. Much of the way we think has a structure to it that is denominational. It is old wineskin, old paradigm. The paradigms have to change.

Of course, the gospel message will stay the same. We are not changing the Bible. We are not changing the gospel message of salvation by the cross and the blood, and of the necessity of grace, and faith, and repentance. The fullness of the Holy Spirit is ours, just as the church has always proclaimed. It is not the historic doctrines of the faith that must change.

A New Wineskin

Concerning the 'wineskin' (the structure and outward form of the church) nothing will stay the same - there is to be a completely *new* wineskin.

It will do no good thinking that you can hold on to much of the tradition and structure, for God is going to change it all. Jesus said you cannot take a patch from a new garment and sew it onto an old one, otherwise you will have ruined the new garment and it will tear the old as well.

The church must have a new garment i.e. a new covering. This is a completely new structure, a whole new way of doing things. We have to take the whole. We cannot take a little of the new and patch it on to the past. This won't work, although some will try to do that. There are those who have *something* of the apostolic truth, something of the apostolic structure, and so they call themselves apostolic. But this is often only the old paradigm with a bit of apostolic truth patched on. To know the power and to be a genuinely apostolic people, we have to 'buy' (accept) it all.

The term 'Apostolic'

At the outset I would ask your patience with the need to use the word apostolic frequently. It is necessary for us to have terms by which we can define what we are speaking of. We are speaking about a change in the structure of the church, a restoration of what should be the right heart of the church, and a better understanding of what our relationships should be like in the ministry. I will be referring to this as *apostolic* Christianity - about what once was, should be, and will be again.

We need terms so that we can define, compare and contrast, for the sake of understanding. But I suggest that a time will come when, these changes having been made, and understood, we will no longer need to heavily rely upon the word 'apostolic'. We will simply say *Christian*. We look forward to that day and bless God for it.

The Mature Church

We do seek to understand what biblical Christianity was like under the leadership of apostles, because it is meant to be even better for those of us who seek it. The Bible says that the glory of the last house will be greater than the glory of the former house. But as great as the New Testament apostolic church was, we are not returning just to that. We must learn what they knew, but press on to '*maturity*'. You can hardly read the letters of the apostles without them telling you we have to go on. They knew we needed more.

To be honest, I do not feel that denominational Christianity is the 'going on to maturity' (Ephesians 4:13, Hebrews 6:1, James 4:1) that is spoken of. Neither is it the face of the church for which Jesus is going to return. Denominational

Christianity is not the bride without spot or wrinkle. There is something better for us. The church has been in a 500 year process of restoration and renewal, begun by the reformers of the 16th century. It is not yet a finished work, but must be completed before Christ's return. Yet Christ is returning, so the work *will* be accomplished.

The term 'Anointing'

For readers not familiar with this term, an *anointing* is the impartation to a believer of the power, the presence and the favour of God to do a particular work, or attend to a specific calling. The anointings of God bring spiritual gifts, impart understanding and abilities, and open doors of opportunity. An anointing gives specific power to prayer, and qualifies the believer for ministry, but only according to God's call. Work done for God without an anointing is done in the flesh, and not acceptable.

This is a biblical term, as in 1 John 2:20, *"But you have an anointing from the Holy One, and all of you know the truth."* Jesus is the anointed one (the 'Messiah', or 'Christ'), and *"God anointed Jesus of Nazareth with the Holy Spirit and power, and ... he went around doing good and healing all who were under the power of the devil, because God was with him" (Acts 10:38).*

Often the scriptures use the terms 'spirit' or 'power' instead of the word anointing, as in Luke 1:17, *"he will go on before the Lord, in the spirit and power of Elijah."* Every believer has the basic anointings, but should pray for the greater anointings and gifts of the Holy Spirit.

Impartation

Finally, there is the grace of impartation. As you read, the Holy Spirit will speak many things to your heart. You have an anointing of the Holy Spirit to understand the ways of God, and the anointing will grow. It will become focussed and specific in various ways. You can drink of the anointing and become a partner with the Holy Spirit in the work and power of that anointing. There are all kinds of anointings available to you by the Spirit of God. Whatever you discern, desire, or believe for, by faith you can receive.

Acknowledgments

*I owe a great debt of gratitude to many
people, in many parts of the world.*

*I would express my appreciation to every
brother and sister in Christ who has loved,
served and supported me.*

*In particular, I wish to acknowledge the
supremely important part played by the
people of the apostolic company,*
Peace Christian Community. *Many have
helped me to explore and live out the
values of apostolic Christianity, and to
understand and come to grips with
the changes which God has brought
to our lives and the church.*

*I have been greatly upheld and loved by
these dear saints. Their sacrifice, to stand
with me in the cause of Christ, has required
great faith and perseverance. I am deeply
grateful for their love, their devotion to
principle, and their commitment to
untiring intercession. These believers
have walked in covenant faithfulness
with me and each other.*

They are faithful servants of Christ.

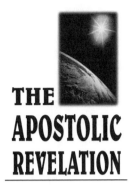

THE APOSTOLIC REVELATION

$\mathscr{C}hapter$ 1

The Apostolic Message:
Reformation for the Church!

The Quezon City Pastoral Movement, a fellowship of some 200 churches, meets every month for fellowship and prayer. Quezon City is a large part of Metro Manila, the capital of the Philippines, a place I have visited for ministry on many occasions.

On the first occasion I preached at a Quezon City Pastoral Movement meeting (in 1997), I was carrying on my heart a message concerning the restoration of apostles to the church — that apostles were to be the spiritual fathers of the ministry. My message was mainly about restoration, teaching that, in the same way many things had been restored to the church from the time of Martin Luther onwards, now in these last days apostles were to be restored.

The Startling Prophecy

The evening before the meeting, I was in my hotel room praying and preparing, and I asked the Lord for a specific prophetic word to share with the pastors of Quezon City. As soon as I made this request in prayer I received a vision, in which a dark black storm struck the city, and then I saw broken buildings and a broken bridge. Immediately I heard the Lord say "An ill wind will blow on the city, and it will shatter the traditional structures of the church."

This was a startling word. But I felt sure, because of the vision, that I had heard God aright. So I determined in my heart that I would speak what God had given me, knowing full well that these men and women could, by the inner witness of the Spirit, judge for themselves what to believe.

The Quezon City Meeting

The meeting that month was at Faith Baptist Church, and we gathered at 7 AM for breakfast in the basement to be followed by the 9 AM meeting in the worship centre. It was a large building, seating over a thousand people, with five aisles, marble floors, and great, high, vaulted ceilings. The side walls were comprised of many fanfold doors (this was the tropics) to let fresh air in. I was the first to arrive upstairs, and was greatly surprised by what I saw before me.

At the head of the centre aisle was an open coffin, with the lectern just in front of it. On either side of the coffin stood eight giant golden (actually, polished brass) lampstands or candlesticks, each over five feet tall, heavily built in with big, wide legs to support them. In a vast semicircle behind the coffin stretching from one wall to the other were some 30 to 40 flower arrangements, each six to eight feet tall. All the candlesticks were alight. Made of solid brass, most of them were electrically lit with multiple lightbulbs, but on each end of the coffin was one that held a single giant red candle, in a glass sheath. This was a light and flower show of tremendous proportions.

> "An ill wind will blow … and will shatter the traditional structures of the church."

I was so taken aback, I thought "it couldn't be". But it was! I went over to inspect the coffin, and sure enough here was a dead body in preparation for a funeral. An elderly member of that congregation had died, and the funeral director had set up early, ready for a funeral service the next day. I would have to stand in front of the open coffin to bring the message of apostolic restoration to these pastors.

I adjusted my mind to the task, and the meeting commenced. When the meeting was handed over to me to preach, I announced what the Lord had given me: that I was carrying an anointing for the apostolic restoration of the church, and when I finished teaching I would release the anointing over Quezon City. The Holy Spirit would go out and begin to effect great change in the church whether they wanted it or not. I then proceeded to teach the apostolic message.

An Enacted Prophecy

About halfway through the teaching, I felt the time was right to share the prophetic word. So I explained the vision I had seen, and stated what I heard the Lord say "An ill wind will blow on the city, and it will shatter the traditional structures of the church."

Suddenly, out of nowhere, a powerful wind struck the building. A great gust of wind blew in just one of the many doors on the side of the building, swept up several of those enormous flower arrangements, and hurled them with great force into one of the giant candlesticks standing at the end of the coffin. This immediately knocked that giant candlestick over, and it fell with a mighty crash across the floor in front of the coffin behind my back. It sounded like an explosion as it crashed down on that marble floor, with the impact reverberating through the high ceilings of that great building. Shattered glass and melted red wax lay strewn across the floor. The suddenness and violence of it all shocked everybody.

All I was thinking about was the need to keep the attention of my audience. Wanting to proceed with the message I said, "Friends, it's OK, we'll clean the mess up afterwards." But immediately one of the young Filipino pastors rose and said "Sir, this is a sign!"

The moment he uttered the word "sign", I realised what God had done. This was an enacted prophecy, not unlike the enacted parable in the Gospels where Jesus cursed the fig tree and it died. I had prophesied an "ill wind" which would be destructive, and as a sign a violent wind struck the building and entered the "church". I had prophesied that it would shatter the traditional structures of the church, and that wind shattered a 'golden' candlestick.

In the New Testament there is one distinctive symbol of a New Testament church — the golden lampstands of Revelation chapters 1 and 2. In Revelation chapter 1, Christ is walking amongst the golden lampstands which are the churches, and in Revelation chapter 2 verse 5 He says, *"If you do not repent, I will come to you and remove your lampstand from its place"*.

From this time I realised two things. Firstly, we are not dealing with just the restoration of things to the church, which can be a simple and progressive work. Rather, we are about to see the *reformation* of the church itself. Up until this time I had preached the apostolic message as a message of restoration, but from this time on, I preached it as the reformation of the church. Secondly, I realised that God is very serious about what He wants for the church; He is about to take the church in hand, and with sovereign power will establish what He desires. He will indeed allow forces, seemingly destructive forces, to shatter the many traditional structures of the church which are not

> God is about to take the church in hand, and with sovereign power will establish what He desires.

of the Holy Spirit, but of men. Chief amongst these traditional structures to be shattered is the *denominational structure*, and the *institutional nature* of the church. Christ is not returning for a denominational bride, nor will the Great Commission be completed by an institutional church. The church of these last days will be an apostolic church — an apostolic people, led by apostles, and under the anointings of Christ that are on apostles and prophets.

> *"I am about to set aside the existing leadership of the church, and raise another leadership."*

I finished the message I was preaching, and came to the time of prayer and impartation. Earlier I had said that, at the end of the message, I would pray and release the anointing for apostolic 'restoration' over Quezon City, and the Holy Spirit would go out and cause change in the church. Reminding them of this, I proceeded to pray and release that anointing. I have never witnessed, before or since, what happened in the following moments. The whole gathering suddenly erupted in spontaneous worship under the impulse of the Holy Spirit, as men and women sang, prayed and cried aloud. This continued for quite some time as one of the most wonderful experiences of our lives. It was a day of signs and wonders.

But surprising revelations were not to end there.

My 'Toronto' Revelation — A New Leadership to Come

Some time later I was in Toronto, and again I was preparing to preach. As I was waiting on God, I suddenly felt the Lord direct me to Psalm 78, verses 65 to 72. The passage explains that there came a time in Israel when God rejected the tribe of Ephraim as leaders of His people, choosing Judah instead, in particular David. It tells that He chose David to shepherd His people, and that David did so with great integrity of heart.

Then clearly I heard the Lord speak: "I am about to set aside the existing leadership of the church, and raise another leadership."

In my heart I knew what this meant. David, the anointed leader who shepherded with integrity of heart, is a type of the apostle. The Spirit of God has been for many years preparing and raising a corporate 'David' to shepherd His people. In every nation, God is preparing apostles for a great move of God. These are not necessarily the existing leaders of the church, although only God is judge of this in the rearrangement of leadership that is about to come. However, He has declared that much of the "existing leadership" will be set aside.

As far as the question of setting aside existing leadership is concerned, God has done this before. This concept has historical precedent. Psalm 78 outlines a change of leadership for the people of Israel, with Ephraim being rejected. Ephraim, a powerful tribe, were the descendants of Joseph, the prince among his brothers. Joseph had the rule over his brothers, and Ephraim had a prominent place in Israel. Nevertheless, there came a time when God rejected them from leadership, and raised another leadership. Why? Ephraim turned back on the day of battle. Further detail in verses 9 to 11 of Psalm 78 states that they did not keep God's covenant, they refused to live by His law, and they forgot what He had done, though He had performed miracles in their sight. All of these problems have an application to many of the institutions of Christianity, and as God Himself alone may know, to the hearts of some or many who claim authority and leadership in the institutions and ministries of the church today.

There is a further example in Holy Scripture of a change of leadership. It was when God was not well served by the leadership of King Saul to whom He had given much grace. The time came when the Lord pronounced that the kingdom had been torn from him, and God anointed David in his place. The change did not come immediately after the new anointing was given (and the old removed), but it came surely.

Apostle Chuck Clayton of Versailles, Indiana, my friend and mentor, is my apostolic covering. One day he heard the Lord speak clearly these words: "I am going to raise a new leadership for the Body of Christ, and this one will have a heart." As the Scripture says, every truth is established in the mouth of two or three witnesses.

Great reformation is coming to the church — apostles will be restored, the apostolic nature of Christianity will be recovered, and a whole new structure for the church will appear. A further witness that alludes to some, if not all of these statements, is Mike Bickle's testimony in his book "Growing in the Prophetic", which relates his experience of God while praying in a hotel room in Cairo, Egypt.

"I knelt on the cement floor by the rickety bed for about 30 minutes when I had one of the most incredible encounters that I have ever had.

"I didn't see a vision, and I wasn't caught up into heaven. I simply heard God speak to me. It wasn't what some people call the audible voice. I call it the internal audible voice. I heard it as clearly as I would have heard it with my physical ears and, honestly, it was terrifying.

"It came with such a feeling of cleanness, power and authority. In some ways I felt I was being crushed by it. I wanted to leave, but I didn't want to leave. I wanted it to be over, but I didn't want it to be over.

"I only heard a few sentences, and it took just a few moments, but every word had great meaning. The awe of God flooded my soul as I experienced a little bit of the terror of the Lord. I literally trembled and wept as God Himself communicated to me in a way I have never known before or since. The Lord simply said, 'I will change the understanding and expression of Christianity in the earth in one generation.'

"I understood that this reformation/revival would be His sovereign initiative. God Himself was going to make this drastic change in Christianity across the world."

- Mike Bickle, "Growing in the Prophetic", (Creation House, 1996) pp 29-30.

My Call to Serve Christ

By the late 1980s I had become puzzled as to the nature of my call. I first preached in 1968, and had entered training for full-time ministry in 1974. My world view of the leadership ministries of Christ centred around pastors of the local church, evangelists, itinerant teachers and missionaries, and my upbringing was evangelical. Throughout the '70s and '80s, with my wife Hazel, I pastored churches, served on the mission field in Papua New Guinea, and then worked in denominational administration and fundraising. I had a strong evangelical background and training, but also fully participated in the charismatic movement. I was 'baptised in the Holy Spirit', and enjoyed the blessing of the gifts of the Spirit in the ministry, especially the use of Christ's authority in deliverance and healing. Healing was a wonderful blessing, as was the message of faith which came to the church with great power during those years.

Now a question stirred within me. I had received a distinct call to the ministry of Christ, and I had enjoyed the affirmation of believers and Christian leaders throughout my Christian life, yet somehow I felt I did not fit the pattern. By that I mean, I did not think I was a pastor, a teacher or an evangelist, but there were no other options. The church circles of which I had always been a part allowed for no other form of ministry. I pondered briefly whether I might be a prophet, and wondered whether there were, or could be, prophets today. But I concluded that I was not a prophet. And that was where I was left, pondering a mystery for which I had no answer, because I was not looking beyond the mindset of centuries of institutionalised Christianity.

I had been raised in a religious system that taught that apostles and prophets were not for today. Preachers and teachers often referred to the ministry as the 'fivefold' ministry of Ephesians 4, but in the ministry there was no room for anything but evangelists, teachers and pastors, who could also serve as missionaries or denominational administrators. The idea of a call to be an apostle or a prophet was shut out by the mindset which we all shared.

The most powerful apostles and prophets ever to serve Christ are yet to arise.

At that time I had no answer to my question regarding the nature of my call, but the Holy Spirit had stirred the questioning in me. Within two years He sent a man from England with the message that was to focus my whole purpose.

A Word Comes

Phil Walters and his wife Esther, both Australians who had been living for many years in England, came to Queensland to plant a church in a town called Yeppoon, near Rockhampton. They were looking for the man the Lord would appoint to be their spiritual covering, and they wanted this vital relationship established before they planted the church. One day Phil sought me out and said "John, you are not a pastor, you are an apostle!"

Never before had I considered the possibility that there could be apostles today, yet his words had the witness of the Spirit, and this caused me to search my heart and the scriptures in a new way. It was then I realised that all the dealings of God with me over more than 20 years pointed to the truth that my call to the fivefold ministry was indeed to be an apostle of Christ.

Compelled by the Spirit to Find Understanding

For the next seven years I searched out the meaning of apostleship — what are apostles, what do they do, what does it mean to be an apostle, what is an apostle's place in the church, how must the church change to accommodate apostles? For at least four or five years I could not speak publicly of myself being an apostle. This was not so much because of shyness on my own part, but because the state of the church in those days, at least in our part of the world, did not allow for apostles — and certainly did not allow for anyone to consider themselves an apostle. Anyone claiming to be an apostle would have been considered deceived, proud and foolish. We had a long way to go to understand the grace of God.

In my own church I commenced teaching extensively on the role of apostles, and of the restoration of the apostolic ministry to the church. I taught about the changes this would bring, and the need to adjust our thinking, our values, our structures and our methods to receive apostolic leadership.

Beginning in the early '90s, the Lord sent me into various nations in Southeast Asia, for the purpose of encouraging and mentoring young apostles. In my heart I knew that, even though there would be many who were called to be apostles, they would have trouble in believing and trusting that call. Yes, the Holy Spirit would be urging upon them vision and faith in accordance with an apostolic call, but they would be hindered in believing because of the prevailing Christian "system" and mindset. Their minds would not allow them to believe what the Spirit of God was urging in their hearts. They needed a father, someone who could speak with a voice of authority and say "You are an apostle."

Then suddenly, there was an advance in my thinking. I realised that this message of Reformation was not just about apostles being restored to the church. It was about the restoration of the apostolic nature of the church itself. *All* of God's people were to be an apostolic people.

This prompted me to ponder a whole new set of questions. What does it mean to be "an apostolic people"? The Nicene Creed, meticulously developed by the church fathers of another age, stated *"We believe in one holy catholic (universal) and apostolic church"*. It was not hard for anyone to preach that the church should be one, holy or universal, but what did it mean for the church to be apostolic? Very few had answers, aside from the idea that the original apostles founded the church. But as I pondered the questions, understanding came.

For years now I have preached and taught these things at conferences, pastors' fellowships, and in churches; throughout Australia and in many other nations. Everywhere leaders and believers alike have responded consistently. They are hungry!

God's people everywhere are hungry for what God is about to do. They are tired of institutionalised Christianity, weary of the old wineskin which no longer produces life, and their hearts have been prepared for a restoration of apostolic Christianity. For this we thank God.

The Glory of the House

God is about to do the greatest and most amazing work He has ever done in the church. The prophet Haggai prophesied that the glory of the latter house would be greater than the glory of the former house (Haggai 2: 7-9). This prophecy is to have a powerful and definite fulfillment in the life of the church. We often look back on the early church and the time of the apostles, as revealed in the pages of the New Testament, as a glorious time which is a model for us. We have all preached from the lives and teaching of the New Testament Christians, upholding their example and quoting their methods and results as the model for the church today. I have good news. Another apostolic age of the church is coming — and this one will be greater than the one before! The greatest stories of apostles and prophets are yet to be told, for the most powerful apostles and prophets ever to serve Christ are yet to arise. The most powerful anointings are yet to be poured out, and the greatest gifts of grace are about to be released to the church.

Let us not think that the greatest or best things God will ever do through men and women He has already done — otherwise that only leaves His second-best for the end of the age. No, the greatest things remain ahead of us, in the days when a restored apostolic church is under the leadership of Christ-appointed apostles, and with anointed prophets in partnership with those apostles.

In this book we shall examine the grace of apostleship, and come to discover the heart of God for the church.

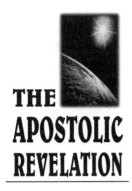

THE APOSTOLIC REVELATION

Chapter 2

The Grace of Apostleship

Apostleship is a wonderful grace from God. Indeed, without grace there can be no apostle. Everything we receive from God, whether gifts of the Spirit, appointments to the ministry, or answers to prayer, all require grace and the power that grace gives. Christ Himself is a gift of God's grace to us, as were the original apostles.

Grace has Great Effect

The apostles of the New Testament were ordinary men, taught by Christ and the Spirit of God, and filled with the power of *grace* (Acts 4:33). Christ had captured their hearts, brought them into submission and brokenness before the Lord, and granted them as a gift of grace to the church and to their generation.

And it is *all* of grace. They began as sinful men, weak in the flesh, but grace was at work. Paul himself testified, *"Through him and for his name's sake, we received grace and apostleship to call people from among all the Gentiles..."* (Romans 1:5). About building the church, Paul stated, *"By the grace God has given me, I laid a foundation as an expert builder"* (1 Corinthians 3:10), and he testified later, *"... by the grace of God I am what I am, and his grace to me was not without effect..."* (1 Corinthians 15:10).

'Grace' has a specific meaning in this context. It means that God will choose ordinary men and women to do what He purposes, and, even though they are ordinary people, *grace* enables and makes them what they are to be. The Scriptures abound with examples, such as Moses, Elijah, Abraham, Jeremiah and a host of others. The New Testament speaks specifically of Elijah, saying *"Elijah was a man just like us."* (James 5:17). Likewise, Peter the apostle to the Jews, and Paul the apostle to the Gentiles, were men just like us.

The point of this discussion about grace is that we certainly may have apostles today! Unfortunately the idea grew in the church that no one today could be an apostle because no one should think of themselves as being like Paul or Peter or John. We attach some kind of 'super-men' status to these, and think that in some way they must have been different from the rest of us. This thinking, which we are all prone to, is of a 'religious' mind rather than a spiritual mind. These men were ordinary men, surrendered to Christ, possessed by the Holy Spirit, called and appointed to the ministry of Jesus Christ whom they loved — and they were granted grace to be a gift to the church. The church needs apostles, and Christ appoints them from among His people, as He has always done.

Apostles are an Ongoing Grace

Despite the fact that the established church has often assumed a theological position that said there are no apostles today, the teaching passages of the New Testament give, without exception, a permanent and important place to apostles in the life and leadership of the church.

We've all heard the old negative arguments about apostles that suggest there can be no more apostles today, because there can only ever be the twelve. Another false argument often presented was that once the Bible was written (i.e. once the canon of scripture was completed), apostles were no longer required. This argument claims that the scripture of the New Testament replaces the apostles, who are not needed now because we only need the Bible.

It is easy to see that these arguments do not contain the truth. They are certainly not based on what the New Testament teaches, but are the reasoning of man. A common fault in our thinking is to assume that what is around us in the church is normal and biblical, and then interpret the Bible to support our current practices. There are several teaching passages in the New Testament which we shall examine (1st Corinthians 12:12-31, Ephesians 4:7-13, and Ephesians 2:19-22) to give us a clear position on our doctrine of apostles for today.

God gives First Place to Apostles

"Now you are the body of Christ, and each one of you is a part of it. And in the church God has appointed first of all apostles, second prophets, third teachers, then workers of miracles, also those having gifts of healing, those able to help others, those with gifts of administration, and those speaking in

different kinds of tongues." (1 Corinthians 12:27-28)

In Chapter 12 of 1st Corinthians the apostle Paul laid down a strong argument for the unity of the body of Christ, stressing the importance of every part. During the course of this appeal, he states a number of practical applications: 1) No one in the church can say "because I am not like you, I do not belong to the body" 2) Conversely, no one can say of another "because you are not like me, you are not part of the body", and 3) God has arranged the parts of the body as He wanted them. He continues his instruction by saying that no one in the body can say to any other part "I don't need you!" (v. 21).

These are strong and definitive statements that lead to his conclusions in verses 27 to 31. He says, *"And in the church God has appointed first of all apostles, second prophets, third teachers, then...".* We have here an order by which the body must function. These are not parts of the body which are spread out in time over a long history — they must all be currently serving parts of the body, in relationship with one another, or the idea of the church being a body is a farce. All these parts of the body must be in a current relationship with one another, or we have something less than the body God said He wanted in verse 18.

> The New Testament gives, without exception, a permanent and important place to apostles in the life and leadership of the church.

The clear implications of the passage are these: apostles must always be present in the building of the body in every place, by divine order they must have first place or the body has not been structured properly, and no one may say of the apostle "we don't need you". This teaching passage applies to the structure of the church at all times and in all places — it does not just apply to the initial apostles. Thus we always need apostles, and as we shall soon see, Christ continues to appoint them.

In the body there is a divine order (v.28) which God has appointed. Men should never try to appoint a different order for the church. If we want *"the full measure of the blessing of Christ" (Romans 15:29)* on the church and the believers, we must honour the Lord's appointments. Unfortunately, in the wisdom of men and church traditions, the institutional church has long departed from this divine order.

"God has appointed first... apostles, second prophets, third teachers, then workers of miracles, also those having gifts of healing, those able to help others, those with gifts of administration, and those speaking in different kinds of tongues" (1 Corinthians 12: 28). This list is very revealing. Notice that

administrators do not appear near the top of the list, but well down. In terms of church government and leadership, administrators are meant to be servants, to apostles firstly, and to the other ministries. But in the institutional church, administrators and teachers usually end up in the power positions of leadership, with apostles and prophets excluded from all influence, usually squeezed out altogether. Biblically, it is the apostles and prophets who are the foundation of the church, and apostles the governing authority of the church. Administrators and teachers should serve, submit to and be in partnership with, these apostles.

When administrators or teachers become the principal leadership of a Christian movement or denomination, the essential life or momentum of that movement dies. It becomes dependent on its tradition, and the real anointings that provided the life of Christ to cause fruitfulness and growth are no longer in place.

We establish then that for the life, effective functioning and building of the body, apostles must have a permanent place, and it must be first place. This is not because the apostle is more important than other people or gifts (all parts of the body are equally important) but because in divine order this is the way the body must function. Therefore honour must be given to the apostles, especially at this time, because (v.24) *"God... has given greater honour to the parts that lacked it".*

Grace Gifts of the Ascension

"But to each one of us grace has been given as Christ apportioned it. This is why it says: 'When he ascended on high, he led captives in his train and gave gifts to men.'...It was he who gave some to be apostles, some to be prophets, some to be evangelists, and some to be pastors and teachers, to prepare God's people for works of service, so that the body of Christ may be built up until we all reach unity in the faith and in the knowledge of the Son of God and become mature, attaining to the whole measure of the fullness of Christ. " (Ephesians 4:7-13)

In Ephesians chapter 4 we discover that there are certainly more apostles than the "twelve". It is also revealed just when it is that Jesus appoints apostles, and for how long He continues to appoint them.

Paul teaches that grace is given to each one of us, and by grace Christ appoints ministry which represents Him to the church. Apostles, prophets, evangelists, and pastor/teachers are grace gifts that represent Christ's anointings, Christ's ministry, and Christ's headship, to the body of Christ. Yes, every member of the whole body is in the ministry of Jesus Christ — every believer is a priest — but there are certain believers who are anointed with some of Christ's anointings to represent Jesus to the other believers from a leadership position and with an equipping responsibility. Thus we have both body ministry and headship ministry. Every one of us is to minister as the body of Christ to the rest of the body and to the world. But some are appointed to represent Christ as head to the body. In particular, apostles carry the essential anointing that connects the body to the headship of Jesus. That is why apostles must become an effective ministry in *today's* church.

Apostles carry the essential anointing that connects the body to the headship of Jesus

To counter the old assertion that there were only twelve apostles, I point out that there are many more apostles named in the New Testament than the twelve. Of course, there are only twelve *Apostles of the Lamb,* and their names are written on the foundations of the New Jerusalem (Revelation 21:14). However we are not talking about apostles of the Lamb, which is a specific title for the twelve. We are saying that in addition to the twelve, there are many other apostles appointed by Christ *in His ascension.* Ephesians 4: 8 says *"When he ascended on high, he... gave gifts to men",* and then in verse 11 *"It was he who gave some to be apostles".* Amongst these are Paul, Timothy, Titus and a host of others. In the New Testament there are very few named as teachers, prophets or evangelists, but there are many named as apostles.

The twelve were not appointed in His ascension — they were appointed from amongst His disciples some three years before. When Christ ascended, He began to appoint *more* apostles. These are the ones referred to in Ephesians 4, whom we often describe as *ascension* apostles. Thus, in His ascension Christ is appointing the fivefold ministry to represent His headship to the body, and as Ephesians 4: 12 says, to equip the saints for the ministry and to build up the body of Christ.

When Christ ascended, He began to appoint *more* apostles

This same passage tells us for how long Christ will continue to appoint apostles and the entire fivefold ministry. Verse 13 uses the word *until.* *"He... gave some to be apostles... until"* (Ephesians 4: 11, 13). Following that word, four things are listed as the results that must be achieved in the church, under the ministry of the fivefold anointings, before Christ will return for His bride.

Grace Gifts Continue Until the Church Comes to Maturity

"until we all reach unity in the faith and in the knowledge of the Son of God and become mature, attaining to the whole measure of the fullness of Christ. " *(Ephesians 4:13)*

No one would assume that the results predicted by Paul in this verse have yet been achieved in the church at any point in history. The church has not yet come to unity in the faith, or unity of the knowledge of the Son of God. The church has not yet become mature, nor does it yet measure up to the stature of Jesus. But, of course, she shall. This is her destiny. It is a destiny to be achieved *in time, on earth,* before Jesus comes.

The maturity here described is not something that will happen after the rapture of the church, or on the day of redemption. The Scripture is plainly stating that the resulting maturity is to come from the work of the fivefold ministry (the anointings of Jesus on chosen ministers) and that Jesus continues to appoint these ministries until the church is fully equipped and mature. This understanding of the text is confirmed as you read the following verses, 14-16. This passage is not describing some state of maturity established after Christ returns, but what the church shall become as we continue to advance toward the end of this age.

> Without the ministry of apostles and prophets the church cannot come to maturity.

We conclude again, as we did when examining 1 Corinthians 12, that apostles have a permanent and important place in the church today.

Without the ministry of apostles and prophets the church cannot come to maturity. For too long we have been trying to build the body of Christ and advance the Kingdom of God with a 'threefold' ministry which we called the fivefold ministry. The church 'system' has effectively shut out, for long ages, the key ministries and anointings that are required more than any other to bring the body to maturity. Without the right leadership, and divine order in church government, the church will never become mature or fulfil its destiny.

However, Christ is coming and the church will be ready. The church will fulfil its destiny, and become mature, measuring up to the stature of Jesus. The beauty, the strength, the wisdom, and the power of Jesus will be the measure of the church. This work will now happen quickly, because Christ is restoring apostles and prophets to the church. You live in a wonderful day, and you will see great things unfold before your very eyes.

God's Ultimate Purpose — a 'Mature' Bride for His Son

When God made man and placed him in the garden alone, that man was the image of Jesus. Adam, the first man, was the anointed one upon the earth. Then God declared, *"It is not good for the man to be alone. I will make a helper suitable for him"(Genesis 2:18).* That statement means 'a helper perfectly matched to him in every way'. From the man's side He made Eve. In the Garden of Eden was portrayed a beautiful picture of Christ and the church.

Where does the church come from? It comes from Christ's side, from which blood and water flowed. He gave His blood for us, and washes us with the water of His Word. When God made woman and put her in the garden, He was from the very beginning speaking prophetically of His ultimate purpose. That purpose was for His Son to have a bride! *'It is not good that he should be alone'* said God, so God is making a helper perfectly matched and suitable for Jesus. You are in the center of His purposes. The Bible tells us we are coming to the place where we will be spotless and radiant as a bride.

From this illustration we see how important it is that the church comes to the maturity spoken of in Ephesians 4. To reach this maturity, the church must have the fully restored ministries of prophets and apostles working with the ministries of pastors, teachers and evangelists. This God has ordained. All of these ministries together represent the fullness of Christ's anointings to prepare and equip the bride.

The Final Reformation

God is about to take the church in hand, because we have a date with destiny. The church for which Jesus returns will be a restored apostolic church, and this one true body of Christ will have completed the Great Commission. This body, in unity, will be holy unto the Lord. Remember the lesson of the Quezon City candlestick — there will be a reformation of the church, and the traditions and structures of men in the church will be broken.

In case you think that God would not do that — that He would not allow destructive forces to touch the church — think again. He has already done this before, both in the history of Israel as God's people, and in the history of the church.

I'm sure that in the year, say 1501, almost everyone assumed that Christianity was the way God wanted it. Was not the church Christ's? Was it not founded on the apostles and the church fathers? Did they not have the Holy Scriptures? Suppose someone at that time had prophesied that there was coming a reformation to the church, because the structure of the church was not what God wanted, and that He was about to shatter the structure of the church. Surely this person would have been denounced as deceived, or burned at the stake as a heretic. Yet every word would have been true. In the year 1517, Martin Luther nailed the paper containing his theses to the church door in Wittenberg. All he sought was to debate the issues. Yet he started a fire, by the grace of God, which burned throughout Christendom, and brought about the great reformation of the church, a work which continues to this day.

However, in Luther's time armies marched, blood flowed, political powers rose and fell, and the map of Europe and the history of the church was violently changed. It was the will of God to change and reform the church. That reform brought about principally a reform of doctrine, a return to the true faith. Since then many other reforms have been added. Today, another reform is required — not principally a reform of doctrine, but rather a reform of the wineskin and the structure of the church. The power of institutionalism and tradition shall be broken, and the church shall be a relational body. We will no longer be bound by the power and money of institutions, but by the bonds of love as we give our hearts to one another and to the apostles who will lead us. And the hearts of the apostles? They shall be knit to one another, and to the believers.

> It is foolish to protest our 'independence'. God has not called us to independence, but to oneness.

The Foundation of God's Household: Apostles and Prophets!

"... God's household, built on the foundation of the apostles and prophets, with Christ Jesus himself as the chief cornerstone. In him the whole building is joined together and rises to become a holy temple in the Lord. And in him you too are being built together to become a dwelling in which God lives by his Spirit" (Ephesians 2: 19 — 22).

We are told in Ephesians 2:20 that God's household is built on the foundation of the apostles and prophets. The question I long considered was whether this Scripture was referring to apostles and prophets in every age, and therefore to apostles today, or whether this was a reference only applicable to the original apostles and prophets. Is there here an important work that must be continued by apostles and prophets in every generation?

This Scripture does have an obvious historical application, but we must also see its powerful current application. Let us examine the text:

"You too are being built together" (V. 22) indicates he is addressing us not as individuals but as a group. The *"you"* is plural, addressed to the present assembly of Paul's day, which was the church of the whole city. So the localised church is a dwelling for God — and He will come in power and be present in His people, the more so as they are built together as one people in unity.

Notice the present tense of Paul's comments here. *"You are no longer", "the building rises", "are being built", "to become",* and *"you are... built"* — all refer to what you, I and all the believers are now. The present church, a living fellowship, is built on the foundation laid in both the hearts of the believers and in the spiritual fabric of the city, by apostles and prophets. The apostles and prophets are to be living ministries with a living, dynamic relationship with the believers.

For the church to really live, the input of apostles and prophets is required, not because all believers are not equal parts of the body, but because we all have differing anointings. Apostles and prophets have anointings that represent Christ in giving a vital life to the body as an organic living entity.

Christ is the source of life. His life flows in various ways and through various means of grace to all His people. But a greater grace (a greater provision, a greater miracle) is required if His people are to have a *corporate* life, especially if the church is to be built together to be the dwelling place of God in a city.

This life flows through the anointings of Christ that are on apostles and prophets, because that is what these ministry gifts are! They are expressions of Christ at work in the body. If you receive them, you receive Christ (Matthew 10:40). If you follow them, you follow Christ (1 Corinthians 11:1). If you submit to them, and to each other, you submit to Christ (Ephesians 5:21).

It is foolish to protest our 'independence'. God has not called us to independence, but to oneness. You are being *"built together, in him",* and *"joined together".* If you will not do this under apostles and prophets, who will you do it under? Would you ever become one with the body? If you are to be what God says, i.e. one with all believers, this can only be because of the 'foundation' of apostles and prophets, for this is what God has appointed — this is Christ in His grace given to His people (Ephesians 4:7 and 3:7).

Again, for the third time, we come to this conclusion. The church must have apostles! And, it must have them today! The Scriptures give a permanent and important place to this crucial leadership ministry.

The reinstatement of the office of the apostle in the church has profound implications. *Nothing* will stay the same! We are talking major restructuring — a reformation of the wineskin. For many years now our prophetic people have heard the Lord tell us repeatedly, "Nothing will stay the same".

Major change is coming upon the body of Christ. Simply assuming that the present leadership structures can be renamed, and then press on with business as usual, will not do! We must have real apostles, and only those who have been appointed apostles by Christ are real apostles!

If someone is a Bishop, or a General Superintendent, or the Senior Pastor of a very large church, this does not imply that they are an apostle. They might rather be a great prophet or teacher, a wonderful minister of Christ in their own calling, but this is not the same as being an apostle.

We must pray for understanding, and for the power of Christ to raise the apostles. We must then allow them to restructure the ministries of the church.

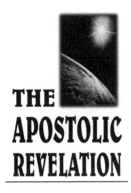

THE APOSTOLIC REVELATION

Chapter 3

What Is An Apostle?

Literally the word apostle (Greek *'apostolos'*) means a 'sent one', a 'delegate', a 'messenger'. In the New Testament the apostle is an ambassador of the gospel, officially a commissioner of Christ, with miraculous powers. Every apostle has a specific commission, and is sent to do the Father's will.

The Apostle of the Father

Christ is the apostle of the Father, for Holy Scripture says of Him *"when the time had fully come, God sent his Son..." (Galatians 4:4)* and *"the Father has sent his Son to be the Saviour of the world" (1 John 4:14, also v. 9-10).* The book of Hebrews tells you to *"fix your thoughts on Jesus, the apostle and high priest whom we confess" (Hebrews 3:1).*

It will be good to think about Jesus as an apostle for a few moments. If we do not understand Jesus as an apostle, we will not understand the ministry He appoints. The text of Hebrews 3:1 calls Jesus *"the apostle and high priest whom we confess"*. Jesus had a specific commission from the Father, and He was sent from the Father's presence into the world to inhabit the body prepared for Him, so that as high priest of a new covenant He could offer an unblemished sacrifice for the sin of man to the Father. Notice that Jesus was not only the high priest offering the sacrifice, He was also the sacrifice being offered. He did this as the apostle of the Father.

This was not Jesus' only task as an apostle. The Father had prepared a body for Him, but Jesus had to make preparations for *another* body that the presence of God would indwell on the earth. This was to be the church, the body of Christ, and for this He had to raise other apostles. He was the apostle of the Father and, other than living the sinless life of obedience to the Father, and giving that life up in sacrifice for the sin of the world, His most important work was to prepare the twelve apostles of the Lamb, to be apostles.

The Anointings of Jesus

As well as being an apostle, Christ was the prophet of the Father. Moses had said *"The LORD your God will raise up for you a prophet like me from among your own brothers. You must listen to him" (Deuteronomy 18:15).* He was speaking of Jesus. Jesus was the great evangelist sent by the Father. He was the one who came to seek and to save the lost, and we see His great love for the lost in His dealing with the woman at the well in Samaria. Then, Jesus was also the pastor and teacher of the Father. Jesus was called Rabbi (teacher) by all around Him, and He taught the crowds as well as His disciples. Jesus was the great shepherd of the sheep — He said *"I am the good shepherd",* and *"I am the door of the sheepfold" (John 10:11,7).*

> With these anointings comes an authority to represent and speak for Jesus

So we see that Jesus had every ministry anointing upon His life, in service to the Father. In the words of John the Baptist, He had the Spirit of God without limit (John 3:34). We must understand then, that when Christ appoints apostles, prophets, evangelists, pastors and teachers, He is placing upon them His own anointings as the Christ (the anointed) of God and the apostle of the Father. Thus the fivefold ministry of the church is the ministry of Jesus distributed effectively through the lives of men and women that God has called to this holy office.

Further, we must understand that with these anointings to do the work of Jesus comes an authority to represent Jesus and to speak for Jesus. Those who are appointed apostles have the apostolic authority of Jesus Christ in the matter for which they are commissioned. Thus, when Jesus sends an apostle, that apostle is Christ to you.

Commissioners of Christ

Apostles have a commission from Christ, and with the commission comes the authority for the task to which they are appointed (Colossians 1:25, 1 Tim 1:12,1 Corinthians 4:1). Included in that is the authority for apostles to appoint and commission others in the service of Christ (Titus 1:5). So the apostle is a *commissioner* of Christ. A commissioner is one who represents a supreme authority, and who has total authority in the matter for which they are appointed.

The structure of The Salvation Army is an excellent illustration of the role of a commissioner. The Salvation Army is a Christian movement that began in England in the 19th century. Before long it adopted a military style, which was inspired by the Holy Spirit as the best means in those days to carry out its evangelical purpose, and it was very successful. The Salvation Army worldwide has one General. Originally this was the founder, William Booth, but there have been a series of successors. The General of the Salvation Army is in total control of the Salvation Army worldwide, but the Salvation Army 'world' is divided into about 40 territories. Each of these territories has appointed over it a Commissioner — a person who represents the General. In the Territory over which the Commissioner has been appointed, the Commissioner has total authority and control. The Commissioner is the representative of the General, is accountable to the General, but is responsible completely for the progress of the work, the appointments of the officers and staff, and the use of the funds and resources in the Territory. The Commissioner is the final authority concerning all matters within their Territory.

This is a picture that illustrates the appointment, the authority and the accountability of an apostle under Christ.

John Eckhardt in his book *"Moving in the Apostolic"* (Renew Books, 1999) points out that before the word apostle was used by the New Testament writers, it was a term used by the Greeks and Romans to describe special envoys who were sent out to expand the empire. He writes, *"Many of these envoys were military generals with authority to go into new territories and fight, if necessary, to establish the Greek or Roman culture in that region. They were also responsible for teaching and training the new subjects in the laws and culture of the kingdom. These envoys were given power and authority from the king to fulfil their mission. They were responsible for fulfilling their commissions and were given everything they needed to succeed. They were highly intelligent and gifted individuals, specially chosen for the task. They were sent to certain territories and charged to subdue, conquer, convert, instruct, train and establish the new subjects in the culture of the empire" (John Eckhardt, 'Moving in the Apostolic', Renew Books 1999, Page 23).*

> The call upon the life of the apostle is, first and foremost, to be with Him.

Thus the word 'apostle', with a meaning well established in the culture of the day, was used by Christ as the designation for those He was appointing to represent Him in building and governing the church. They were to take charge of the advance of the kingdom of God under the leading of the Holy Spirit.

Three Basic Qualifications

The gospel of Mark relates the appointment by Jesus of the initial twelve apostles, and here we find three basic qualifications that must apply to all apostles. *"He appointed twelve — designating them apostles — that they might be with him and that he might send them out to preach and to have authority to drive out demons" (Mark 3:14-15).*

Firstly, *"that they might be with him".* This is surely the first qualification of an apostle. They have spent time in the presence of God; they are constant seekers after Christ; they know what it is to be with Jesus. The call upon the life of the apostle is, first and foremost, to be with Him.

Secondly, *"that he might send them out".* Being sent is central to the purpose of an apostle. Every apostle knows there is a calling, a commission. In some Christian circles it used to be thought that an apostle was someone who was sent overseas as a missionary; that to be an apostle was to be sent to a foreign people. But this is not so. It means to be sent from the presence of God with a commission. An apostle may be sent to his own people, to his own community. The important element is that a commission has been given, just as was given to Moses at the burning bush when he was sent to deliver and lead his own people.

Thirdly, *"to have authority".* Spiritual authority is one of the clear evidences of apostolic grace upon those who are apostles. This authority, however, is a *grace.* It is not controlling, not authoritarian, not overbearing. Rather, apostolic authority brings liberty and impartation to the believers. The apostle has authority to set things in order, protect and govern the church, and pull down principalities and demonic strongholds. In addition, the apostle has grace to impart authority to other ministries and believers. We will discuss spiritual authority at greater length later in this book.

Submission to Christ

In speaking of authority, we must make very clear that apostles are not a law unto themselves. A very real qualification of apostles is their submission to Christ. Indeed, without submission to Christ there can be no real authority. Unless authority flows from submission to a greater authority, then real and genuine spiritual authority is absent.

The genuine apostle has a heart submitted and surrendered to Christ alone. This is in fact the key to their authority, and one of the reasons they have been chosen as Christ's representatives.

Must an Apostle See Jesus?

It is essential to discuss this question, because many of the commentators have entrenched the idea that an apostle must have a physical manifestation or revelation of the resurrection of Jesus. That is, they must have seen Christ in His resurrection to be qualified as an apostle. This has become a commonly accepted evangelical position. But is this what the Bible teaches? I do not think this is the Bible position at all.

The passages of scripture usually referred to are Acts 1:21-22, Acts 22:14-16, Acts 26:16-17, 1 Corinthians 9:1, and 1 Corinthians 15:4-10.

Acts chapter 1 holds a description of the qualification of the one person who was to join the eleven remaining apostles of the Lamb. He was to replace Judas, and complete the required number of twelve such apostles. Acts 1:21-22 quotes Peter defining that the man needed to replace Judas must be qualified by having been with them the whole time from the beginning of Jesus ministry until His ascension, and who was a witness with them of the resurrection. There were many who met these qualifications, and they narrowed the choice down to two men, of whom Peter said on behalf of the eleven, *"one of these must become a witness with us"*. This is not a statement describing a qualification for all future apostles, but only of the one man who was to join the twelve.

The other passages listed above are all personal and narrative passages concerning the apostle Paul himself. None of these teach the requirement that all future apostles must see the resurrection of Jesus. In fact the New Testament on the whole tends to imply the opposite, as I shall illustrate in a moment.

There is no doubt that the appearance of Jesus to Paul was an essential part of his personal qualification as an apostle, but then he was called to an apostolic office of a very specific nature. He was 'the apostle to the Gentiles', a position which no one else held even though there were many apostles that went to the Gentiles (See Chapter 7 on Spiritual Covering).

In 1 Corinthians 9:1, Paul appeals, *"Am I not free? Am I not an apostle? Have I not seen Jesus our Lord? Are you not the result of my work in the Lord?"* It has been assumed that this passage implied that to be an apostle one had to see the Lord, but this is not what Paul is saying. Rather, he is listing his own qualifications in arguing his freedom. In the passage Paul is arguing for Christian liberty, and in listing his qualifications he lists his apostleship, and his having seen the Lord, as separate items. He is not arguing here that one proves the other, but that he has both.

Furthermore, in 1 Corinthians 15:8-9 Paul states that, after Jesus had appeared to the other apostles and to many believers *"...last of all he appeared to me also, as to one abnormally born. For I am the least of the apostles...".* This would imply that there were to be no more resurrection appearances of Jesus, even for future apostles. And there were more future apostles, because the New Testament names some of them. For example, Acts 14:14 refers to *"the apostles Barnabas and Paul"*, Romans 16:7 has Paul speaking of *"Andronicus and Junias, outstanding among the apostles"* and further, in 1 Thessalonians 2:6 we find *"As apostles of Christ, we (Paul is referring to himself, Silas and Timothy)"*. There is no evidence that these apostles required a resurrection appearance of Jesus to be qualified as apostles.

There are to be many apostles, and this office has a permanent place in the life of the church of every age, as we have shown to be the case in chapter 2 where we examined 1 Corinthians 12, Ephesians 4 and Ephesians 2. If Christ requires these apostles to be qualified by a resurrection appearance of Jesus, then of course He will give that revelation. But we should be clear that a resurrection appearance of Jesus is not a *biblical requirement* for someone who has been called and anointed of God to be an apostle. At the same time, with or without resurrection appearances, apostles the world over will look to God to obtain an ever greater experience of Christ, as Paul did, and as every believer should do (Philippians 3:7-15).

The Bible position is that *no* Christian actually needs to see the resurrection of Jesus. The initial Christians were eyewitnesses of His resurrection, and the rest of us are called to faith in believing the word of God that has been preached. The apostle Peter said, *"though you have not seen him, you love him; and even though you do not see him now, you believe in him and are filled with an inexpressible and glorious joy" (1 Peter 1:8).* There is an implication here that those of us who believe without seeing have a greater faith, or at least some significant blessing, as in Jesus' statement to the apostle Thomas, *"Blessed are those who have not seen, and yet have believed" (John 20:29).*

Having said that, every apostle must know the significance of Christ being formed in them, and of being called and appointed by grace to apostleship. There will be significant experiences of Christ, for the apostolic anointing is a revelation of Christ. Wherever I have been on my journey to seek understanding and revelation of apostolic ministry and the restoration of the apostolic church, I have come face-to-face with Christ. The whole journey has been a constant call to intimacy with the Father and the Son.

When I woke one Friday morning in February 1997 to find Christ standing by me, He spoke and gave several instructions. One of them was to go to the nations with an apostolic message — but the final instruction was to keep looking into the eyes of Jesus Christ.

A Friend of the Bridegroom

John the Baptist said to his disciples, *"A man can receive only what is given him from heaven. The bride belongs to the bridegroom. The friend who attends the bridegroom waits and listens for him, and is full of joy when he hears the bridegroom's voice. That joy is mine, and it is now complete. He must become greater; I must become less" (John 3:27, 29-30).*

John spoke of himself as the friend of the bridegroom. This is a very apt metaphor, and is very much the role of the apostle. Concerning John, Jesus said he was *"more than a prophet" (Luke 7:26).* In the Gospels we read, *"There came a man who was sent from God; his name was John" (John 3:6).* John the Baptist is a type of the apostle, as were numerous Old Testament figures, such as Adam, Abraham, Moses, David, and Elijah.

The Old Testament ends with a promise and a prophecy, *"I will send you the prophet Elijah before that great and dreadful day of the Lord comes. He will turn the hearts of the fathers to their children, and the hearts of the children to their fathers;" (Malachi 4: 5-6).* John was a specific fulfillment of this Old Testament prophecy, and his role was to prepare the people of God for the coming of Christ. He came in the spirit and power of Elijah, just as the angel of the Lord had foretold when speaking to his father Zechariah. *"And he will... turn the hearts of the fathers to their children and the disobedient to the wisdom of the righteous — to make ready a people prepared for the Lord" (Luke 1:17).*

Apostles today now have this vital work to do. In the same way that John was sent in the spirit and power of Elijah before the first coming of Christ, many are now being sent to every nation, in the spirit and power of Elijah, to prepare the people for the coming of Christ again. The scriptures must be fulfilled.

The apostle has grace from God to prepare the bride for Christ. Christ is returning for a mature and spotless bride, a people made ready for the Lord (Ephesians 4:13, 5:25-27). The apostle knows that the bride is not his — the apostle must never 'touch' the church in an inappropriate way. But the apostle does have a commission from Christ to bring the church to the place of readiness for the wedding supper of the Lamb.

The apostle Paul wrote to the Lord's people who had been entrusted to him, *"I am jealous for you with a godly jealousy. I promised you to one husband, to Christ, so that I might present you as a pure virgin to him"* (2 Corinthians *11:2)*. Every true apostle will have this passion, this jealousy, that the church would be what she is called to be, and measure up to the stature of Christ. Every apostle has a great love for Christ and for the church, and longs for the church to come to spotless maturity. This passion, and the understanding of Christ's desire for the church, is upon the apostle because of the apostolic anointing.

> The heart of the true apostle is for the WHOLE body of Christ — not just for a denomination or a movement

Note also that the heart of the true apostle is for the WHOLE body of Christ — not just for a denomination or a movement. In the past there may have been apostles who expressed themselves denominationally, but this will no longer be the case. The current anointing will no longer allow that. This is the day when apostles will build according to Ephesians 4 and 1 Corinthians 1 — no longer is Christ to be divided, no longer shall we say 'I am this' or 'I am that'. The church shall go beyond the unity of the Spirit (Ephesians 4:3) and will come to the unity of the faith (Ephesians 4:13). Every apostle must believe in the power and the intent of Jesus' prayer recorded in John 17, and wholeheartedly devote themselves to the purpose of visible and obvious unity for the true body of Christ. Otherwise, they are something less than Christ's apostle.

See here the heart of the true apostle. Paul wrote to the church, *"I rejoice in what was suffered for you, and I fill up in my flesh what is still lacking in regard to Christ's afflictions, for the sake of his body, which is the church. I have become its servant by the commission God gave me to present to you the word of God in its fullness... We proclaim him, admonishing and teaching everyone with all wisdom, so that we may present everyone perfect in Christ. To this end I labour,..."* (Colossians 1:24-25, 28-29).

Here is proclaimed the apostle's commission to present the church to Christ perfect. And here is revealed the apostle's passion for the task, with an apostolic willingness to suffer for the sake of Christ and the church. Thus, like John the Baptist, the apostle is 'the friend of the bridegroom', the trusted friend commissioned to prepare the bride for that great day.

A Spiritual Father

To the Corinthians Paul wrote, *"... my dear children. Even though you have ten thousand guardians in Christ, you do not have many fathers, for in Christ Jesus I became your father through the gospel. Therefore I urge you to imitate me" (1 Corinthians 4:14-16).* This is an extensive subject and will be treated separately in chapter 7. We need to note that the true apostle always has the heart of a father for those about him in the church, and for the churches themselves. Such is the purity of his love for the believers, and the focus of his own heart in following Christ, that he is able to say *"imitate me"*.

> The key to apostolic authority is death, and apostles have more authority because they have faced more death.

In the past many believers and churches have been unable to recognise apostles because they have been looking for *"super apostles"* (2 Corinthians 11:5, 12:11) who would come with signs and wonders, when they should have been looking for a father. The apostle will usually appear first as a father, rather than a miracle worker, to those pastors and churches who are praying for God to provide them with an apostle. Signs and miracles have their place, but it is not usually first place. God will give them according to His will to confirm His word, but an apostle is primarily concerned with relationships, building the house of God to be a true household — i.e. a family.

It is a father who gives identity, and it is the voice of a father that gives permission to succeed into the heart of every believer and every young minister of Christ. More on this later.

Master Builders of God's House

I have a friend in Rockhampton, a member of my church, who has built over 700 houses, yet he himself did no painting, no plumbing, he did not drive one nail or cut one piece of timber, or lay any of the bricks. All these things were done by others, called sub-contractors. He was, however, the builder who understood and controlled the master plan, and directed every step of the building process.

In like manner Paul calls himself an expert builder, but he states he only laid the foundation, and someone else is building on it (1 Corinthians 3: 10). We find another reference to this in Ephesians 2:20, where we are told that God's household is built upon the foundation of the apostles and prophets.

In the house of God, these are spiritual foundations that have to be laid in both churches and the hearts of the believers. This is the regular ongoing work of apostles and prophets. An apostle carries an anointing to set the house of God in order, and to speak into the spiritual fabric of that house, as well as into the lives of the believers. The apostle also has authority to address the spiritual realm over the cities and communities where these believers live. Apostles have specific authority that relates directly to principalities and powers of darkness — the apostle is a spiritual weapon in dealing with high-level forces that oppose the establishing of the church.

The apostle does not do all the building. Every believer helps to build the house of God, and every pastor or teacher is an important 'sub-contractor' in the building of the house. Each one should be building upon foundations that have been laid by apostles. I remember visiting a small town in Central Queensland some years ago, to preach on a Friday night at a small church that had been operating for a couple of years. After preaching I proceeded to pray for them corporately, and felt led by the Spirit to make a proclamation over them, and declare that they were a church of the Lord Jesus Christ. In the very moment that I declared them to be a church, in the Lord's name, something shifted. It was as if something that had been missing was put in place, something needed was sheeted home in the spirit realm. It was of course, an apostolic blessing, and an apostolic recognition of what they were corporately. It was an apostle supplying missing foundations.

We feel the same principle applies to house churches and church cells. Where they are on their own, they will struggle. When an apostle visits the house church, and claims it for Christ, and blesses the house church and the leaders, it will thrive. No house church should ever remain without the apostolic covering of a spiritual father, just as no evangelist, prophet, pastor or church should be without the covering and the love of an apostle.

Authority over the Church

Notice that when Christ prepared a leadership, which would take His place when He ascended to the Father, He prepared apostles. All other ministries have come from what apostles have established. Success in ministry comes from being under the blessing of the apostle's anointing, and this is still a powerful principle today. As prophets, teachers and other elders were developed and appointed, they took their place alongside the apostles in leadership of the church, but they remained subject to the apostles. Apostles are, rightly and properly, the final leadership authority in the church. This is the work for which they have been prepared and anointed by Christ.

Without apostles in the church, we lack the proper functioning of Christ's headship ministry. This is the reason there is so much division — there are many ministries at work building the body, but without apostles there is no unity, and no master plan. Apostles bring together the body in unity, because their role is to bring the body of Christ into proper relationship with Christ, the head of the body. Christ, the head of the church, relates fully and properly to the corporate body on earth through apostles and prophets, for He speaks through both and lays foundations through both. However, it is the apostles who exercise authority over the church and its ministries, and in partnership with prophets and the other elders, set all things in order and bring the body to unity and maturity in Christ.

We will expand our understanding of this when we discuss Spiritual Covering in chapter 6, Fathering in Ministry in chapter 7, and the City Eldership in chapter 9. For now we make the point that every ministry in the body of Christ is meant to be under authority — and it should be the relational authority of a man of God, not of a committee or an institution. Every church and every senior minister should have a primary relationship with an apostle, and each apostle also must be in an accountable relationship, under the covering of another apostle.

The Key to Apostolic Authority

The key to apostolic authority is death, and apostles have more authority because they have faced more death. The death referred to here is death of self, death to the world, and death to the fear of man and the praise of man. It was, I believe, Dietrich Bonhoeffer who said, "When Jesus calls a man, He bids him come and die."

A graphic description of this death being worked in an apostle is supplied by Paul, when he wrote, *"it seems to me that God has put us apostles on display at the end of the procession, like men condemned to die in the arena. We have been made a spectacle to the whole universe, to angels as well as to men. We are fools for Christ, but you are so wise in Christ! We are weak, but you are so strong! You are honoured, but we are dishonoured! To this very hour we go hungry and thirsty, we are in rags, we are brutally treated, we are homeless. We work hard with our own hands. When we are cursed, we bless; when we are persecuted, we endure it; when we are slandered, we answer kindly. Up to this moment we have become the scum of the earth, the refuse of the world" (1 Corinthians 4:9-13).*

This is one of the reasons that no one should carelessly claim to be an apostle, or seek to place apostleship on someone who is not called or anointed for that office. It can be very costly. If Christ has chosen and anointed someone to be an apostle, the anointing will protect and equip that believer. Without the anointing, no one would want to be exposed to the things that are in the spirit realm against those who are named apostles.

I still remember the events of March and April 1996, when I had been praying over a promise that God had given me. Through a dream, the Lord had said that He was going to bring me into a specific relationship with the body of Christ. The next day a fellow apostle brought me a prophetic word that promised I would have the heart of David in being a shepherd of integrity over God's people. I was sitting at my desk praying over promises in Holy Scripture that related to these ideas, when I heard the Lord speak to my heart, "With respect to this promise, you have to die!"

Immediately I knew this meant trouble. But I had promised the Lord, again and again, that He could do with me whatever He wanted, and no matter what it was I would not pull back. The strange thing was, I thought I was already dead. Through many experiences of the dealings of God, I had kept a humble and submissive heart. Nevertheless, I had to face more death. The following four years were the most difficult of my entire life, because God was preparing us (me and others) for something better. Was it worth it? Oh yes, a thousand times so! Now there is something, on the inside, which is different — a better heart. I thank the Lord sincerely for those difficult times.

So the Holy Spirit prepares the heart of the apostle. As with Jesus, there will be those who betray, and deny, and mock. Like David, there will be an Absalom.

There will also be rejection. Jesus experienced rejection, and anyone who would become like Jesus will also taste rejection. I think no apostle will ever be raised to apostolic authority who does not go through a season of rejection. This is a crucial part of the preparation. We must face misunderstanding, accusation and opposition, and yet still have a right heart and a sweet spirit. We must love and we must forgive. An apostle must come through these experiences without bitterness, without resentment, without self-pity, and without regret. Notice that Jesus never felt sorry for Himself. The apostle likewise must have a right spirit — he must live and love in the Spirit of Jesus, who taught us to love and forgive our enemies. Without passing this test, we cannot stand in the ministry of Christ as an apostle.

The Spirit of Jesus

Indeed, this is the spirit of apostleship — to have the heart of Jesus. Part of this is a willingness to suffer, if only the Father's will may be done. The apostle will have a heart to drink Christ's cup — which is often a cup of suffering. Jesus said to His young apostles, *"You will drink the cup I drink and be baptised with the baptism I am baptised with" (Mark 10:39).*

For the apostle, Christ is all. The apostle has one heart, an undivided heart, and it is Christ's alone.

Where Do Apostles Come from?

The prophet Malachi recorded this word from the Lord, " *'I will send my messenger, who will prepare the way before me. Then suddenly the Lord you are seeking will come to his temple; the messenger of the covenant, whom you desire, will come,' says the Lord Almighty" (Malachi 3:1).*

This prophecy must have a fulfillment for both the first and second comings of Jesus. We have already seen that John the Baptist was the messenger 'sent' to prepare the way for Jesus 2000 years ago. Now God is raising many apostles who will go before Him in the spirit and power of Elijah, as was prophesied, before the coming of Christ for His bride.

We said an apostle is a 'sent one', and the Lord has said, *"I will send my messenger".* Notice that word 'send'. You will see these little apostolic signals sitting everywhere in the Bible. *"I will send my messenger."* This raises the question, where does He send him from? The answer is, they arise in our very midst.

They always arise in our midst.! Yet because of that, often we do not have eyes to see that they've been sent from God. The Bible says of John the Baptist, *"There was a man sent from God whose name was John."* But John had been born right there. They didn't respect Jesus either, and least of all in Nazareth. Why? Because He had played with their children.

> Something in our hearts has to change with respect to the ministry. God is raising mighty ministers amongst us, but we despise them.

Something in our hearts has to change with respect to the ministry. God is raising mighty ministers amongst us, but we despise them. Why do we despise them? There are many factors, but one is that we have been culturally trained to do that by denominationalism and by the 'religion' we have adhered to all our lives. We are locked into the religious attitudes that surround us, and that are within our own hearts. Nevertheless, grace is *grace*. If only we will walk in the light, we can walk free from this bondage to religion. We must come to the place where we honour and respect the ministry which God chooses to raise.

Interestingly, today we look back at Elijah and think, 'What a wonderful man of God'. Or Elisha, 'Oh how wonderful'. Or Moses, 'What a mighty man of God, every word he spoke was of God'. It's all very well for us in hindsight. Had you been there on the day, what is the chance that you would have been the Joshua or the Caleb? All the others died because they grumbled and grizzled, disobeyed and complained. That is the human tendency and none of us are very different.

This is precisely the issue that Jesus took up with the Pharisees. The Pharisees tended the graves of the prophets. They made much about the wonderful prophets of Israel, and upheld the writings of the prophets. As in Matthew 23:29-32, Jesus told them, "It was your fathers that killed the prophets and you've tended their graves so you have the same guilt as they do." Jesus was seeing something they never saw, and if we are not careful, it will be as true of us today as it was of the Pharisees in Jesus' day. We also tend to look back at Christ's servants in history and recognise them as mighty men and women of God, but fail to recognise what God is doing today.

If Hudson Taylor were alive today, how many would recognise him as having such a tremendous anointing to go and put those foundations for the work of God in China. William Booth was one of the most amazing Christian leaders who has ever lived in 2000 years, but in all the early decades of him building that ministry he was despised and vilified. He was spat on in the street. By the time he died, kings and queens attended his funeral. We all want to be part of the action when the 'glory' is on something. When the world honours something, we rush to be in the middle of it. But when the world does not recognise the honour and the glory of God, we tend to fail to be there.

Now we must do better than that. If we are going to be an apostolic people, we must be prepared to discern what God is saying and doing, and put ourselves in agreement with Him in the centre of His purpose. It will be essential to make room in our churches for apostles and prophets to rise. What does that mean? It will mean to honour the ministry, to give them their place, and to accept the authority that God has placed on them.

Apostles Identify Themselves

Every time Paul wrote a letter, he identified himself as an apostle. Peter did the same (1 Peter 1:1, 2 Peter 1:1). It is obvious from the writings of the New Testament that apostles were honest and forthright in the declaration of their call to the apostolic ministry. Even false apostles claimed to be apostles, obviously because that was the normal practice of the apostolic church.

But institutionalised Christianity has developed in us a culture where we think no one should claim to be an apostle or a prophet — and that such a claim would come from pride, arrogance, manipulation or deception. It is true that false claims to the apostolate can and do come from these evils, but the church is meant to test those who claim to be apostles, and reject the false. Meanwhile, true apostles will need to establish apostolic ministries in the name of Christ.

In the early 90's, I was trying to build an apostolic ministry without naming it as such, and without naming myself as an apostle. There was both unbelief and cultural resistance in the church to the idea of anyone seeing themselves as an apostle, and I was being cautious. At that time I wondered why things seemed to be slower than they should be, and why the money to support the ministry was not flowing as it should. I sought the Lord, and He informed me I had things back to front. I was trying to do apostolic ministry without naming it, in the hope that other people would recognise the ministry, name it for me, and thus declare me to be an apostle. The Lord said it does not work like that. He said I was to stand up and declare this to be apostolic ministry and myself an apostle of Christ, and then He would bless the ministry.

So I did, and He did! Consequently, for years now, I have been around the world again and again and again, and not lacked the dollars to do it. And for the last four years, I have taken no salary from my church, because the Lord told me to give it up and He would keep me. I have a wife and eight children, missions to support in various nations, and the expense of extensive travelling, and He supplies it all.

His provision for me and this ministry is an ongoing miracle testifying to the validity of my call to be an apostle of Jesus Christ.

THE APOSTOLIC REVELATION

Chapter 4

The Nature of an Apostle

If apostles are not in place (first place) in the leadership of the church, the 'machinery' of the church does not work properly. The church of Jesus Christ needs and must have the authority, the wisdom and the gifts for government and leadership that are on apostles by the anointings of Christ. But gifts alone are insufficient — we *also* need, and must have, <u>the apostle's *heart*</u>.

Suppose someone was to take up leadership in the body of Christ — someone who had wonderful leadership gifts, and great ability to organise, plan, manage and govern. Suppose they had these strengths in abundance, but did not have the apostle's heart. Would this work for us? No! Leadership authority has to be married with the heart of an apostle!

The Heart of an Apostle

The heart that is to be in an apostle takes time to establish. You can be born with gifts, abilities and talents, even motivations, but there are some things that simply take time. There are certain lessons that apostles have to learn, and particular qualities of attitude and heart that need to be developed. Even then, the apostle will need to be tried and proven in them.

As I see it, there are two ways to make progress in these ministry anointings to the point of being established in Christlike authority as an apostle (and this principal holds true for advancement to maturity in *all* ministry). There is the long way and the short way. The *long* way is when someone called to the apostolic ministry makes their way alone (i.e. they do not have a spiritual father) - this could take 20 or 30 years. Long years of learning are required, in the "University of Struggle and Pain", and will continue until a "Master's degree" has been obtained.

We have no better example of this than the apostle Paul. Paul did not have an apostle as a spiritual father, and instead he walked the sometimes lonely and always difficult path of a pioneer. He had to break new ground, and fight the war in new territory. He was sent to the Gentiles at a time when no other apostle had any real vision for the Gentiles. Paul was entrusted with great revelation concerning the gospel. To keep him in a right state of heart and mind, he was given, over and above his suffering, struggle and hard labour, a thorn in the flesh (2 Corinthians 12:7). It was his accountability mechanism, a reality check.

By the grace of God there is another way, an easier way, to obtain the heart and spirit that an apostle should have, and that is to submit to such an apostle as your spiritual father. You then learn from him, and catch his spirit. You won't necessarily have to go through all the things he went through, because you will learn from him and not make the same mistakes he made. Your heart will become instructed in the attitudes and values of apostolic grace, and you will walk in the humility, simplicity and gentleness of Christ required for the apostolic office. If a young apostle serving under a spiritual father does not have a submitted heart, the process is going to take longer, and there will be more pain.

A Different Spirit

You will not qualify for this office unless there is something about your spirit that is substantially different to what we have known of religious, institutional, denominational Christianity. We are not here to build our own kingdom, or the 'kingdom' of our favourite religious institution. We are not here to build an organisation in the image of man. We are here to pay whatever price must be paid for Christ to be established and honoured in the heart of all people, and for His kingdom to be established and advancing in every place.

Willingness to Suffer

There is one particular thing that will be in the heart of the true apostle. He will have a heart to accept the cup of Christ. He will be willing to drink Christ's cup for the sake of the church (Colossians 1: 24). Part of the 'qualification for the job' is the willingness to suffer. Was not this the heart of Jesus? Was the Son of God not willing to suffer so that the Father's will may be done? This is the spirit of Jesus, and the spirit of apostleship.

Remember when those two young apostles James and John, with their mother's help, put a request to Jesus about sitting at the right and left hand of Christ when He came in His glory. What was Jesus' answer? *"Can you drink the cup I drink or be baptised with the baptism I am baptised with?" "We can,"* they said. He replied, *"You will drink the cup I drink... but to sit at my right or left is not for me to grant"* (Mark 10: 38-40). Notice He never took the cup, His cup, from His apostles, even though they had no understanding of it. Every apostle, in some way small or great, will share the cup of suffering, although not every apostle will suffer to the degree that Paul did. It will depend on the call of God, the need of the apostle's own heart, and the need of the times. Every apostle will be proven by trial and suffering, but note that every apostle will make great inroads into the kingdom of darkness by the same trials and suffering, for which grace will be given. As the great apostle made clear, *"I want you to know, brothers, that what has happened to me has really served to advance the gospel"* (Philippines 1: 12).

When God spoke to Ananias to send him to pray for the future apostle Paul, God said, *"I will show this man how much he must suffer for my name"* (Acts 9: 16). Paul was appointed by God to this high level of suffering, and was given the power of grace to suffer according to the will of God.

Paul wrote, *"I served the Lord with great humility and tears, although I was severely tested by the plots of the Jews"* (Acts 20:19). No matter how much was brought against that apostle by the schemes of the enemy, which God allowed, Paul would never yield from his total devotion to take hold of Jesus at any cost. Again he wrote, *"I want to know Christ and the power of his resurrection and the fellowship of sharing in his sufferings, becoming like him in his death"* (Philippians 3:10). That is the spirit of apostolic Christianity.

I am attempting to define the spirit or the nature of apostolic Christianity. The issue here is not the degree to which an apostle may be called to suffer. The issue is that an apostle should have the same spirit as Jesus, who was willing to suffer so that the Father's will would be done. He was willing to pay the price, *whatever* the price, if only the Father's will may be done. That is the spirit of apostleship.

Servants of the Church

The apostle's great heart is especially directed toward the benefit of the church. The apostle will love what Jesus loves, and Christ loves the church. Christ gave Himself specifically for the church because of His great love for her, and Christ's heart for the church will be formed in every apostle. Paul wrote *"Christ loved the church and gave himself up for her to make her holy, cleansing her by the washing with water through the word, and to present her to himself as a radiant church, without stain or wrinkle or any other blemish, but holy and blameless" (Ephesians 5: 25-27).*

Paul's description here of Christ's purpose is also the apostle's purpose. The apostle is called to **give himself for the church**, to **cleanse her through the word he brings**, and to **present her to Christ perfect**. We discovered in chapter 3 that this is the apostles purpose, but here we note that this passion is in the apostle's heart because of Christ.

Every believer in the church is called to be a servant. All are meant to have a servant-heart. Jesus said that if any amongst us desired to be the greatest of all, he should be the servant of all (Matthew 20:26). The church needs leadership, and it is as *leaders* that apostles *serve* the church. When an apostle exercises authority, instructs and corrects, provides vision and appoints the ministries and other leadership of the church, he is serving Christ and the church. We are not to think that a servant to the church has no power or authority. An apostle serves by the right use of authority over the house of God. The church needs such leadership, and Christ gives what we need by providing, firstly, apostles.

Paul said that he was commissioned by Christ to serve the church in this way. His commission, to be the church's servant, (Colossians 1: 25) was to present the word of God in its fullness to the church, proclaiming Christ, admonishing and teaching everyone, so that he could present everyone perfect in Christ (Colossians 1: 25-28). For Paul this meant suffering, affliction and hard labour but all enabled through a powerful spiritual energy given by the grace of God.

He said, *"I rejoice in what was suffered for you, and I fill up in my flesh what is still lacking in regard to Christ's afflictions, for the sake of his body, which is the church" (Colossians 1: 24).* What could this possibly mean, because we all know that Christ's suffering is complete? His work upon the cross for our redemption is a finished work. No one can add value to what Christ has done. He alone has carried our sins and borne our sorrows. Yet the apostle says his own sufferings are important in completing Christ's afflictions. This is a mystery indeed.

The explanation is this, I believe. Christ's sufferings are for your redemption, and this is indeed a finished work. You need no other Saviour, and no one else can by suffering make you more acceptable to God, pay the price for your sins, or provide your eternal redemption. Christ has done this for you, and He has done it completely and perfectly. Paul is referring to something else. He is talking about the pain and hard labour that is involved in bringing the church to maturity. All of us are called to share the sufferings of Christ in this world, and much of that suffering and pain is for the sake of the body. There is a price to be paid by every apostle to help bring the church to maturity for Christ.

The Grace of Apostleship

This takes us further in our understanding of apostolic grace. The grace of God is not just kindness or mercy, and grace is not just God's value system. Grace, when it reaches men and women, is always power. For example, in the gift of salvation, grace is the power that changes our hearts and delivers us from bondage. Every miracle, every answer to prayer, is grace received as power.

Thus apostles are empowered by grace, just as they were chosen by grace. *"We received grace and apostleship to call people from among all the Gentiles to the obedience that comes from faith"* said Paul (Romans 1: 5). With that apostleship was grace (power) that *enabled* them to bring the Gentiles to obedience.

Grace from God meant that the apostles not only had the power to do outwardly the things their ministry called for, but even more importantly there was an inner grace that kept their hearts and gave them the will and the passion to do what had to be done. Thus grace enables every apostle to endure. Consider the following descriptions of the apostolic life:

> *"We put no stumbling block in anyone's path, so that our ministry will not be discredited. Rather, as servants of God we commend ourselves in every way: in great endurance; in troubles, hardships and distresses; in beatings, imprisonments and riots; in hard work, sleepless nights and hunger; in purity, understanding, patience and kindness; in the Holy Spirit and in sincere love; in truthful speech and in the power of God; with weapons of righteousness in the right hand and in the left; through glory and dishonor, bad report and good report; genuine, yet regarded as impostors; known, yet regarded as unknown; dying, and yet we live on; beaten, and yet not killed; sorrowful, yet always rejoicing; poor, yet making many rich; having nothing, and yet possessing everything"* (2 Corinthians 6:3-10).

> *"We were under great pressure, far beyond our ability to endure, so that we despaired even of life. Indeed, in our hearts we felt the sentence of death. But this happened that we might not rely on ourselves but on God, who raises the dead"* (2 Corinthians 1:8-10).

"But we have this treasure in jars of clay to show that this all-surpassingpower is from God and not from us. We are hard pressed on every side, but not crushed; perplexed, but not in despair; persecuted, but not abandoned; struck down, but not destroyed. We always carry around in our body the death of Jesus, so that the life of Jesus may also be revealed in our body. For we who are alive are always being given over to death for Jesus' sake, so that his life may be revealed in our mortal body. So then, death is at work in us, but life is at work in you" (2 Corinthians 4:7-12).

An 'amazing' grace is at work in these apostles, and here we find principles of apostolic ministry. The apostle will not always look successful in the eyes of others, and success is neither the test nor the proof of just who God may be raising to be an apostle. Of greater significance is this; the power of grace that keeps an apostle is also at work in their hearts producing character and Christlikeness. This is of very great value to the church, and of great significance for the advancement of the kingdom. As a result, we are able to have apostles who are trustworthy stewards of the authority of Christ in the church. Thus Paul could write the following definitive statement, *"men ought to regard us as servants of Christ and as those entrusted with the secret things of God"* (1 Corinthians 4:1).

The Hallmark of an Apostle: GENTLENESS

The 'hallmark' of an apostle is gentleness. This may seem a surprising statement, since most people have been taught to think of signs and wonders as the mark of an apostle. Paul did say that signs and wonders are things that mark an apostle (2 Corinthians 12:12), but these are not obligatory proofs that apostles must give to prove themselves. Jesus went to Nazareth and could do no mighty miracles there because of their lack of faith (Mark 6:1-6). The problem was not with Jesus the apostle, but with the hearts of the people the apostle visited. On many occasions Jesus was asked for a sign to prove who He was, and He refused. He said, *"No sign will be given this generation except the sign of the prophet Jonah"* (Matthew 16:1-4). That sign was His death, burial and resurrection. Jesus refused to give signs to unbelieving people when they demanded them as proof of who He was.

Likewise, apostles today are under no obligation to provide signs and wonders for unbelieving Christians, and especially not if they demand them. Furthermore, the Spirit of Jesus in them will not be willing to give signs in such circumstances.

But wherever apostles minister and are received by humble Christians looking to Christ, the Lord Himself will confirm the word preached, with sovereign acts of God in accordance with Hebrews 2:4. For example, when I first went to India to build relationship with some ministry leaders, at their invitation, we prayed for many needs and saw various healings. On that visit I was not promoting the idea that I was an apostle, since there was little understanding there, and it would have been premature. But a miracle occurred of which I had no knowledge – a six year old girl who had never walked, began to walk from the day I prayed for her. On my next visit, the leader of the ministry told me that he wept with joy every time he saw that little girl, and he knew in his heart that God had sent them an apostle.

But we are here speaking of another kind of mark — a hallmark. A hallmark is the official symbol stamped into gold (and silver) which marks the standard of the gold, and is a sign of its quality and authenticity. As applied to apostles, there is a mark pressed into their character and ministry as a sign of their authenticity. That hallmark is gentleness — the gentleness of Christ.

Both Jesus and Paul have modeled this truth for us. Jesus said, *"Take my yoke upon you and learn from me, for I am gentle and humble in heart, and you will find rest for your souls" (Matthew 11:29).* No apostle, nor any minister of Christ, can afford to overlook the importance of these words. Jesus was specific in telling us that when yoked in partnership with Him, we were to learn His ways and walk in them. In particular we are to take upon ourselves His gentleness and humility. Notice that this is also the key to rest, as His words make plain. In the ministry, without the gentleness and humility of Christ, spiritual rest will be hard to obtain.

Jesus spoke these words publicly, but His most important students were His own apostles. If Christ the 'apostle and high priest of our confession' must of necessity minister from a position of gentleness, how much more should those He commissions as apostles to represent Him and carry His authority. This is a matter of such importance that, in those years when I was developing teaching about the role of an apostle, Christ woke me one night in the Philippines to impress upon me the importance of 'the hallmark of an apostle'.

Paul is repeatedly very clear about it. In his first letter to Timothy, he lists a number of things that Timothy, as an apostle, must pursue diligently. Gentleness is one of these (1 Timothy 6:11). He writes again to Timothy and reminds him that the Lord's servant must not quarrel, but instead must be kind, able to teach and never resentful. Then he adds, *"Those who oppose him he must gently instruct..." (2 Timothy 2:25).*

When Paul wrote to the Corinthians, he appealed to them, *"by the meekness and gentleness of Christ" (2 Corinthians 10:1).* The Philippians he instructed, *"Let your gentleness be evident to all" (Philippians 4:5).* And, in his letter to the Galatians we have that well-known listing of the *fruit of the Spirit* which every believer, especially the leaders who are to set an example for all, must be pleased to mature in. Gentleness is one of those important graces.

Possibly the best example of Paul's apostolic grace in gentleness is expressed in his first letter to the Thessalonians:

> *"As apostles of Christ we could have been a burden to you,* **but we were gentle among you, like a mother caring for her little children.** *We loved you so much that we were delighted to share with you not only the gospel of God but our lives as well, because you had become so dear to us. Surely you remember, brothers, our toil and hardship; we worked night and day in order not to be a burden to anyone while we preached the gospel of God to you. You are witnesses, and so is God, of how holy, righteous and blameless we were among you who believed. For you know that* **we dealt with each of you as a father deals with his own children, encouraging, comforting and urging you to live lives worthy of God,** *who calls you into his kingdom and glory" (1 Thessalonians 2:6-12).*

Having gentleness as a quality of heart does not mean an apostle is never strong, or does not take charge and exercise the authority of Christ, or does not discipline his 'children' and the church as a whole. Quite the reverse. The true apostle has such *love* that he is faithful to correct, to rebuke and to discipline wherever there is a need. *"I write these things when I am absent, that when I come I may not have to be harsh in my use of authority-the authority the Lord gave me for building you up, not for tearing you down" (2 Corinthians 13:10).*

The Great Love of the Apostle

The love of an apostle's heart will have been established and deepened through tribulation. As mentioned earlier, an apostle will face rejection as part of his preparation to be an apostle. There are those who will have vilified him, there may have been attempts to destroy him. Certainly there will have been much false accusation, and the undermining of false brethren. Often the apostle will have been made to look foolish or a failure.

Through it all, the apostle forgives. An apostle must learn to experience rejection, and even the hatred of others, yet have no bitterness in his own soul. He must come through these experiences with a sweet spirit, carrying no unforgiveness or resentment. He must not only forgive, but in his heart extend a mercy which goes beyond forgiveness, walking in what the Bible calls a mercy that triumphs over judgement (James 2:13). It is these very experiences that purify his love and deepen his intimacy with Christ. The Spirit of God is establishing in the heart of the apostle a genuine humility and a faithful love, upon which can be built an apostolic ministry that exercises great authority.

The love of an apostle is a significant grace. The apostle is given a love that encompasses large numbers of people and churches, and which longs for faithful relationships to be built in the body of Christ. Personal relationship with other ministries and all the believers is the motivating desire that touches every aspect of an apostle's ministry.

The true apostle is always thinking of you, praying for you, longing to see you. His heart is with you. He is joyful over you and burdened for you at the same time. There is upon his heart the sense of a constant care for you. All of these qualities we see plainly displayed in the letters of the apostles of the New Testament.

To the Philippians Paul wrote, *"In all my prayers for all of you, I always pray with joy... It is right for me to feel this way about all of you, since I have you in my heart;... God can testify how I long for all of you with the affection of Christ Jesus" (Philippians 1:4,7,8).*

For the apostle, loving the believers and churches is not simply a function of his job description — not just obedience to the commands of Christ. It is the passion of his heart, built into him by the anointing he has been given and by the work of the Spirit within him over many years. And so, whenever Paul writes, he reveals his heart, *"We loved you so much that we were delighted to share with you not only the gospel of God but our lives as well, because you had become so dear to us" (1 Thessalonians 2:8-9).*

For three years in Ephesus, Paul never ceased personally warning and exhorting the elders of the church, night and day, and with tears (Acts 20:31). And when he met them at Miletus to bid them a final farewell, *"They all wept as they embraced him and kissed him. What grieved them most was his statement that they would never see his face again" (Acts 20:37-38).* They loved him, and knew that in Paul they had a father who loved them.

This is always the way it should be in the church. The whole church of Jesus Christ is meant to be based on such relationships. The church is not meant to be an institution — the church was never meant to be an institution — or as we have today, a series of institutions. In this book I will seek to show the true relational nature of Christianity. Meanwhile, if we bear in mind the picture we have of the relationship between Paul and the Ephesians elders, then we have something which will help us see what the church is meant to look and feel like for every believer.

Everyone Paul knew he loved, and longed to see them. *"Night and day we pray most earnestly that we may see you again and supply what is lacking in your faith" (1 Thessalonians 3:10)* he wrote to one church, and likewise to Timothy he bares his heart, *"Recalling your tears, I long to see you, so that I may be filled with joy" (2 Timothy 1:4).*

At one point Paul found it necessary to 'boast' to defend his ministry, in a context where to defend his own ministry was to defend the purpose of God for the gospel and the Gentiles. He listed an incredible array of punishments and violent opposition he had experienced against himself, including floggings and beatings, as well as shipwrecks and a multitude of dangers. On the list is the danger of false brethren, and many other struggles and privations. But he crowns the list with this, *"Besides everything else, I face daily the pressure of my concern for all the churches. Who is weak, and I do not feel weak? Who is led into sin, and I do not inwardly burn?" (2 Corinthians 11:28-29).* This is the spirit of every apostle.

We should not think that Paul was an exceptional case, and the rest of us are excused from such excellence in apostolic ministry. Rather, Paul was to be the model from whom many would learn of the grace that is available to *every* apostle. And Paul's example to the end of his life was, *"I press on..." (Philippians 3:12).* No apostle can be satisfied with what has been achieved, nor his own progress in the faith. He cannot settle where he is. There will be a constant looking for more of Christ, and a constant cry of the heart for the church to be conformed to Christ's image.

An apostle is generally unhappy if he goes to some place on ministry but cannot find genuine heart-to-heart relationship with the leaders in that place. The apostle is unsatisfied without meaningful relationship being the basis of all ministry, because this is what God Himself is looking for in the church.

A Heart to Discipline

The point has already been made that because of *love* the apostle will discipline. Often in the institutional church discipline has been avoided by those who should have applied it. Sometimes this is because of vested interest, and sometimes because of fear of man (people pressure), or because the spirit of the age is on the church.

But an apostle is motivated by a different spirit. Since he has the heart of a father, full of love for his children, he will discipline them. He fears the outcomes that will result from error or sin, in both the lives of believers and the life of the church, if he does not correct and discipline them. The love of God the Father and the wisdom of Christ are in the authority of the apostolic anointings that are upon him. This gives him something many leaders lack — the heart to discipline.

Hebrews 12: 5-13 gives the foundational truth we need. Discipline is always given to those regarded as sons, and it produces a harvest of righteousness and peace. Sadly, many churches have experienced a field of sorrows instead of a harvest, because they lacked the discipline of the Lord, which should have been brought by the spiritual fathers. Jesus Himself said, *"Those whom I love I rebuke and discipline" (Revelation 3:19).*

The apostle knows this is wisdom. Paul instructed his junior apostle, and every apostle today, *"Preach the Word; be prepared in season and out of season; correct, rebuke and encourage — with great patience and careful instruction" (2 Timothy 4:2)* but he had written earlier to Timothy to advise him *"Do not rebuke an older man harshly, but exhort him as if he were your father" (1 Timothy 5:1).* To Titus, his other faithful son in the apostolic ministry, he sent this instruction, *"Encourage and rebuke with all authority. Do not let anyone despise you" (Titus 2:15).*

To apply discipline requires courage. No one I have met in ministry ever really wants to do this, but those who fear the Lord and have a great love for the church and the saints will make wise decisions in the face of difficult choices. They will choose in favour of the holy commands of the Lord, and put the holiness and welfare of the church ahead of their own feelings and the selfishness of individuals.

An apostle will not allow the pressure of the opinions of others to keep him from applying discipline or bringing the commands of the Lord to the church. The New Testament refers in many places to the authority that apostles have for building up the church. Paul wrote to the Corinthians, *"Some of you have become arrogant... What do you prefer? Shall I come to you with a whip, or in love and with a gentle spirit?" (1 Corinthians 4:18, 21).* In a later letter he added, *"I write these things when I am absent, that when I come I may not have to be harsh in my use of authority — the authority the Lord gave me for building you up, not for tearing you down" (2 Corinthians 13:10).*

Humility

Enough has been said already to establish that we will find important character values being worked out in the life of every apostle by the Spirit of grace.

Admittedly, these are values and character attributes that are urged upon all Christians, not just apostles. In fact, if we are not growing in these graces we would need to go back to the cross, and test ourselves to see if we are in the faith at all (2 Corinthians 13:5). But when Christ appoints apostles, who must be an example to all believers, to exercise authority over the church, it is essential that the character of Christ be formed in them.

It is a myth of Christianity to think that we cannot recognise humility in ourselves. Both Jesus and Paul could speak honestly of their own humility, and they are our examples.

Jesus said to take His yoke upon us and learn from Him, and added, *"for I am gentle and humble" (Matthew 11:29)*. Thus we are to learn humility from Him, and walk in it. Jesus would not have commanded us to do this, if it was not something that an honest heart, with grace and faith, could do. Therefore it is possible to serve Christ in genuine humility, and to have some honest understanding of one's progress without being proud of it.

Paul, who has said to us all, *"I urge you to imitate me (1 Corinthians 4:16),* gave the following testimony before the Ephesian Elders. *"You know how I lived the whole time I was with you, from the first day I came into the province of Asia. I served the Lord with great humility and with tears..." (Acts 20: 18-19).*

Humility is the foundation upon which gentleness, the hallmark of the apostle, is built.

Patience

Patience becomes well-established at an apostolic level when the heart is at rest in Jesus Christ. That rest comes from learning gentleness and humility from Jesus, but also as a result of understanding *the way of grace* (rather than the way of works) in obtaining results in the lives of believers and building the kingdom of God. The apostle knows to trust and allow God to work, and to look for the way in which God will work.

The best results (and the only results that count), are obtained by looking to God for what He wants to do, and then cooperating with Him. Far too many rush out to try and do something for God. Too many others are doing something in Christ's name, but doing it for themselves. No grace attaches itself to man's methods.

Only by grace can the church and the kingdom be built. Any work done by any believer, including apostles, that is not carried along by a momentum of grace will achieve nothing of eternal spiritual value. There are many things done by believers and fivefold ministers which are done in their own strength, and sometimes these things look good in the eyes of man. However, if they have not been established by the grace of God, they will not stand the test of eternity, nor bring about a genuine maturing of the church.

Each of us needs to find a *flowing* of God's grace through our lives. We must enter rest to find this. Hebrews chapter 4 tells us that we enter the sabbath-rest of God through faith, obedience, and by ceasing from our own works. When we enter this rest, we are no longer relying on our own works but on God who works. Then grace flows, which is the *power* of God at work.

When we rest in Him, God works — but when we 'work', God quits.

Foundational to everything is the truth of grace. It is the foundation of the Gospel itself, and therefore must be maintained in purity in all aspects of the life of the church and the believer.

Paul was very strong in commanding the believers and the churches to follow the way of grace. He made it clear there is no middle ground — you either teach, believe and live the message of grace, or you have returned to the law. If you have departed from grace, you have departed from the gospel, and Christ is of no benefit to you. (See Galatians 1:6-10, 3:1-5, 3:10, 3:17-20, 5:2-12)

Patience does not mean that anything and everything in the church must be 'tolerated'. Paul showed no patience whatever with those who would bring falsehood into the church, nor with believers who followed such error. Paul was very quick to condemn the error, and very quick to correct those who had been deceived. This is because such things are contrary to the gospel, and entirely destructive of the work of the Spirit in the lives of believers and churches where such error takes root.

Paul was grieved about what happened in Galatia, because the lives of his sons and daughters were being destroyed by a great evil. The mixing of 'works' with grace is an evil, but most fail to recognise these important distinctions, even today.

I have included this teaching so that no one will get the impression that because gentleness, humility and patience are inherent in the nature of an apostle, the apostle is therefore soft, without backbone or strength, and overlooking weaknesses and problems. An apostle is no pushover. If you want the model for an apostle, think of Christ or Paul. Jesus, for example, was always quick to correct and rebuke His own disciples (Luke 9:55), as He did when they discouraged children (Mark 10: 13-16), and as He rebuked Peter for resisting

His statement that He would go to the cross (Matthew 16:21-23). Jesus entered Jerusalem on a donkey, which was a sign that He came as a humble servant, but He proceeded straight into the temple and, with great aggression turned over the tables and drove out the money changers with a whip (Matthew 21:5, 12). Paul also threatened to come to one church with a 'whip' (1 Corinthians 4:21).

A clear distinction must be made here. The discipline, rebuke or anger of Jesus or His apostles does not come from a heart that is angry, controlling or intolerant. Rather, it comes from a pure and sincere heart. The strength to correct, discipline and set things in order is actually rooted in the gentleness, humility and patience of the heart of the apostle.

The New Testament tells us that Christ has *"unlimited patience" (1 Tim 1:16)* so we should not be surprised when we find it a great, and greatly needed, quality of apostles. Paul's letters to Timothy and Titus were those of a senior apostle instructing young apostles who were members of his apostolic team. These letters are full of instructional training for apostles. Paul's life itself was, by and large, the training manual to be read by future apostles. He wrote, *"You... know all about my teaching, my way of life, my purpose, faith, patience, love, endurance, persecutions, sufferings..." (2 Timothy 3: 10-11).* One of the qualities listed here alongside his *"way of life"* and *"purpose"* was his patience. A few verses later he instructs Timothy to preach, correct, rebuke and encourage *"with great patience and careful instruction" (2 Timothy 4:2).*

In discussing the patience of an apostle, so far we have mainly implied that this is a patience with people, but of course patience in the scriptures is more often concerned with *perseverance.* When you consider the biblical material concerning the patience of Job, and the patient waiting of Abraham, we realise this to be a major part of the work of faith in obtaining from God all that He has promised, and seeing the work of God established in the land. Holy scripture says, *"imitate those who through faith and patience inherit what has been promised" (Hebrews 6: 12),* and the writer to the Hebrews goes on to speak specifically of Abraham who, *"after waiting patiently,... received what was promised" (Hebrews 6: 15).*

Apostles are called to build up, by grace, the work of God in the nations. Every apostle can expect a great work of patience in faith and perseverance to be established in him by the Holy Spirit.

Trustworthiness

It is the heart of God to prepare and appoint faithful sons as trustworthy apostles of Christ over the church. It is a grief to the heart of God if these servants are not trusted by those they are sent to serve. Paul made it plain, *"So then, men ought to regard us as servants of Christ and as those entrusted with the secret things of God" (1 Corinthians 4:1).*

It has never been God's method to appoint committees or institutions to carry His anointings and watch over His works — it has always been *individuals* that He has entrusted with every purpose He has brought to the earth. He entrusted Moses, and the testimony of scripture is that Moses was faithful in all God's house (Hebrews 3:2,5). He entrusted Abraham, and Abraham became our father in the sight of God, and the father from whom came the promised seed that would bless all nations, because he obeyed God's voice (Genesis 22:18). He entrusted David, the one who was the man after God's own heart (Acts 13:22). These are but a few examples from the many.

Where would salvation history be if God did not entrust individuals with authority, power and purpose? Where would we be without Joshua, or Gideon, or Jeremiah, or Nehemiah, Elijah, Elisha, John the Baptist, or Peter, John, and Paul? There would be no salvation history, and no church of the Lord Jesus Christ, without those individuals who have yielded to God, who not only received a trust, but who gave up all, entrusting themselves to Him, as Paul shows by his testimony. *"I know whom I have believed, and am convinced that he is able to guard what I have entrusted to him for that day" (2 Timothy 1:12).*

Where would we be without Augustine, for example, or Wycliffe, or Luther, Knox, Wesley, William Carey, Hudson Taylor, Watchmen Nee, David Livingstone, Count Zinzendorf, and William Booth? These are just a few from amongst a great host, both men and women. God has always used anointed individuals for His purposes, and He is not about to change.

It is true that some falter, and a few fall, like Adam, Balaam and Judas. Yet all the while God knows exactly what He is doing. He places trust where He chooses, and expects His people to trust Him by believing His word, and with submitted obedient hearts, trust and submit to those He anoints to lead them.

Tell me this is not what God required of the children of Israel under Moses, or the Jews under Nehemiah. Tell me this is not what God ordained for the early church under the apostles. The work of grace can only ever be built on trust, which is why the believers are called to walk in intimate relationship with one another. God calls us to know well, to love, to serve, and to be committed to, those He places over us in the Lord. *"Now we ask you, brothers, to respect* (to know intimately) *those who work hard among you, who are over you in the Lord and who admonish you. Hold them in the highest regard in love because of their work" (1 Thessalonians 5:12-13).* Every believer must have the same heart for his leader (his pastor, his apostle) as Paul did for his fellow workers and the churches. Nothing else is genuine Christianity.

When we trust and give our hearts to the one over us in the Lord, we will come into a better place — a place of greater blessings — because the one God places over us will have the very thing we need. Developing a right relationship with them will be the catalyst to bring the change of circumstances or the blessing we need. Often the relationship with our leader will be the key to the things for which we have been praying.

Read now the following passage with eyes to see these principles — that God anoints an individual human vessel to carry forward His purposes, and relationship with that person is for your personal good:

*"Surely you have heard about the administration of God's grace that was **given to me for you**, that is, the mystery made **known to me by revelation**, as I have already written briefly. In reading this, then, you will be able to understand **my insight into the mystery of Christ**, which was not made known to men in other generations as it has now been **revealed by the Spirit to God's holy apostles and prophets**. This mystery is that through the gospel the Gentiles are heirs together with Israel, members together of one body, and sharers together in the promise in Christ Jesus.*

*I became a servant of this gospel by the gift of **God's grace given me** through the working of his power. Although I am less than the least of all God's people, **this grace was given me:** to preach to the Gentiles the unsearchable riches of Christ, and to make plain to everyone the administration of this mystery, which for ages past was kept hidden in God, who created all things. His intent was that now, through the church, the manifold wisdom of God should be made known to the rulers and authorities in the heavenly realms, according to his eternal purpose which he accomplished in Christ Jesus our Lord. In him and through faith in him we may approach God with freedom and confidence. **I ask you, therefore, not to be discouraged because of my sufferings for you, which are your glory"** (Ephesians 3:2-13).* See also 1 Timothy 1:10-11, and Titus 1:3.

Those whom the Lord anoints to be apostles are trustworthy, and God intends that we should trust them. It is to the glory of God that the saints trust those He sends, and God's purposes are enabled to be advanced. When loved and trusted, apostles are helped to be even more successful in the progress of their stewardship. They will have the benefit of agreement, the saints standing with them, to advance the kingdom of Christ.

The saints are not to be full of fear, worried about giving authority and trust to individuals. Jesus Christ is an individual, and is represented by individuals. This is ever God's method, because *"God is love" (1 John 4:8)*. God will never work except personally through individuals. If you want to see the greater glory of God in the world, you will need to look for God in personal relationships with other believers and especially with those who are over you in the Lord.

The New Testament witness is that apostles are trustworthy. The scriptures do say there will be false apostles, but we are meant to test those who claim to be apostles, and reject the false. (We are also told there will be false Christ's, and false teachers. This information does not cause us to reject Christ, or the teachers we know to be godly.) Once we understand who the apostle is to whom we should relate, and have the witness of the Holy Spirit, we are meant to trust God and give the apostle our love from the heart.

The following passage is the biblical position on the heart motivation of the true apostle:

"You know, brothers, that our visit to you was not a failure. We had previously suffered and been insulted in Philippi, as you know, but with the help of our God we dared to tell you his gospel in spite of strong opposition. For the appeal we make does not spring from error or impure motives, nor are we trying to trick you. On the contrary, we speak as men approved by God to be entrusted with the gospel. We are not trying to please men but God, who tests our hearts. You know we never used flattery, nor did we put on a mask to cover up greed-God is our witness. We were not looking for praise from men, not from you or anyone else.

As apostles of Christ we could have been a burden to you, but we were gentle among you, like a mother caring for her little children. We loved you so much that we were delighted to share with you not only the gospel of God but our lives as well, because you had become so dear to us. Surely you remember, brothers, our toil and hardship; we worked night and day in order not to be a burden to anyone while we preached the gospel of God to you.

You are witnesses, and so is God, of how holy, righteous and blameless we were among you who believed. For you know that we dealt with each of you as a father deals with his own children, encouraging, comforting and urging you to live lives worthy of God, who calls you into his kingdom and glory" (1 Thessalonians 2:1-12).

This passage of Holy Scripture instructs us that these are *"men approved by God to be entrusted"*, whose *"appeal ...does not spring from error or impure motives"*, and who are not motivated by *"greed"* or *"praise"*. They are *"gentle"*, they *"love"* the saints, they *"work hard"*, and they live *"holy righteous and blameless lives"*, constantly *"encouraging, comforting"* and exhorting the saints according to the will of God. We must accept that these statements of scripture represent what God does in the heart of every apostle anointed by Christ and sent by God to the church today.

To fellow apostles, I would address these few words. We have been given a great trust, a great authority, and a great opportunity. To us is being given also, great power and freedom. This is not freedom from accountability, but it is freedom from the control of institutionalised vain religion.

Remember that it is Christ who gives the power and freedom, but Christ will judge. In answer to Peter's question, *"Lord, are you telling this parable to us, or to everyone?" (Luke 12:41)* Jesus gave a clear response to His apostles which included the following, *"From everyone who has been given much, much will be demanded; and from the one who has been entrusted with much, much more will be asked" (Luke 12:48).*

Paul was well aware of the need to maintain the discipline of his calling in his own life (1 Corinthians 9:27), and for his followers to guard their own hearts. To his faithful son in the apostolic ministry he wrote this appeal, *"Timothy, guard what has been entrusted to your care. Turn away from godless chatter and the opposing ideas of what is falsely called knowledge, which some have professed and in so doing have wandered from the faith" (1 Timothy 6:20-21).* In his later letter to Timothy he reminded him again, *"Guard the good deposit that was entrusted to you - guard it with the help of the Holy Spirit who lives in us" (2 Timothy 1:13-14).*

This discussion of trustworthiness began with a statement from Paul, *"So then, men ought to regard us as servants of Christ and as those entrusted with the secret things of God" (1 Corinthians 4:1).* His following statement was, *"now it is required that those who have been given a trust must prove faithful".*

Are there Other Kinds of Apostles?

It is important to discuss this question, because in recent years there have been increasing references to 'apostles to business'. The idea that some apostles are called to minister in the business world, some to government etc., has become a popular feature of some apostolic and prophetic conferences.

This raises the question of whether this is a different kind of apostle. Is the heart of this apostle motivated differently? Does this kind of apostle have a different agenda? Does this kind of apostle have a separate purpose from the apostles of the New Testament, or is the passionate love for the church, and the anointings and call to build the church, the same?

There are apostles who carry a great anointing to minister to businessmen, and who have the wisdom of Christ concerning finance. Actually all apostles have an anointing to handle finance and speak to businessmen and government, but there are those who have exceptional anointings and a specific function to serve in this area.

Such an apostle I have, I am glad to report, as a very good friend.

Dr Sim Jek Choo had been a dentist in Malacca, Malaysia. This great brother and his wife Siew Hong lived an amazing life of faith and generosity — loving people, witnessing for Christ, and always giving obediently. They were constant financial sowers into God's kingdom, and they were always quick to hear His voice in the distribution of their money.

The time came when Christ appointed them to establish a new ministry in another land. They were called to leave their business and profession, and relocate their family to Brisbane, Australia. They have been ministering out of Brisbane as their base since 1989.

I consider Dr Sim to be the most wonderful of brothers. He is a big 'teddy bear' with a gravelly voice. He is full of love, has a passionate heart in the things of God, and I love to hear him speak. I am always overjoyed to see him, and the sound of his voice even on the telephone blesses my heart. It is a pleasure to sit under his exhortations in a meeting.

Dr Sim has a powerful anointing in financial matters. Listen to him speak for a few minutes, and you know that here is a rare gift of God. His closest friends are Chairmen and Managing Directors of national and multinational businesses in Singapore, Malaysia and Australia. He is a regular speaker at meetings of businessmen in Southeast Asia, and he will often help businessmen set affairs in order, or bring an apostolic word of grace that releases a businessman.

Visiting a church to preach on one occasion, a businessman approached him to say that he would like to start a business, his purpose being to sow his profits into the Kingdom of God. He sowed an initial gift to Dr Sim, and God blessed him with one hundred and eighty thousand dollars within two weeks.

God has sent Dr Sim to many churches in Singapore and Malaysia to help to raise finances for the pastors, and also for their building projects. Once when in Kuala Lumpur, a pastor was desperately in need of $56,000 to pay for his building renovation. Dr Sim told him to arrange a special meeting on a Monday night, where he shared the word of God with that pastor's congregation and received an offering from his people immediately afterwards. That night the pastor could not sleep, and he wept all night, because they collected $58,000, two thousand more than he needed to pay the debt.

Recently Dr Sim was invited to speak in two days of meetings in Penang. There he felt led by the Lord to receive an offering for the pastor of the church, which amounted to $19,000. The pastor later shared that she had been praying for $17,000 for the renovation of the church, and rejoiced that God sent more than she needed. God is a God of miracles, and signs and wonders confirm the word of God.

But Dr Sim and Siew Hong walk with Christ on a very challenging path of faith. They live by faith in God, trusting God for everything. Dr Sim returned recently from several weeks ministry, with gifts and offerings of $22,000. He had preached and poured his heart out for weeks on a gruelling schedule, and came home tired. He stepped off the plane looking forward to being home, and needing sleep. When he arrived home, he went straight to bed.

As his head touched the pillow, he heard the Lord speak, "Sow out $50,000." This is the last word any of us would have wanted to hear. No longer would there be that satisfaction of money in hand. But Dr Sim and Siew Hong live by this kind of faith. He immediately began to send out thousands of dollars. By the time I saw him a few weeks later, he had already sown over $35,000 in progressive obedience to the guidance of the Holy Spirit.

Financial Grace Imparted

Dr Sim receives financial miracles, and imparts the grace of God for them to others.

Some time ago, he wanted to buy the acreage next door to the ministry property he already owns. The price being asked was $320,000. At that time he had $45,000, which he wanted to use as a deposit, but he heard the Lord speak "Give away the $45,000." In obedience he sowed the money, the price on the land dropped to $280,000, and within six months the Lord had provided the full payment for the property.

In his fellowship is a widow who badly needed a new car. Under Dr Sim's leadership she had for years understood the principles of sowing and reaping, and had been walking in them by faith. She had also been saving towards a new car, and had managed to save $10,000. One day Dr Sim brought a word to the meeting of the fellowship. The Lord had said, "Sow your *precious* seed". She understood this to mean she was to sow what was dear to her heart, her savings of $10,000. In obedience she sowed — and within two weeks she was given a brand new car, and $20,000 cash.

Earlier this year I was visiting his ministry to speak in a meeting. For two days I shared conversations and meals with Dr Sim, and slept in the guest accommodation of his ministry centre. At that time I needed a new car for the ministry, and I had arranged a very good deal — I could buy a new $35,000 car, for only $25,000. I was to pick it up the day I left Dr Sim's, but because I had no money for a car (I had not one dollar in the ministry budget for another car) I was arranging finance. A loan had been approved.

While at Dr Sim's, the Spirit of the Lord came upon me to believe for financial provision. I felt the Lord was saying not to take the loan, but write a cheque for the full amount and believe God for the money. This I did the next day, and the finances of the ministry were released, as the Lord had promised.

I also needed finance for the preparation and publishing of this book. That night in the meeting, Dr Sim arose and declared that the Lord had, just then, told him to give me $5000 for the publishing of the book. He proceeded to take an offering for that purpose, and included the additional $5000 of his own.

Do All Apostles Have the Same Nature?

I have taken time to illustrate the financial anointing that is on such an apostle, so that we could answer the questions we asked above in a more informed manner. Do apostles to business have the same passions, the same calling, the same values, the same anointings, and the same purpose, as the apostles that I have described in this chapter? In short, do they have the same *nature*?

The answer is, they do, and they must! I told how Dr Sim had been called to Australia to establish a new ministry. What was that ministry? It was to build the unity of the body of Christ! And when you hear him speak, his passion is for the church, and the maturity of the believers.

Every apostle, without exception, has this heart! The things that are described here apply to all apostles, regardless of any specific task they are given, or any particular anointing that is at work through them by the grace of Christ. There will be apostles to nations, to people groups, to cities and regions, and there will be apostles to the poor and downtrodden, to outcasts, and to every corner of the planet.

Should anyone claim to be an apostle, but not have an apostle's heart, the claim is to be questioned. There will be Christians who will be greatly blessed by God in business, and who will be a blessing to others in business — they may be very generous, and sow large sums into vital ministries — and they may provide great leadership both in business and in the church. Still, all of that does not make them an apostle. Every apostle to business or to government or to whatever other special focus of ministry, will have the nature of an apostle as laid out in Holy Scripture, and will have the apostle's calling and passion for the body of Christ.

The Benchmarks of Every Apostle

Here we introduce a new term, another kind of 'mark'. A benchmark is a surveyor's mark indicating a point in a line of levels. A series of these benchmarks describes a level. The term benchmark has come to mean a 'criterion'. A criterion is a principal taken as a standard of judging something.

In this chapter on the nature of an apostle we have discovered a series of benchmarks. They are the principles upon which we judge what an apostle is, and what an apostle is not. This sets for us a level by which we can measure the true apostolic ministry.

There will be no exception to these benchmarks, because this is the biblical revelation concerning the nature of an apostle. Outside of the biblical revelation, we have no authority to propose a different kind of apostle. We must not bring upon the church the mistake of attaching to other useful and powerful gifts of ministry the term apostle. Let us be very clear about what an apostle is.

The Power Anointing is about to be Poured Out

For years I have believed and preached that the full anointing, the greater power anointing for apostles and prophets, has not yet been given.

The church has been in a season where for many years the Lord has been preparing and raising apostles and prophets in every nation. Many are ministering publicly as apostles, and providing a leadership and spiritual covering to churches as apostles. This is a wonderful progress towards the restoration of the apostolic church for the last days, and towards the building of the new wineskin of the church.

However a greater and more specific anointing is coming. Apostles and prophets are not yet functioning in the full capacity of these offices, because we have been in a time of training, transition and preparation. On the whole, many apostles are still being trained for a future role.

Recently I was invited to preach again at the monthly meeting of the Quezon City Pastoral Movement. I taught on spiritual covering — that apostles are the covering of Christ for the body of Christ. In preaching, I illustrated the apostolic covering being built by the Lord for the body of Christ today with reference to the clothing of Jesus. When Jesus was crucified, the soldiers gambled for His tunic, because it was a valuable garment and they did not want to divide it.

The tunic of Jesus fitted the description of the garment of the high priest, which Aaron wore first as high priest. It was to be woven in one piece, and especially strengthened at the neck because the garment of the high priest was never to be torn. As an apostle, Jesus was sent to fulfil His duty as our great high priest to which He had been appointed, and He wore the symbolic garment of the high priest. His tunic was woven in one piece from top to bottom, and at the cross the soldiers fulfilled the Lord's requirements for the symbol – *"Let's not tear it"*, they said (John 19:24).

That day I preached that this garment of Jesus was a sign and an illustration of the spiritual covering that is required for the body of Christ (see chapter 7). A covering of seamless unity, woven from the top down by God, and which must not be divided. This is clearly meant to be symbolic of the apostolic covering for the church, which God is now building.

The next morning I was alone, when the Lord asked for my attention. He said, "I have something for you today". When I sat He directed me to Psalm 133, and I read these words:

How good and pleasant it is when brothers live together in unity!
It is like precious oil poured on the head, running down on the beard,
running down on Aaron's beard, down upon the collar of his robes.
It is as if the dew of Hermon were falling on Mount Zion.
For there the LORD bestows his blessing, even life forevermore.
(Psalm 133:1-3)

I had read these words for years, and knew them well from memory. Yet for the first time in my life I noticed that it was specifically the collar of *Aaron's* robe that was to be touched by an anointing of amazing proportions that would come as a result of unity. Suddenly I realised that this Psalm had an application to the apostolic anointing specific to the *covering* of Christ for the body of Christ. As I was reading the Psalm, the Spirit of the Lord spoke, and said, "The apostolic anointing is about to be poured out."

I knew that those of us who were already established in apostolic ministry should not take for granted our portion in this anointing. It would be foolish to think that with the greater anointing about to be poured out, we would automatically be recipients. Humbly and sincerely I look to God to include me in what He is about to do — to grant me also this greater anointing.

An Undivided Heart

Finally, an apostle has *one* heart, and it is *Christ's*. By that I mean an apostle has an *undivided* heart, and it is completely given over, surrendered, submitted, yielded, to Jesus. Grace has brought this about — Christ has 'captured' the heart of the apostle, and granted grace to stand. This is also the secret of the apostle's authority.

The apostle has one love and it is Christ. You would not expect to find in an apostle a love of the world mixed with a love for righteousness. The prayer of the psalmist was *"...give me an undivided heart, that I may fear your name" (Psalm 86:11).* The true apostle walks in the fear of the Lord. There is an uprightness in him, a pure heart, that looks to Christ, points others to Christ, and yields all to Christ.

This undivided heart that yields all is the spirit of apostleship. It should be the heart of every believer, for the whole church is meant to be an apostolic people.

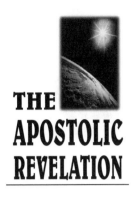

THE APOSTOLIC REVELATION

Chapter 5

The Authority of an Apostle

The question of authority is one of the pivotal issues for the reformation of the church. As we often say, "this is where the rubber hits the road". Either apostles do have authority over the church on behalf of Christ, or they do not.

If apostles do have authority, then the church needs to listen to them. If there is no apostolic authority, then it remains for every church, movement or denomination to establish their own authority and leadership systems — they may do what is right in their own eyes. That is precisely what we *have* had, creating an inordinate amount of disunity in the body of Christ. A divisive, denominationalistic spirit has often ensnared the church, and the world sees it as both a mess and a joke. Jesus said that when we are one, as the Father and the Son are one, the world will believe (John 17:20-23).

If a church or denomination rejects apostolic authority, they have closed their hearts to much of what the scriptures say about the leadership and structure of the church; especially the means by which Christ exercises *His* leadership and authority in the church. Such groups are operating on a foundation of limited understanding. Any denomination or ministry built on a limited view of the biblical revelation of leadership, must by definition be something other, or less than, what Christ really wants.

This is not to say they are not good people — not great Christian ministries in other ways. But *apostolic* authority is lacking, and therefore the body is disjointed. According to Ephesians chapter 4, the problem of the body being disjointed, disunited, infantile, and unstable (Ephesians 4:14-16) is precisely the problem to be addressed and overcome by the ministry appointments of Christ *which must include apostles and prophets* (Ephesians 4:11-13).

All Authority

Undisputed amongst believers should be the truth that Christ holds all authority, given by the Father. He Himself said, *"All authority in heaven and on earth has been given to me" (Matthew 28:18)*, and the apostle Peter explained that, *"...Jesus Christ, ...has gone into heaven and is at God's right hand - with angels, authorities and powers in submission to him" (1 Peter 3:21-22)*. Paul made it even clearer, with passages like Ephesians 2:20-23, and Colossians 1:15-20, and 2:9-10.

Even earlier, there was a noticeable change in the authority structure of ministry as soon as Jesus began to teach. Everyone noticed that He taught as one who had authority, so unlike the religious leaders of the day (Matthew 7:28-29) — and this authority He immediately began to divest to others, beginning with the apostles (Mark 3:15, Luke 9:1,10:1,10:19).

To be vested with authority will be the first manifestation of an apostle's commission. When the twelve were appointed by Jesus to be apostles, He sent them out to preach and *"...to have authority to drive out demons" (Mark 3:15)*. At this point the authority was over demons, but the authority of the twelve was progressively expanded. By the time we come to Matthew 28 and the Great Commission, Christ bestows His complete *"authority in heaven and on earth"* upon the apostles, and ultimately, to the church through them. We see this because He says *"therefore go"*. There is a clear implication in Jesus' words: the authority of Jesus over all things has been placed upon the apostles. In that authority they will go to all nations to bring a people to obedience to Christ, and in exercising this authority Christ will be with them.

The authority of Christ is to be exercised on earth through His body, the church. *"And God placed all things under his feet and appointed him to be head over everything for the church, which is his body, the fullness of him who fills everything in every way" (Ephesians 1:22-23)*. The scriptures abound with such amazing statements, and the intent is for us to understand our high position in Christ. God placed everything under Christ's feet, but the verse is specific in its reference to the church. We are His feet under which all things have been placed, and we are the fullness of Christ who fills everything. This shows us the extent of the authority we are meant to exercise.

No Authority without Submission to Authority

But wait! There can be no authority without submission to authority. Unless they are in submission to another, no one in the church has any *genuine* authority.

Many scriptures call us into this place of submission, to one another as well as to Christ. When we find this right spirit of submission, true spiritual authority can flow to us and through us.

This is why there must be apostles, or the fullness of Christ's authority does not come upon the church. Only through submission to apostles under Christ will the church have *apostolic* authority.

The goal for the whole body is to function in *apostolic* authority. Every believer may have this apostolic power, as was common in the New Testament. Examples abound. Stephen, though not an apostle, was *"a man full of God's grace and power, (who) did great wonders and miraculous signs among the people" (Acts 6:8)*. Philip the evangelist went to a city in Samaria, proclaimed Christ, and the signs and wonders God gave were incredible. The whole city was brought to faith (Acts 8:4-13).

Understand that these believers were in submission to the apostles (Acts 8:14), and the secret of their power was in this submission. This is the most basic principle of biblical authority, being clearly laid out in the Gospels.

Here we find this foundational concept, *'The centurion replied, "Lord, I do not deserve to have you come under my roof. But just say the word, and my servant will be healed. For I myself am a man under authority, with soldiers under me. I tell this one, 'Go,' and he goes; and that one, 'Come,' and he comes. I say to my servant, 'Do this,' and he does it." When Jesus heard this, he was astonished and said to those following him, "I tell you the truth, I have not found anyone in Israel with such great faith" ' (Matt 8:8-11)*.

Jesus was amazed to find someone with such perfect insight into Christ's own authority. Jesus had authority over all things and could freely exercise God's power because He was so completely submitted to the Father. The Centurion rightly understood that only someone in submission to authority can have authority rest on them. He knew instinctively that Christ's submission was the secret of His power. And that is how apostolic authority flows to the church.

Apostolic Authority Flows Down

Apostles are called into complete submission to Jesus, and those who yield their will to Him will carry great authority. The other leaders and ministries of the church are meant to recognise the authority of Christ on the apostles, and give the willing submission of their own hearts to Christ *and the apostle whom Christ sends* to them. By extension of this principle, apostolic authority will then flow upon the whole ministry of the church, and to every believer.

Each individual believer is meant to be in submission to the authority of the leaders that are over them in the Lord. The beautiful writings in the book of Hebrews sets it plainly before us, *"Obey your leaders and submit to their authority. They keep watch over you as men who must give an account. Obey them so that their work will be a joy, not a burden, for that would be of no advantage to you" (Hebrews 13:17).*

There Must Be an Authority in the Church

Christ's headship must have expression in the church, but it is not through leadership systems that have been established by human processes, such as the election or selection of popes, bishops, general superintendents, or whatever else. Neither is it through institutional boards and committees. Christ Himself chooses, anoints and sends apostles.

Apostles are appointed by Christ, not man. The church is not meant to select its own leaders, although we must be diligent in 'testing' them so as to recognise them. Some may object by saying that in the early church when the deacons were needed, the apostle Peter said, *"Brothers, choose seven men from among you" (Acts 6:3).* I point out that they were not choosing the spiritual leaders of the church. Rather, they were looking for good stewards to take responsibility in addressing a need, and Peter exercised an apostolic authority in delegating the responsibility.

Clear authority is needed in every household, and the church is the household of God (Ephesians 2:19). There are to be clear lines of authority in the church, and God has plainly told us the way He wants them. When the church is in divine order and we function according to the wisdom of God, the blessing, grace and power of God flowing to the church greatly increases. When apostles are received and allowed to speak with authority into the life of the church, apostolic grace blesses the church. When the church is in submission to apostles, apostolic authority and power is available to the believers.

Authority and power is much needed *by* the church, therefore apostolic authority is needed *over* the church!

A Different Style of Authority

Note at this point that Christ's leadership and authority is expressed with a different spirit, and with different motives compared to the leadership and authority systems of this world. Jesus explained this to His apostles, *"You know that the rulers of the Gentiles lord it over them, and their high officials exercise authority over them. Not so with you. Instead, whoever wants to become great among you must be your servant, and whoever wants to be first must be your slave - just as the Son of Man did not come to be served, but to serve, and to give his life as a ransom for many" (Matthew 20:25-28).*

No one should think that these words of Jesus mean that leaders in the church do not have authority over the believers, or over the church as a whole. This would be to argue that Christ has no authority over the church or the believers, because in this teaching He gives Himself as the example of how those in church leadership are to lead.

Now Christ also referred to *"whoever wants to be first"*. The New Testament says that God has set the apostle *"first"* in the church (1 Corinthians 12:28), so this instruction applies then, first of all, to apostles. They are slaves to the church, but make this careful distinction. They are slaves *to*, but not slaves *of* the church. They are bond-slaves of Jesus Christ, and He sends them to serve the church. They will serve the church, as His slaves (and His friends), to provide leadership and government, and to exercise His authority on His behalf for the good of the church. The spirit of the apostles will reflect the nature of this arrangement, i.e. the nature of their relationship with Christ and His bride.

Apostles Give Freedom

Apostles are not controlling. This is not the purpose of their authority. The whole focus of the ministry of an apostle is to bring the believers and the churches into the liberty of the Spirit (2 Corinthians 3:17) and the freedom of Christ (Galatians 5:1). This must be clearly understood or we will create great misunderstanding. Paul referred twice to *"the authority the Lord gave us for building you up rather than pulling you down" (2 Corinthians 10:8, 13:10).*

Christ does not send apostles to create bondage, nor to make the church subservient. The apostle will not make the church dependent on himself, nor keep the church in a place of weakness for his own benefit. This would be the work of a false apostle, or a 'hireling', or a leader who was insecure or motivated by fleshly ambition.

The true apostle comes to bring the church to maturity in Christ, to raise 'sons' to be 'fathers' in their own right, to commission others with authority for the work of Christ, to impart gifts, grace and opportunity to every believer whose heart is right before God. The apostle will lift up and honour; the apostle will release and give freedom. The apostle's goal is the freedom and maturity in Christ of every believer, every minister, and every church, and to see each one clothed with apostolic anointing and power.

The apostle's commission is to present every believer perfect in Christ, and to present the church mature and spotless to Christ (Colossians 1:22,24-25,28-29, Ephesians 5:26-27). For this purpose the apostle works to build up the strength and freedom of the believers, that they may stand. When a true apostle becomes the spiritual father of a pastor, and the principal apostle of a congregation, his purpose will be to bring them into better things. His heart's desire is for that pastor and those people to succeed, and that as his own dear children they will have an even greater success than he himself has enjoyed.

The Specific Authorities of an Apostle

A review of the New Testament shows us a clear pattern for the exercise of apostolic authority in the life of the church. Again, Paul and his relationship with the churches is the apostolic model given by inspiration of the Spirit of God and recorded in Holy Scripture.

By examination of the biblical revelation, we are able to see how the relationship of the apostle and the churches functioned. We can see the specific areas of church life and leadership over which the apostle exercised direct authority. We also recognise areas of church life over which the apostle is not seen to exercise authority at all.

In this chapter we are speaking in general of the authority of all apostles, but we are dealing especially with the relationship between what we shall call a 'primary apostle' and the churches over which he has been appointed, or developed God-ordained relationship. I will further define this term a little later. Paul was the primary apostle for Corinth, Ephesus, Galatia, Philippi, Colossae, Thessalonica, Crete and other places, but not for Rome or Jerusalem.

We see that the apostles exercised complete authority in matters of doctrine. No local church could go its own way on doctrine, or else the apostle would quickly deal with them, as Paul did with the Galatians. In addition, the apostle always had an authority to speak concerning the spiritual life of the church. He would call the church to order, and instruct them how to live both personally and corporately. In matters of church discipline, he had final authority — if the church did not discipline itself, he acted.

Furthermore, the apostles appointed the elders of the churches (see the definition of New Testament eldership in chapter 8) and maintained an authority over those elders. The apostles also addressed relationships, the attitudes of the believers to their leaders, and the attitude of the church to the apostle. And, the apostle was entitled to their financial support, as well as their love, prayers and honour. All of this was the apostle's province.

However, certain things you will not find addressed as matters of authority when the apostle wrote to the churches. Aside from appealing for generous offerings, and with an acknowledgement that they owed him his own support, the apostle did not govern the finance of the local church. He did not control their offerings. Nor did he own their property, or tell them what to do with property. Neither did the apostle control the constitution of the local church. He made no comment on how the church should be internally structured, or what should be their internal rules for order or government. Finally, the apostle did not set the vision for the local church.

Paul, at least in his letters, never spelt out specific local goals and objectives, or any immediate purpose, but focussed on great spiritual goals. For example, he pursued the great goal of presenting everyone perfect in Christ (Colossians 1:28), and the need for the believers to be of one heart and one mind (Philippians 1:27, 2:2, 1 Peter 3:8), advancing in the love of Christ (Philippians 1:9), and to be built together to be a dwelling in which God will live by His Spirit (Ephesians 2:22).

Naturally, however, today's apostles will certainly be advisors to the churches on every matter of church life.

The 'Local' Ministry

The local church is meant to be autonomous and self-governing. If, as we say they should, the leaders of the local church have authority over the finance, the property, the constitution, the vision and the local government of the church, then that church is indeed autonomous.

Still, the apostle has a key role, where in love and before Christ he holds the senior minister, the leadership team, and the church accountable. There is a general accountability in all things, but he has direct authority to hold them accountable in the *big* things — like unity, for example, and purity of heart, relationships, morality, discipline, doctrine, attitudes, holiness, love, Christlikeness, and passion for Christ.

However, the relationship between the pastor/leaders/church and the apostle is far more than accountability. This is a personal, caring, loving and mutually honouring, mutually helpful relationship. There is a great empowering which takes place for all ministry through apostolic relationships. We will deal with this more extensively elsewhere. It is also a fun relationship — usually there is great delight on both sides of the equation.

What we call the 'vision' should be established by the anointed leader or leaders of the local ministry. This is not usually the apostle, except of course in his own ministry. The local leader has the immediate authority over the ministry, but remains in an accountable relationship with an apostle.

The way in which churches and ministries govern themselves may vary greatly. The New Testament does not establish 'rules' concerning this, aside from the fact that the apostles appointed elders over the church in every town or city, and maintained an accountable relationship with those elders as well as with the church is a whole. There is a great deal of liberty for every ministry or congregation to be themselves.

Authority in Doctrine

From the beginning the believers *"devoted themselves to the apostles' teaching" (Acts 2:42-43).* The true Christian faith has always been the *apostolic* faith, and the church the *apostolic* church. The apostle Peter instructed, *"I want you to recall the words spoken in the past by the holy prophets and the command given by our Lord and Savior through your apostles" (2 Peter 3:2).*

Church doctrine is not just the special domain of theologians, and it is not theological colleges that determine by some scholastic process what true doctrine is. Of course the church has been blessed with many truly great teachers, theologians and authors. But apostles have anointing from Christ to clearly understand the truth of *"the apostles doctrine" (Acts 2:42 KJV),* and the responsibility to keep the church in the purity of it. It was apostles who set the doctrine of the church with authority. This is not suggesting that apostles in this day will change doctrine. We cling to the great historic doctrines of the Christian faith that were established by those first apostles, and which have been recorded faithfully and accurately in the Scriptures of the New Testament. As Paul said, *"What you heard from me, keep as the pattern of sound teaching, with faith and love in Christ Jesus" (2 Tim 1:13).*

Apostles today do have two primary responsibilities in the area of doctrine. One, to teach and maintain the doctrinal purity of the church and correct error, and two, to bring out of the Holy Scriptures the things we have not been able to see before. The apostles of the New Testament were given great revelation (2 Corinthians 12:7) and taught many things that are not fully understood today (Ephesians 3:2-5). These are alluded to in Holy Scripture, but the church does not always see or understand what is written. Apostles and prophets will help to *"enlighten"* the *"eyes of (our) heart" (Ephesians 1:18).*

The Holy Spirit is constantly bringing enlightenment to the church through many parts of the body (1 Corinthians 14:26, 30). Apostles hold final authority to determine that what enlightenment comes to the church is truly biblical and truly Christ. The following is an example of that authority. *"As I urged you when I went into Macedonia, stay there in Ephesus so that you may command certain men not to teach false doctrines any longer nor to devote themselves to myths and endless genealogies. These promote controversies rather than God's work - which is by faith. The goal of this command is love, which comes from a pure heart and a good conscience and a sincere faith" (1 Tim 1:3-5).*

Notice that the apostle has authority to *"command"*, an authority referred to repeatedly throughout the epistles. Note that this 'authority to command' is not only Paul's, but also Timothy's, who is here being instructed to command, not only the believers, but also those who are in error.

Paul encouraged his apostolic team in other responsibilities of the ministry also. In the same letter he urges, *"Command and teach these things. Don't let anyone look down on you because you are young, but set an example for the believers in speech, in life, in love, in faith and in purity" (1 Tim 4:11-13).* To Titus, his other faithful son, he writes, *"These, then, are the things you should teach. Encourage and rebuke with all authority. Do not let anyone despise you" (Titus 2:15).*

So we see that once the apostles have established doctrine, subordinate apostles maintain the pattern of that doctrine. They are not constantly recreating the pattern, but they cling to what has been revealed (1 Timothy 4:16, 2 Timothy 1:14).

Authority in Appointing Elders

The elders of the church should be appointed by apostles, not elected by the believers. We can say this because there is only one pattern given in scripture for establishing elders in the church.

Of particular significance is that Paul never wrote to any of the churches with instructions for the selection of elders — Paul wrote those instructions only to his apostles. Two passages in the New Testament outline the criteria by which elders are to be chosen — one was written to Timothy and the other to Titus. This was because it was not the responsibility of the believers or even the local leaders of the church to choose and appoint elders. It was the specific work of the apostles.

In the book of Acts, the apostles went to many places pioneering churches. We read that they revisited those churches, and *"Paul and Barnabas appointed elders for them in each church and, with prayer and fasting, committed them to the Lord" (Acts 14:23)*. We could argue that they would have done this in complete cooperation and harmony with the local leaders and believers, and in thinking that we would be right. This is precisely the way apostles would work. But the revelation remains — it is the apostles who must judge the suitability of someone for the ministry, and it is the apostles who have the authority to set them apart and lay hands on them, appointing them to be elders over the church.

Confirmation of this truth was given when Paul clarified Titus' purpose. *"The reason I left you in Crete was that you might straighten out what was left unfinished and appoint elders in every town, as I directed you" (Titus 1:5-6)*. Paul proceeded immediately to define the qualifications of those elders. This was instruction for the apostle he had left in charge. In Paul's first letter to Timothy, he not only sets forth a similar set of qualifications for elders, he also gives instructions for the honouring and remuneration of the elders, the protection of elders from false accusation, and for dealing with any elder who sins (1 Timothy 5:17-20). This is because apostles have authority over elders, and elders are to be accountable to apostles.

To understand exactly who these elders are, you will need to read chapter 9 of this book, since the elders will be defined as something quite different from what most of us have known in denominational Christianity.

A further insight comes from Acts chapter 20 wherein is recorded Paul's farewell to the Ephesian elders, whom he had called to see him (Acts 20:17-38). He told them, *"I know that after I leave, savage wolves will come in among you and will not spare the flock. Even from your own number men will arise and distort the truth in order to draw away disciples after them. So be on your guard!" (Acts 20:29-31)*. The telling words are "after I leave". Without the apostle, the covering authority would not be in place to protect the church and to help the elders guard their own spirit so as to remain humble and accountable. Paul instructed them to watch over themselves and each other, yet nevertheless this would prove to be insufficient. An apostle was needed.

Every church needs an apostle to be such a father to the elders. The apostle has the love and authority of a father to bless and to honour, to love and correct, and if necessary to discipline.

We have a great advantage today over those early apostles. They were greatly limited in travel and communication, but we have the telephone, the internet, fast cars and the jumbo jet. Apostles and pastors can be in constant contact with each other, which must greatly help in developing effective relationships, mutual encouragement, supporting one another in building the house of God, and helping each other by means of our grace gifts.

Authority over Church Life, Order, and Spirituality

"For even if I boast somewhat freely about the authority the Lord gave us for building you up rather than pulling you down, I will not be ashamed of it" *(2 Corinthians 10:8).* Even to his own, Paul sometimes had to argue his case. There were times when he had to state plainly his authority, and command a good hearing. He would insist that they accept his authority where Christ had given him authority, and he was not prepared to allow anyone to undermine what God had given him.

In writing to Timothy and Titus, he told them to not let anyone look down on them, to allow no one to despise them, and to teach, correct and rebuke with authority. There were good reasons for this. He was not prepared to let anyone take from him the ground of his apostolate, which God had given him. Paul always gave his reason for taking this stand — it was not for his own sake, but for the sake of the church and the gospel. (1 Corinthians 9:23)

When you read these letters to the Corinthian church, it is obvious that we have here the pure, passionate heart of Christ's apostle crying out for righteousness and godly order in the church.

Paul is writing to an established church with an established eldership, yet he is claiming that he holds the Lord's authority to build up that church. Later he refers to this again. *"...I write these things when I am absent, that when I come I may not have to be harsh in my use of authority - the authority the Lord gave me for building you up, not for tearing you down"* *(2 Corinthians 13:10).* The point is that the apostles claimed and took a stand upon the authority that Christ gave them over the life of the churches, even though those churches had elders and other leaders.

And the authority was *personal*! There are many passages which, whilst showing the apostle's heart and great love for his people, also show the apostle held a *personal* authority over those churches. For example, he writes, *"I urge, then, first of all, that requests, prayers, intercession and thanksgiving be made for everyone..."* *(1 Timothy 2:1-2).* Observe the personal pronoun, *"I"* . This is not "God gave me this command so I am passing it onto you".

No, the apostle has his heart full of the divine pattern, and has a commission from Christ to define what is required. A few sentences later he explained *"for this purpose I was appointed a herald and an apostle - I am telling the truth, I am not lying - and a teacher of the true faith to the Gentiles" (1 Tim 2:7).*

All apostolic authority is personal. It is not received from committees or institutions, nor can any denomination impart the apostolate to anyone, no matter how sincere. Neither does Christ give this apostolic authority to organisations, institutions, missions, or denominations. It is always given to *individuals.* It is these individuals who bring Christ's authority to the church.

Of course apostles will empower others, and so we often end up with empowered movements and anointed missions. But without the apostle, or someone who inherited the genuine apostolic succession (as Joshua did from Moses, Elisha from Elijah, Timothy from Paul, and the twelve from Jesus) the movement will 'dry out'. In place of power, there will be tradition — and in time it becomes only a monument to a past greatness. So the church must ever continue to pray for Christ to raise and send His apostles. Why? Because apostolic authority is personal!

The apostles are the master builders of the church. All others are to build on the foundations that apostles lay in the church. Paul said *"I laid a foundation as an expert builder, and someone else is building on it" (1 Corinthians 3:10).* When he says *'someone else'*, he actually means every person who is at work in the church. Today, apostles must *continue* to lay foundations in the lives of believers, in towns and cities, in missions and ministries and congregations. All other leadership in the church is in fruitful partnership with the apostle (through personal relationship) to build on those apostolic foundations.

In the Pauline epistles we see the apostle addressing every matter of spiritual importance, and exercising the clear authority of Christ to issue commands, make judgements, and give advice and instruction. Paul summarises this for us, *"...brothers, we instructed you how to live in order to please God, as in fact you are living. Now we ask you and urge you in the Lord Jesus to do this more and more. For you know what instructions we gave you by the authority of the Lord Jesus" (1 Thessalonians 4:1-2).* The apostolic instruction had behind it the full authority of Christ, yet it was always urged upon the believers with the care and personal concern of a true father, which apostles are.

Even so, the apostle expected that the believers and the church leaders accepted his authority in Christ, and understood that when he spoke, he spoke for God. Paul confidently expected that every prophet and every spiritually discerning believer would have a clear inner witness of the validity of his words. *"If anybody thinks he is a prophet or spiritually gifted, let him acknowledge that what I am writing to you is the Lord's command. If he ignores this, he himself will be ignored" (1 Corinthians 14:37-38).* In fact, Paul seems to make a judgement here that anyone ignoring the word of God through the apostle would be set aside, it would seem, from being fruitful in the life of the church.

Despite such warnings, and the serious words of correction and discipline which the apostle needed to speak, the relationships were always buoyant, cheerful, and full of good hope and expectation. The apostle had confidence in those he loved, and they had confidence in him. He assured them, *"We have confidence in the Lord that you are doing and will continue to do the things we command. May the Lord direct your hearts into God's love and Christ's perseverance" (2 Thessalonians 3:4-5).*

In the exercise of this authority, the apostle was careful to make a distinction between commands, allowances for freedom, and general good advice. Take for example the following three statements, all of which occur in the same passage of Holy Scripture:

- *"I say this as a concession, not as a command"*

(1 Corinthians 7:6-7).

- *"To the married I give this command (not I, but the Lord)"*

(1 Corinthians 7:10).

- *"Now about virgins: I have no command from the Lord, but I give a judgment as one who by the Lord's mercy is trustworthy"*

(1 Corinthians 7:25).

These statements indicate that the apostolic authority extends not only to church order, and the moral life and holiness of the individual believers, but further. It extends to order and discipline in the personal lives and relationships of the believers, as we see here. *"In the name of the Lord Jesus Christ, we command you, brothers, to keep away from every brother who is idle and does not live according to the teaching you received from us. For you yourselves know how you ought to follow our example" (2 Thessalonians 3:6-7),* and again, *"We hear that some among you are idle. They are not busy; they are busybodies. Such people we command and urge in the Lord Jesus Christ to settle down and earn the bread they eat" (2 Thessalonians 3:11-12).*

My purpose here is not to identify every issue of church life to which the apostle speaks, but rather to demonstrate the extent of the apostle's personal authority in speaking to churches and believers regarding the will of God. The apostle holds an authority to call the church to follow Christ, and to follow also the apostle's own example (1 Corinthians 11:1).

Authority in Church Discipline

The local church (specifically the elders or leaders), does have all the authority needed to deal with matters of discipline and correction. The senior minister and the leaders should be carefully guarding the life and holiness of the church, by the grace of God and the authority of Jesus. But they are, or should be, accountable to an apostle. That apostle should hold them accountable for good church discipline, and will need to act if discipline is wanting.

No doubt you remember the very strong position taken by Paul in dealing with the Corinthian church over the extreme immorality of one of the members. Paul was distressed that they had not dealt with it appropriately themselves. Here is part of that passage:

"And you are proud! Shouldn't you rather have been filled with grief and have put out of your fellowship the man who did this? Even though I am not physically present, I am with you in spirit. And I have already passed judgment on the one who did this, just as if I were present. When you are assembled in the

> Apostles will work to maintain the spirit of holiness and the purity of the faith in the life of the church

name of our Lord Jesus and I am with you in spirit, and the power of our Lord Jesus is present, hand this man over to Satan, so that the sinful nature may be destroyed and his spirit saved on the day of the Lord. Your boasting is not good. Don't you know that a little yeast works through the whole batch of dough? Get rid of the old yeast that you may be a new batch without yeast - as you really are. For Christ, our Passover lamb, has been sacrificed"(1 Corinthians 5:2-8).

Notice the exercise of apostolic authority. Alone he passes judgement and says that in the meeting of the church he will be with them in spirit, and the power of Christ will be present. He commands that they are to hand the man over to Satan so that his sinful nature (the flesh) will be destroyed, in order that his spirit may be saved on the day of the Lord.

Why did Paul take such a strong stand? Because the church did not do its job, and the sin, left undealt with, was very dangerous — in time it would affect the whole church with a weakness for moral sin, as he reminded them — *"Don't you know that a little yeast works through the whole batch of dough? Get rid of the old yeast that you may be a new batch without yeast"*

(1 Corinthians 5: 6-7).

Some years ago I returned to my home church to discover the pastors and elders struggling with a serious problem. Here is what occurred.

A man in the district had been excommunicated by the leaders and members of a sister church, because he was a serious troublemaker who had filled the town and the churches with false accusations and terrible stories about the pastor and the church. This man had a history of arrogance and stirring up trouble, and now he had sworn himself to destroy that church and my church, as well as both the pastors.

During my absence he had telephoned my senior associate pastor and issued all kinds of threats — he was going to come to the church, he would expose the church, he would bring the media, etc. The leadership team met in my absence to discuss what to do, and agreed on the following course of action. They informed him that because of his excommunication from a sister church, he was therefore also excommunicated from us, and was as a result forbidden from attending our church. If he did so, we would call the police to remove him, if necessary.

(Note that the whole purpose of church discipline is undone if someone under correction or excommunication can simply walk into another fellowship. The purpose of discipline is to bring the person to repentance, and to then restore them to the fellowship of the church they are meant to have relationship with.)

The next Sunday morning I arrived in time for the service, to be informed about what had transpired. The troublemaker was there too, sitting amongst the believers, waiting for the meeting. I told my associate pastor that I would begin the service, and that since he had been dealing with the man, he should invite him into the library for discussion, and advise him to leave. So abusive was this man that he carried a portable tape recorder that he would hold in front of you to record whatever you said. It was another form of threat. He claimed also to be recording telephone conversations.

Whilst the church service proceeded, he argued at great length and refused to leave. The police were finally called to the library and ordered him to leave the property. The police advised him that this was our legal right, and if he did not obey our request, the police would be obliged to remove him forcibly. He left full of threats, and declared that the following Sunday morning he would return with the media to film and report him being forcibly removed.

On Tuesday night the leadership team met again. We prayed and sought the Lord's grace and wisdom. Then we discussed what we should do if he came again the next Sunday. The brothers felt it was better to ignore him — better, they thought, than having his accusations exposed in the media. There seemed no real answer. But the Lord always has an answer, and we had prayed for grace.

I woke on Wednesday morning with the Lord speaking a very clear word — "Exercise the provisions of 1 Corinthians 5 against him," and by the wisdom of the Spirit, I then knew exactly what to do.

The next Sunday morning he arrived half an hour early, and sat in the auditorium ready for the meeting. I arrived early to prepare and explain to the staff, the leaders, the worship leader and the sound system operator what to expect, and what to do to support me.

I then went and sat with this divisive brother, looking him in the eyes, but speaking very softly and slowly. I quietly advised him that he was to leave, in accordance with all previous discussions. He replied that he was refusing to leave. So, I advised him further; if he refused to leave and chose to remain, then in accordance with Christ's instructions to me I was going to exercise the provisions of 1 Corinthians 5 against him during the service. He knew very well what this was — it had been part of his threats against others for many months. I then left him to consider what I said, but reminded him that if he remained I would act against him in accordance with the scriptures.

I waited until the end of the praise and worship period, receiving the microphone from the worship leader at the climax of the final song. The power of God was greatly present at this point, and I addressed the church.

I advised the church of the circumstances of 'a particular brother who is present', and briefly explained the meaning and purpose of 1 Corinthians 5 and excommunication. I also advised the church that I had explained to him personally what I needed to do, by the grace of God. Once I had explained the position, I named the brother before the church, and went to God in prayer.

In prayer, I handed him over for the judgement of God, and finished the prayer by making this declaration "...and so now, in the name of Christ Jesus, he is excommunicate!"

In the very moment I spoke those words, it was reported by a number of the believers, there was heard a loud "Crack!"- something in the spirit realm was rent - and the man who had been so much noise and trouble simply rose and left the building. He has never returned, and we have never heard from him again.

Paul refers to the authority that is given the apostle for the purpose of discipline when he warned the Corinthian church that he would deal with the arrogance of some of them on his next visit. *"I already gave you a warning when I was with you the second time. I now repeat it while absent: On my return I will not spare those who sinned earlier or any of the others, since you are demanding proof that Christ is speaking through me. He is not weak in dealing with you, but is powerful among you"(2 Corinthians 13:2-4).*

This can only mean the apostle had *power* at his disposal to carry out the disciplinary actions that were needed – not political or institutional power, but the actual power of God.

This is a right use of apostolic authority, for the sake of the church, the believers, and the individual who is under judgement. It is usually the means of saving them — rescuing them from their darkness. In most cases it is the one means remaining of restoring them to faith, repentance and Christ. In the case referred to in the Corinthian letters, that man too was saved from his sin and restored to the fellowship of the church (2 Corinthians 2:6-8).

Apostles are not afraid to exercise discipline, and will work to strengthen the resolution of the elders and the believers to maintain the spirit of holiness and the purity of the faith in the life of the church. *"For there are many rebellious people, mere talkers and deceivers, especially those of the circumcision group. They must be silenced, because they are ruining whole households by teaching things they ought not to teach - and that for the sake of dishonest gain... Therefore, rebuke them sharply, so that they will be sound in the faith..." (Titus 1:10-11,13).*

General Authority as an Apostle

We have identified *specific* areas of authority for an apostle in relationship with specific churches, and we also made note of areas in which an apostle does not exercise authority, but gives freedom to the leadership and vision of others. There is, nevertheless, a general sense in which an apostle of Christ can speak with authority over all things.

The letter to Philemon records Paul's appeal to a dear brother to receive back his runaway slave in a spirit of mercy and forgiveness. The slave, Onesimus, had become very dear to Paul — Paul refers to him as *"my son... who became my son while I was in chains"*. Paul had been greatly helped by Onesimus, but because he was a runaway slave, he felt obliged to send him back to Philemon. Paul's concern was that Onesimus would be received and treated well, and so he writes, *"...although in Christ I could be bold and order you to do what you ought to do, yet I appeal to you on the basis of love" (Philemon 8-9).*

Here we see an example of the general authority of an apostle. There is a sense in which he could truthfully command the believer to do anything needful that is in accordance with God's will — anything right and holy in God's sight. Yet the church does not function by rules and regulations; it can never thrive on orders alone. The real heart of the church is love; our real strength as God's people is in relationship, and the apostle will function more by appeal than command, even though it is within his authority to speak boldly.

The apostle lives and works with this tension, knowing he holds far more authority than he can usually display, and humbly loving, encouraging and exhorting the saints.

On the other hand, with regard to preaching the revelation of Christ, the grace of God, and an appropriate response to it, boldness remains! There are times when the apostle and every minister of grace must be bold, as we see here: *"Command those who are rich in this present world not to be arrogant nor to put their hope in wealth, which is so uncertain, but to put their hope in God, who richly provides us with everything for our enjoyment. Command them to do good, to be rich in good deeds, and to be generous and willing to share. In this way they will lay up treasure for themselves as a firm foundation for the coming age, so that they may take hold of the life that is truly life" (1 Tim 6:17-19).*

The 'Rule of Thumb' for Authentic Authority

A rule is a principle or a standard by which we measure things. When we speak of a 'rule of thumb', this usually means measuring something based on experience or practice, rather than theory.

A rule of thumb is a simple, quick, easy and reasonably accurate way to measure something. It is a way in which we can tell quickly if something is genuine, and if it measures up to what it should be. Such a 'rule of thumb' is needed to help us in assessing the validity of the authority or authorities that are in the church.

Two such 'rules of thumb' I feel are to be applied to the use of authority. These principles would apply to apostles and to any church or denominational leader.

Firstly, "*no authority without relationship*". Personal, committed and loving relationships are the heart of what the church is all about, and these are the true foundations for genuine authority in leadership. We have seen too much *institutional* Christianity, or churchianity, and it is time that this should no longer be the nature of most of the visible church. We have seen religious leaders make decisions that affect churches from a position of institutional authority, yet have no real relationship with those churches.

True apostolic authority requires heart relationship. As Paul, who exercised great authority, described it, *"I became your father"(1 Corinthians 4:15)*. This is simple really. If you do not have relationship with the pastors, the churches, the elders, the cities, etc., you do not have authority over them.

Secondly, "*no authority without responsibility*". No one should be making decisions or exercising authority affecting the believers, and not also feel responsible for how it works out in the lives of the people.

An apostle who relates to a local church and is in relationship with the leaders will feel a concern and responsibility for their wellbeing. He will care about them *personally*. When he makes a decision, he knows it will directly affect the people to whom he relates.

As Paul declared, *"I promised you to one husband, to Christ, so that I might present you as a pure virgin to him" (2 Corinthians 11:2)*. That's the burden that must be on the heart of everyone serving as an apostle. An apostle will have a caring responsibility for the results of every decision.

In summary, it is the *relationship* and *responsibility* factors which will largely determine whether authority is genuine or spurious. The apostle will have relationship with Christ, and responsibility to Christ. The apostle will likewise have relationship with, and responsibility for, the leaders and believers.

Apostolic Authority over Finance

Apostles have grace to handle finance for the Kingdom of God. In reading about the church in the New Testament you come across what might seem a curious idea. The believers laid their gifts at the apostle's feet (Acts 4:35, 37,

Acts 5:2).

From the beginning apostles were trusted with finance, and in the church of the coming days apostles must also be trusted. The apostles have authority to handle finance for Christ, and He will be placing in their hands very large resources for the work of the coming days. Apostles should be directing the available resources of the church according to the greatest need and opportunity in the world today.

There are principles of ministry here. The resources of the church should serve the vision of the church, and those who are not the authorised leaders should not have final control of the finance or property of the church. Unfortunately, too often, subordinate leaders such as deacons or the treasurer use the financial levers of the church to control the pastor and the life of the church. This should never be.

In many places, once the constitution is established, the church is subservient to the constitution, and once the budget is drawn up, the church is bound to the budget. On the contrary, the constitution and the budget should serve the vision of the church and the leadership of those who are responsible for the implementation of it.

We have made this very clear in the ministry of our church. The leader of the ministry, and the vision given by God, and the leading of the Holy Spirit are to be served by the finance and the personnel in charge of financial management and administration. The treasurer is to be a servant to the leaders and does not dictate policy or make final decisions on the use of finance. That is the prerogative of the authorised leaders of the church.

In the coming days we will again see very significant amounts of money laid at the feet of the apostles. Wealth is about to flow into the Kingdom of God for the sake of the gospel. It will flow to those apostles who have the calling and anointing to handle millions of dollars for the cause of Christ. New works will be raised up across the nations. The apostolic ministry and those in submission to it will prosper, even in days when the world is in financial recession.

A Heart for the Poor and for Mission

Apostles are seen to take up specific responsibility both for mission and for the poor in the Gospels, in the Acts of the Apostles, and in the Epistles.

A regular activity of Jesus and His disciples was evangelistic mission, and giving to the poor. Everyone in the church is called to these responsibilities by the love of God, but apostles will always have it on their hearts as an area of need to which they must devote leadership.

When Paul went to Jerusalem to confer with James, Peter and John, the poor of Jerusalem were on their hearts. *"All they asked"* he explained to the Galatians *"was that we should continue to remember the poor, the very thing I was eager to do" (Galatians 2:10).* Notice here the word *"continue"*. Something dynamic had already been happening amongst the apostles in ministry to the poor. The apostles had taken up the burden — and this was a financial burden.

Paul devoted two whole chapters (2 Corinthians 8 & 9) to his financial appeal to the Corinthians. He wanted them to keep their promise, and to follow the example of the Macedonians in giving very generously to the Jerusalem poor. Paul needed a major offering, and because of that we have been blessed abundantly with the teaching in these two chapters about the power of the offering.

All pastors and every Christian leader will serve and give for missions and the poor, but apostles have specific authority and responsibility to address these needs from a leadership perspective.

Different Kinds of Apostles

One might have been inclined to think that all apostles are the same, but this is simply not so. Apostles will not only vary greatly in personality, gifting, leadership style, emotional makeup and so on, but also in many of the features of the specific calling to which Christ sends them.

Some will be household names, being called to great prominence and worldwide influence on the church. Their impact on the world will be more obvious. Others will be unknown by the church at large, but will nevertheless fulfil a vital and important role.

Even now, there are many 'hidden' apostles. The Spirit of Christ is preparing large numbers of apostles for the coming days, but most of these are hidden at this time, not just from the world but also from the church.

Indeed, it would seem that the majority of the greatest apostles to come are amongst these 'hidden' ones. They look unimportant, even in their own eyes. They are in insignificant places, working with small numbers of people, with no great influence and no apparent way of impacting their world. Sometimes they look like failures, because they have been put through fire and water (Isaiah 43:2, Psalm 66:12). While being prepared in the furnace of affliction, and their hearts humbled by 'insignificance', they are being kept by God in readiness for another day.

Strangely, there has seemed to be an assumption on the part of some that the leaders of the more significant public ministries and churches must be apostles - even to the suggestion that anyone with a church congregation above a certain number is really not a pastor, but an apostle. This is not necessarily so. Having success, including church growth and large numbers in the congregation, does not prove whether one is an apostle or not. Many wonderful ministers with great influence and large churches are great *pastors*, or great *teachers*, or great *prophets*. Remember, these ministries are also church leaders with Christ's anointings and calling.

Many great apostles will actually arise from the ashes of defeat! I have heard that the early church fathers did not trust a man in leadership of the church, unless he had known failure. I have learned that one cannot teach success if one only knows success — for that produces shallowness and immaturity.

So wait! Great apostles will arise, for God is about to reveal them. This is not to say that the church is not being presently served by some great apostles, but God is about to bring forth a greater anointing upon this ministry, and many great apostles and prophets will arise from seemingly insignificant circumstances. Like John the Baptist, many are being prepared in the wilderness.

Some of these will be apostles to whole nations, many to smaller regions and cities, and some will have international authority. Amongst these, there will be those who are, at least for a lengthy season, the 'junior' partners in the ministries of senior apostles.

Senior and Subordinate Apostles

We should not be surprised at the idea that some apostles will serve, not in their own right, but under the authority of another apostle. Surely this is a legitimate biblical pattern. This is what we see in the relationship of Titus and Timothy to Paul, and the Bible refers to James, Peter and John specifically as the pillars of the church in Jerusalem. There were other apostles serving under them, at least in the many years before they went in different directions to other nations.

It is very plain from Paul's letters that Timothy and Titus were his beloved 'sons' in the ministry. When he could not go, he would send a son to represent him (1 Corinthians 4:17). When he had to move on from Crete, he left Titus as the apostle in charge of all the work — yet still under Paul's own instruction, guidance and authority (Titus 1:5). They were members of the same apostolic team, and while Paul lived he had authority over them.

Sooner or later a subordinate (associate) apostle is likely to come into their own ministry. If nothing else happens, the time comes when the senior apostle goes to be with the Lord. When Paul was martyred, Timothy and Titus and others had the responsibility for the ministry — they had inherited the ministry as sons. Of course this is not the only pattern. A fathering apostle will raise sons to maturity and can release them, as the Lord leads, into autonomous ministry. There are no hard rules here. This is family.

On another issue, *every* apostle without exception needs to be in personal relationship with, and under the spiritual covering of, another apostle. No apostle today should go it alone. Christ is not leading anyone, apostles included, to see themselves as being above the need for a submitted, accountable relationship with other Christians. This important idea is further addressed elsewhere in this book.

The Primary Apostle

Every senior pastor and every church (every ministry leader and every Christian ministry) should be related to a primary apostle.

The primary apostle is the spiritual father, the one who carries an apostolic authority and who provides the apostolic covering in relationship to the pastor and the church. This is the picture we have of Paul in relation to the churches for whom he was the spiritual father (1 Corinthians 4:15). There can be only one such primary apostle in relationship to a church and the pastor.

The primary apostle is the most important apostle in the life of the pastor personally, and in the covering of the church. The more ongoing relationship between these parties, the better and richer they all will be in walking in the inheritance they share in Christ. This apostle provides protection and security for the pastor, for all the leaders, and for the church generally. A proper relationship with this apostle prevents trouble in the church, and if trouble does arise it is more easily addressed and resolved.

As a result of the relationship between the church and the primary apostle, pastors will no longer come and go on the whim of a few believers. Someone's research showed that when churches have trouble and division, and pastors are rejected and thrown aside, this is usually caused by an average of only six individual members. Often terrible disruptions are caused by very small groups that do not represent the whole, yet work to obtain an illicit influence. The primary apostle is the authority that prevents injustice and false accusation having influence in the church. He could correct or discipline the church, or the leadership team, or the senior pastor, depending on just who may be at fault. Further information on how this works is to be found in the appendix where I have placed a section from our church constitution as an example.

There will be other apostles who also have ongoing personal relationship with the senior minister and the church as trusted friends and associates. Sometimes another apostle represents the primary apostle in his absence personally, as Paul said Timothy was to do when he wrote to the church in Corinth, *"I urge you to imitate me. For this reason I am sending to you Timothy, my son whom I love, who is faithful in the Lord. He will remind you of my way of life in Christ Jesus, which agrees with what I teach everywhere in every church" (1 Corinthians 4:16-17).*

Apostolic councils can be formed to extend the ministry of covering and protection through a team, in which the primary apostle is the leader. The members of an apostolic council will each be in a fruitful personal relationship with the pastor and the other leaders and believers of the church. All are of a like spirit, and have a covenant relationship of the heart towards one another. With these 'secondary apostles', there is always ongoing relationship in place.

In addition, every church is meant to be open to receive of the wider fivefold ministry that Jesus provides. No local church should ever be isolated from the greater ministry of the body of Christ. Jesus will often want to speak to the church through visiting ministers. Amongst these are pastors, teachers, prophets, and evangelists, as well as apostles. Jesus said to His apostles, *"He who receives you receives me, and he who receives me receives the one who sent me" (Matt 10:40).*

There should always be a place for the visit of other apostles. Paul had this kind of relationship to Rome. Although he had no direct authority over the church, he wanted to visit and minister out of the apostolic gifts and anointings that were upon his life, and have them help him as well. He wrote to them, *"I long to see you so that I may impart to you some spiritual gift to make you strong - that is, that you and I may be mutually encouraged by each other's faith" (Romans 1:11-12).*

Authority over Principalities

There are other areas of apostolic authority which are beyond the scope of this present book, since we are concentrating here on the reformation of the church, and the relationship between the apostle and the church. Nevertheless we need to make note of the apostle's specific authority over principalities and powers of darkness.

The anointing to rule (over principalities) and to exercise authority in Christ's name, is on apostles

Principalities are dark areas of spiritual authority ruled over by 'princes' of darkness. In the church there is an anointing to confront them and deal with them in Christ's power. To serve in that anointing is part of the apostle's call. The anointing to rule, the anointing to exercise authority in Christ's name, is on apostles. There is a sense in which they are the modern-day 'princes of Judah', the sons of David the mighty warrior king. For anyone to claim to be an apostle if they are not is foolishness — there is the risk of exposing themselves to powers of darkness for which they have not been equipped by the Spirit.

Yet all churches and believers are called to a place of prayer and warfare against principalities. According to Ephesians 6: 10-18, we are all to be dressed together in Christ's armour, taking a stand in prayer specifically against principalities and rulers of darkness, the powers of the air. Each church and the whole body of Christ should stand in this war against the powers.

With the help of praying saints, apostles will succeed and break through against high-level demonic powers, and annul their claims over territories and people. The apostle is not necessarily the only one who can do this — teams of prophetic intercessors achieve amazing results all the time. Still, the apostle does have a specific authority, whereby in humility of heart and with Christ's hand upon him, he will struggle with and defeat principalities.

Whenever I travel, I find it necessary to bind the principalities over the place where I am to minister — over regions, cities, states and nations. This is because the principalities would otherwise resist me because of the apostolic anointing — these are opposing anointings.

There are many places I go where I must claim the ground if I am to have freedom when ministering. In prayer, I humbly submit to Christ, then in His name take authority over and bind the principalities and powers, commanding them that they are to be subject to me in Christ's name. This always makes a difference. If I fail to do this, the preaching and the meetings are resisted.

When I do this, I am able to minister freely and progress toward breakthrough.

I went to preach in a city where an emerging apostle was building a new ministry — but he was being strongly resisted. He had been going through a great struggle for some time. During the course of the meetings the Holy Spirit instructed me to lay hands on him and publicly declare him to be an apostle before the principalities and powers. By the mind of the Spirit I understood that the powers were resisting his appointment as an apostle, i.e. they were disputing with him and his people that he was an apostle.

I called him forward before all the people, and declared him to be an apostle. Laying hands on him and commissioning him as an apostle, I rebuked the principalities for opposing him, commanded them to cease their resistance to his appointment, and declared that they were subject to him and me in Christ's name. This made an immediate difference — to him, to the ministry and to his people. He informed me in the following weeks that much opposition had fallen away and there was a noticeable increase in the authority of the ministry. I thank God for His grace. Such experiences illustrate principles that will be effective anywhere.

Empowerment: Impartation with Authority

In writing to Rome, Paul said he longed to impart some spiritual gift to them. This is one of the most significant, consistent and enjoyable aspects of the apostle's ministry. Whenever there is an opportunity to pray for another — a pastor, the church, a believer — there is an opportunity to give a gift. Anointings are imparted, gifts are activated, blessing and increase and success released, and authority established and built-up.

> Whenever there is opportunity to pray for another, there is opportunity to impart a gift

This is what I love the most, and find the easiest of all. It is not hard to teach the saints how to exercise faith to receive the impartation of gifts, and it is easy to exercise faith to release these impartations of God's grace to others. Whether in private prayer with individuals or in corporate prayer over congregations, what God is willing to do never ceases to amaze me. Quite apart from the standard impartations of gifts of the Spirit such as prophecy, it seems there can be an impartation of grace as a special gift for just about any need or opportunity. I have seen impartations of grace for marital blessing, for financial increase, and even for humility, imparted as an anointing from Christ. An amazing and tangible anointing of peace is also a very powerful impartation that is easy to obtain. Often it is the impartation of spiritual authority.

The anointing for impartation and blessing is a significant apostolic grace, although all fivefold ministers surely have inheritance in this work. The grace of impartation begins with apostles however, because of the principle of authority through submission.

When an apostle ministers, whether to churches or individuals, he is looking to give gifts and grace and blessing in Christ's name. Those who have the benefit of being under the covering of an apostle's ministry can expect a genuine empowerment from his prayers and his blessing. This is the way of Christ.

The Apostolic Blessing

The blessings of the Abrahamic covenant rest on apostles, as they do for every believer in Christ (Galatians 3:14). God said to Abraham, *"I will bless those who bless you, and whoever curses you I will curse; and all peoples on earth will be blessed through you" (Genesis 12:3).* These words are resting on all believers, and apostles walk in the power of them. Everyone who walks with God and has faith may know this power, but for apostles it is an established part of what they are in Christ.

To receive God's blessing through an apostle, you honour the apostle. It was the Lord who said, *"I will bless those who bless you."* This is a spiritual principle and there is no exception to the rule. If you want to be blessed, you must honour the source of blessing. Resentment will drive the blessing away from you. Anything you resent cannot be a source of blessing to you.

When you honour God and honour the apostle, by receiving him, the blessings of God that he carries are available to you. In accordance with the word of the Lord *"all peoples on earth will be blessed through you".*

It is therefore not surprising that sweet blessings, and release, and favour, spring up in people's lives in response to the prayers of an apostle. These blessings were always intended for every believer, because they are the blessings of Abraham. They are the spiritual blessings that are said to have been lavished on us in Christ (Ephesians 1:3, 8). The apostle is the key that releases many of these blessings, because he is our modern-day Abraham, the one God is pleased to use as our present father in the faith.

The whole of Christianity is meant to be relational, but in particular the relationships are of a family nature. From the beginning it has been father and son. Abraham the father of faith was promised a son, and it was over that son that all the tests of Abraham's faith were carried out. Father/son relationship is important to us because God has revealed Himself as God in Father and Son. This is the essence of apostleship.

Every church, every ministry, every pastor and every believer needs the apostolic blessing. You cannot be independent. In looking to Christ you must receive the one He sends. You need the apostle, because Christ will send with the apostle many of the blessings you desire.

Abraham is the model for your faith and obedience, and Abraham himself needed the blessing of another person who represented Christ to him. And so we have this example: *"Melchizedek... blessed him who had the promises" (Hebrews 7:1-10)*. In this, Melchizedek represents Christ (*"king of peace"*, etc) and Abraham is typical of every believer (*"him who had the promises"*). We are all exhorted to imitate those who have inherited what was promised (Hebrews 3:12-15).

For the apostle, to function in this ministry is a stewardship which has been entrusted to him (1 Corinthians 4:1, 9:17, 1 Peter 5:2-3, 2 Corinthians 3:5-6).

THE APOSTOLIC REVELATION

Chapter 6

Women in Apostolic Ministry

Many of the Lord's greatest servants are women. This has been true in every generation. Amongst them are pioneers, missionaries and leaders — ministers of grace for Jesus Christ, who have gone anywhere He has sent them.

I often seriously consider that my own wife Hazel is likely to have a far greater reward in eternity for her faithfulness, love and sacrifice than I will. Even though I have been entrusted with an extensive public ministry and a greater authority in Christ, and carry many responsibilities for Christ and His people, position on earth does not determine our ultimate position in the body of Christ or the level of our *eternal* authority. Neither does it determine, nor reveal, the level of our intimacy with Christ.

Women Are of Great Significance in the Church

It is likely that women are in the majority of those believers who have pleased the Lord the most, and who in eternity will have the greatest rewards, the greatest authority and the greatest recognition. It has to do with what goes on in the heart between each of us and the Lord, rather than the positions we hold and the importance we may seem to have in the church while in this world.

I consider there to be a wonderful grace upon women in the church, and all my life I have greatly appreciated the worship, prayer and faithfulness of these great saints, many of whom have lived sacrificial lives in service to others. Most churches, if not all, have more women than men, and usually far more women are faithfully involved in the critical work of prayer and prophetic intercession.

However, we are to here consider the specific question, "Are there women

---

apostles?" And we will consider this in the context of the place of women generally in the leadership ministries of the church.

A 'Positive' Answer about Women in Leadership Ministry

I am making an endeavour to achieve the 'impossible'. No one has ever produced an answer to the question of the place of women in leadership ministry that has satisfied the whole church and ended the argument. It does not seem possible to take the angst out of this for everyone, but I think the answer is not to be found in a formal doctrine. The subject is very emotive, and the New Testament itself does not seem to leave us without some confusion and cause for debate. The most difficult passages in the Bible to understand and interpret correctly are some of those concerning the place of women in the church.

There is no limit to the height to which a woman may aspire in service to Christ

For those who look for a way ahead, we can be confident that God does not leave us without a clear word. If I cannot find a position that satisfies someone else, at least I need a position that satisfies me, and those I work with. In the ministry I have to give leadership and make decisions that are honouring to all Christians, and give freedom for the Holy Spirit to use every believer as He wills — and I must be able to do so out of genuine conviction regarding the biblical position.

Then, any answer to this question must be a *positive* answer. There needs to be a biblical and spiritual answer that is truly satisfying, one that is positive for every person, man or woman, whose heart is called to serve Christ. I will here share what I believe the Lord has given me.

At the outset I would like to state plainly to all women, my sisters both older and younger, that there is no limit to the height to which you may aspire in service to Christ. For me, the ultimate goal is the release of women to serve Christ with freedom.

We are not to artificially put the lid on anything. For years I have said that a woman can function in any spiritual gift and any ministry, because there is no justification for hindering any woman from serving Christ in accordance with any genuine heavenly call. As long as, of course, her heart is full of love for Christ and His people, motivated by purity and not self. The question that remains to be answered is the question of what roles may women fill.

The Church 'in Community'

In the church fellowship at Peace, almost all our worship leaders, over many years, have been women. We make cell pastors from amongst the women, and basically anything in the church is the domain of the women as well as the men. The leader of my intercessory team is a godly woman, and almost all of my personal confidential intercessors are women.

A great deal of our work is done in prophetic intercession, and most of the clear directions for the church come from prayer retreats or other expressions of the fellowship which involve a free interaction of both men and women. We function as a community rather than an institution with committees and programs. It is inconceivable that the church should operate without the freedom for interaction of every person who has a right spirit and who is seeking God to take us forward as a people. In practice, this involves many more women than men, especially with the work of prophetic input and intercession.

This does not mean there are not those with authority to watch over the whole, and to make final decisions on matters. We have a number of anointed leaders who have responsibility, and as the leader of the ministry I have an overall governing authority. We do not have a democracy, but we do have community. Democracy cannot produce community, but community is what the church must be. In community there can be equality, but democracy produces striving. In democracy everyone has rights, but in community we do not cling to our rights but love and accept one another in a spirit of mutual submission. The Bible tells us that this is the attitude we should have, like Christ, who although He was God did not cling to His rights as God but took the nature of a servant (Philippians 2: 5-7).

Understanding the Simple Pattern in Scripture

The following is what I believe the Lord gave me as a simple method to understand the place of women in the ministry of Jesus Christ. We take our understanding of this from the Scriptures, which contain a simple pattern that is helpful for everybody.

There are two separate and opposing ideas I seek to harmonise. Many believe that the senior spiritual leadership of the church is for men alone, and that women should not be in positions of authoritative leadership over men. Others believe that women should be in the ministry of leadership as well as men. Both these viewpoints are based on Scripture, and both contain truth. I hope to show how these fit together. Following is my understanding of the ways of God as shown in the biblical pattern.

The Old Testament Pattern

In the Old Testament, as a rule, all anointing for ministry was for men. Men had all the leadership, men had all the authority and all of the anointings. Men were placed in all of the offices — all the kings were men (i.e. there was no anointed queen), all the priests were men, and generally all the prophets. In the main, God's dealings were exclusively with men, and leadership was always upon men, *unless God made an exception*.

So the pattern for the Old Testament was **all anointed leaders were men — unless God made an** *exception*. God could, and God *did,* make a few exceptions to this pattern. The obvious exception to the rule is that of Deborah, the prophetess whom the Lord made a 'judge' (a leader or deliverer) of Israel (Judges 4:4). Another exception is that of Miriam the prophetess (Exodus 15:20), Moses sister, who had a significant role of influence and example in the community under Moses. There was also Huldah the prophetess (2 Kings 22:14) and Anna the prophetess who, although her story occurs in the Gospel of Luke (2:36), lived under the Old Covenant. Except for Deborah, none of these were ministry leaders as such.

Of further significance are a number of references in the Old Testament about daughters who received inheritance along with their brothers. Normally it was only the sons who received a share of their father's estate, and it was of special note when daughters were honoured and blessed by receiving inheritance along with their brothers. One example of this is that of Job's daughters (Job 42:15. Another is that of Acsah, the daughter of Caleb, who was given land by her father, so she asked for springs of water as well, and her father gave her the upper and lower springs (Joshua 15:18). There are symbols here of great significance — consider the keywords like inheritance, father, land to possess, and springs of water.

(When we talk of exceptions, this is not a discussion about the *significance* of women. All through the Old Testament the Lord honoured women highly — He cherished and loved and cared for them — their stories are told with great feeling, stories such as Ruth's, and Naomi's, Esther's, and others. Many women had a significant place in the history of God's dealings with His people. Our discussion of 'exceptions' has only to do with the anointing to exercise authority over the people of God. It is not a question of our worth, or whether God will use us to be a blessing to His people.)

So the Old Testament contains these exceptions. Some are 'exceptions' in ministry leadership like Deborah, while others have more subtle messages hidden in the symbolism. What is the message there? That the clear mandate for anointed leadership is upon men, and will remain upon men, but women have an inheritance amongst their brothers, and God will use them in the same anointings as He wants to and needs to.

We could summarise the message from the Old Testament pattern as follows: Men have the responsibility for leadership, but women are not excluded from leadership.

A Promise of Change Comes Forth

During this Old Testament period where ministry anointing for women was an exception, a promise comes forth. It heralds a coming change in the way God is going to do things.

The prophet Joel made this announcement for the Lord, *"And afterward, I will pour out my Spirit on all people. Your sons and daughters will prophesy"*, and more, *"Even on my servants, both men and women, I will pour out my Spirit in those days" (Joel 2: 28-29).* On the day of Pentecost, when the Holy Spirit anointed the church with power for ministry, the apostle Peter declared that these prophecies of Joel were being fulfilled. From now on, the anointings and power for ministry was being poured out on *all* flesh. From this time every believer would have anointings of the Holy Spirit for service to Christ.

> The anointings and power for ministry has been poured out on all

The New Pattern of the New Covenant

In the New Testament, all anointings are for men and women equally, unless again, God makes an exception.

Everything in the church is for both men and women, unless God makes an exception — and it so happens that *there are* some apparent exceptions. But of those exceptions, which we will discuss in a moment, God can also make exceptions. Just as the Lord made exceptions to His general method in the Old Testament, He is as free and well able to make exceptions to the usual rule of the New Testament.

What is the usual rule, or pattern of the New Testament? *All leadership and ministry anointings are for both men and women, unless God has made specific exceptions — and He has made some specific exceptions — but God is free to make exceptions to these exceptions.*

The 'Exceptions' of the New Testament

There are two things that the New Testament does make 'exceptions' of, for women — things that the Lord does not normally put upon women as a burden and responsibility. To these duties they are not normally called and appointed. These are ministry roles for which the Lord normally requires men to carry the responsibility, and from which women are normally free.

One is the **eldership,** where the eldership is the spiritual covering over the church of the city. This we discuss in Chapter 8. The other is **apostleship,** especially where the apostle is a covering apostle. This concept is taught in Chapter 7. The great common element in these two responsibilities is the spiritual covering.

Concerning covering, remember that this is not the old and false idea that a woman needed a man's supervision - not at all. Spiritual covering has to do with an anointing, which must rest on someone who has been prepared for that purpose, which sets in place a power for high level protection in the spirit realm, and keeps open the way for power and blessing to flow. Whilst we may not fully understand this, there is something about the nature of this spiritual covering that usually requires a man to be in place, like Adam or Abraham or Paul.

This has a great deal to do with the specific authority that God has placed on men to carry the responsibility for the care and protection of others. Thus, in a family, while both husband/ father and the wife/mother are equals in a partnership, and both are leaders in their home and family, only one is the head of that home - and it is always the man who is the head of the home. Of course even here you have exceptions, like for instance if a husband has an accident that leaves him alive but mentally incapacitated - the wife will assume total leadership responsibility, and rightly so. But that doesn't mean it is necessarily easy for her, or the ideal plan for their lives. Yet the outcome can be very successful, and many women in these situations do very well.

Similarly, apostles and elders are those prepared by God to stand in the place where they carry the anointing and the responsibility, and the pressures of the spiritual war at that level, for the protection and blessing of the people and the work under their covering. Because this involves standing in an authority which, whether known or unknown, is in direct resistance to dark powers, this is usually, almost always, the calling of men. This requires a headship authority, and men in general have been appointed by God to fulfill this specific headship role.

The Elders

Do we find this idea (that the elders should be men) consistent with the New Testament Scriptures? There are two passages that define the qualifications for eldership in the apostolic church. These are found in 1 Timothy chapter 3 and Titus chapter 1. Both passages are consistent in saying that an elder must be the husband of only one wife, a man who manages his household well, and that his children obey and respect him. The Greek word translated in Titus 1:6 and 1 Timothy 3:2 as *'husband'* actually means *'an individual male'*. The practice of the apostolic church, as revealed in the pages of the New Testament, everywhere fitted this pattern. We are not to think this was because the church was following the cultural norms of the day. Rather, under apostolic revelation, this was the normal requirement to meet the need for the spiritual covering of the church.

Therefore, the eldership as the spiritual covering of the church in any given town, city or region, should normally be comprised of spiritually qualified *men*. This does not mean that their wives, or other godly women, are not with them in the ministry. Ideally their wives should walk with them in the ministry, but it is the men who carry the anointing for the spiritual covering. At the same time, this releases the women to function in their gifts and ministries with great freedom, without carrying the burden for the spiritual covering to which they were not meant to be yoked. This principle of appointing men to the eldership is not meant to restrict women from ministry, but to liberate them in ministry.

The Apostles

The same principle applies to apostles, but in particular where the apostle provides an apostolic covering over other works of God.

Most apostles are not just pioneers or travelling ministries. Most will provide spiritual covering through fathering and accountable relationships with pastors and churches, and with prophets, evangelists, Christian schools, and in fact over every form of Christian ministry, including other apostles. This means that on the life of the apostle is an anointing that works to protect and bless those under them. This is why, in general, apostles also are men.

It should be noted that a covering apostle is, by default (this means automatically), one of the elders. The apostle Peter wrote, *"To the elders among you, I appeal as a fellow elder"* (1 Peter 5:1).

Can There Be Women Apostles?

I have said that I believe a woman can function in any anointing and any ministry in the church. It is quite possible to have an apostolic call upon a woman, as we often discover when in ministry about the churches. This means they have been, or are being, prepared by the Lord for a specific task, and they will have a duty under God for which they have authority and responsibility. That qualifies as being apostolic in nature. Women will serve on apostolic teams, and be seen to have apostolic gifts, apostolic anointing, and apostolic purpose.

So far, so good. You would say that women are *"among the apostles" (Romans 16:7)*. But women travelled with Jesus and His apostolic company, as His disciples, without ever being apostles, and they were an important and appropriate part of the overall ministry (Luke 8:1-3). Paul records the names of women as his faithful co-workers, but these were not apostles (Philippians 4:3).

So can we consider the idea of a woman being a primary apostle? What about a woman providing spiritual covering for pastors and churches? What basis in Scripture do we have for an answer to these questions? And we must remember that anointings such as apostolic and prophetic anointings can rest on believers for service to Christ without them actually being apostles or prophets. For example, there are many in the church who prophesy, and some have very powerful prophetic anointings — but this does not make them a prophet. In the same way many believers will have apostolic anointings and exercise apostolic gifts without being apostles.

> Many believers will have apostolic anointings and exercise apostolic gifts without being apostles

In the book of Romans there is recorded a greeting from Paul to Andronicus and Junias, his own relatives who had been in prison with him. Of them he makes this comment, *"They are outstanding among the apostles" (Romans 16:7)*. Many have pointed out that Junias, here referred to as an apostle, is a woman.

Unfortunately, it cannot be finally proven that Junias was a woman, since this was a name common to both men and women. However, the weight of evidence would suggest that in fact Junias was a woman, and in the main the early church fathers believed that Paul was referring to a woman.

The Doctrinal Issue

Now here is the issue. If we are to determine that it is normal for the church to have both male and female apostles, there must be a scriptural foundation for that position as a teaching of the church. This truth would need to be established on the basis of clear scriptural evidence and precedent. The biblical rule that applies is that there must be a minimum of two or three witnesses to establish every truth. If we were to establish as truth for the church the teaching that it was normative to have female apostles, we would need two or three 'witnesses', i.e. scriptural statements of truth, as evidence that the teaching was valid.

If you search the New Testament for evidence of female apostles, you will not find the two or three witnesses that we require. Therefore we cannot establish a doctrine that says there must be female apostles. And in the case of Romans 16:7, this is really only 'half' a witness, because it is not 'cut and dried', it is not clear. There is still theological argument across the church as to whether a man or woman is referred to here, so this is not a very clear witness. However, if we count it as one good witness, we lack the other witness. Interestingly, I think the Holy Spirit, in inspiring Scripture, has done this on purpose.

We are here comparing the difference between something which is established by the Lord as being normative for every church and every apostolic ministry in every place, against that which the Lord is free to do in the moving of His Spirit among the people. There is enough biblical evidence for women to be accepted amongst the apostles — to let God do what God wants to do, to accept that God can and does raise holy women to do wonderful things in ministry — but there is not enough biblical evidence for us to make a doctrine that says we must have women apostles, or that we must raise more women to be apostles.

Instead, Grace Aplenty

However, the biblical pattern we are following gives us a simple position. God may certainly anoint a woman to do whatever He desires whether there are usual 'rules' or not. Therefore He can send a woman as an apostle to the church, or appoint a woman to the eldership, by special grace. Like any man of God, a woman has what God gives, although the church will test every claim to the apostolate.

There is grace aplenty for women to rise up and do whatever God calls and appoints them to, even though there is not a biblical position that says that women are elders and apostles as a matter of course.

In this the church is not to take a position of affirmative action by saying, "We have men as apostles and elders, now we need women apostles and elders, so who are we going to appoint?" As soon as we do that we are back into man's religious ways, and falling for a trap set by the spirit of the age which locks us into striving and institutionalism.

I believe there is a good reason why the Lord has left this very grey area for the church. The only way to have an answer to these questions in each place where the church meets, is to have a heart that is such towards God and our brothers and sisters that in the end it doesn't matter, it just doesn't matter. We are simply going to work together. We are partners in the Lord. We all have a share in this work, so whatever grace gift is on you, and whatever grace gift is on me, we are going to build together. In the end we are not concerned with lording it over each other — and, with the apostolic 'revolution' of the church, the whole nature of the church is going to change in favour of acceptance of each other and vitality in relationships.

Wherever the Lord places calling and anointing upon a woman to fulfil these special roles, grace will have been given in which that woman may walk. By definition, this must be a special grace. Wherever grace is upon a sister to serve Christ in any capacity, we must honour the woman and accept with appreciation the ministry of Christ that is upon her.

Female Apostles in Practice

We have been speaking of these issues in principle. When it comes down to the practical specifics, apostles can only effectively be apostles in relationship with other people, and with actual churches and ministries. If someone is a primary apostle (an apostle providing apostolic covering to pastors and churches) it will mean there are pastors and churches who have determined that this person is an apostle, and is the one that has been appointed for them. It follows that they trust that person, and have the kind of heart relationship with them that receives from them. They will be satisfied that Christ has provided for them an apostle. The real test of whether a woman is an apostle or not will be in the acceptance of her *as an apostle* amongst those who serve Christ with her (1 Corinthians 9:2).

For every senior pastor and church, it will all come back to the issue of recognising their spiritual 'father'. Normally, most pastors and leaders are looking for a man to be the spiritual father who will stand in that position of authority and spiritual covering in relation to them. A majority of pastors would find it outside their perception of the right order for their own ministry to submit to, and relate to, a woman as their apostle and spiritual 'father'. And they would not be wrong. God has not called the majority to this arrangement, and it is not the scriptural norm.

These observations have nothing to do with sexism or prejudice. It is the way we relate, the way our needs are met, that is important here. It should be obvious to every one of us that it is normal and healthy for both men and women of all ages in the leadership of the church to relate to a man as their spiritual covering and father in the ministry. Therefore, in the main, we should expect that the church will continue to follow the biblical norms as far as covering ministries are concerned.

If the Lord raises a woman to be an apostle in her own right, grace will be given. Firstly, grace for the woman to stand in this responsibility and carry apostolic authority, then also grace to the ministry leaders and the believers who are meant to recognise her leadership as God's grace to them.

So then, it will come back to the recognition of spiritual fathers. If the senior pastor of the church, and the church as a whole, recognizes a particular woman as their apostle, they will know in their hearts that this is real for them. They will know that in this way God is going to bless them – and it is not for others to make rules for them.

Honouring Women in Ministry

There are certain ways in which I, as an apostle, would feel free to promote men, because they have specific God-given responsibilities — and with an attitude of "You fellows, get up and do your job." On the other hand, when God wants to raise a godly woman, and anoint her for great and specific leadership roles, who are we to deny or resist that?

Where God has anointed a sister for a particular ministry, we will honour what God has done, and we will honour the woman, both as a woman and as a minister of grace.

Equal in the 'Rules'

I would speak a word to all godly women who feel called to the ministry. In this you need not fear, and there need be no limit on what you can believe God for. As long as you are certain about what God is calling you to, and as long as you have fellow believers, and someone you are accountable to in the anointing, who also can recognise and affirm this grace in you. Take notice, this is what we say not only to women, but to everyone who claims a call to the ministry.

In ministry leadership, there are no 'rules' that apply to women that do not also apply to men. There should not be any special rules for women. The

Women have the same freedom to obey God as men

principles that govern ministry apply to everyone in ministry. For example, *"Every woman in ministry should be under apostolic covering"*. This 'rule' or principle is true, but this is what we say about every man, whether apostle, prophet, evangelist, pastor or teacher.

Another example: *"If a woman aspires to leadership she needs to have a right spirit"*. What is meant by this is she cannot be striving for recognition or demanding a place in ministry. Unfortunately, as soon as you operate that way, the spirit of it is wrong. Again this same rule applies to men. If a man demands his place, his spirit is wrong, and he does not qualify for leadership. Every true leader should be raised by the Spirit of the Lord, and we each must look to God to bring us into our calling.

Do you see what I mean? There are no rules that apply to women aspiring to ministry that do not also apply to men.

Neither should it ever be said or thought of a woman in the ministry that God probably gave her a position because a man refused. This assertion is sometimes thrown up at women, because of something in the story of Deborah. Deborah told Barak that because he would not lead the battle without her going with him, the Lord would not give him the honour for the victory over Sisera, but instead the honour would go to a woman. The other story commonly heard in the church is that of Kathryn Kuhlman, who apparently declared that the Lord had told her that He had called 60 men to do what He had given her to do, but they would not obey.

The Kathryn Kuhlman story above is a personal anecdote, not biblical teaching or precedent, and therefore is not an illustration of biblical doctrine. As for Deborah, she was never a replacement for a recalcitrant man, but was always a prophetess and judge of Israel in her own right. It is wrong to make such an assumption about any woman in the ministry.

In any case, it was only recently that someone in a prophetic utterance told me that the Lord had called several other men in Australia to do what I was now doing. Again, any ministry principles that are true for women are also true for men. Even if and when this might be the case, this does not make the present obedient minister second-class. Remember that King David was the replacement for the disobedient King Saul. Which one would you rather serve under?

Equal in Freedom

There is no sense in which the church should ever forbid a woman to step out in ministry just because she is a woman. There should be freedom in the church. Women have the same freedom to obey God as men do — to evangelise, to plant churches, to preach, and to write books, for example.

Just recently I was in India, in the state of Andhra Pradesh, where amongst the ministers of the churches I met an older woman, a grandmother. She was a gracious and godly woman with a noble heart and a sweet disposition. They called her an evangelist. For years she had been planting churches, and her method was this. She would spend time in a village, gather people together for Christ, and form a church. When she had built a faithful company, she would put a young man in charge as the pastor, and then she would go on to another village. She did this without any fuss, no institutional Christianity supporting her, and no one telling her whether she could or couldn't do this work.

When men give themselves to the ministry, they succeed depending on whether they were called and anointed, and whether they persevered despite the enemy's attempts to resist their efforts and nullify their faith. Women likewise will succeed, or fail, on this basis. There is no rule and no authority that says a woman cannot do by faith and grace what a man may do. If a woman is mistaken about her call, or has been presumptuous, this will become apparent and the ministry will not succeed — but men can and do make the same mistake, and suffer the same results.

Some New Testament 'Norms'

Can you name some New Testament exceptions to the 'men in apostolic and eldership ministry' principle? Only Junias, and no mention of her role. That is why the evidence for women in covering ministries is a bit thin.

You might ask, "What about Priscilla and Aquila?" No, that is not an exception, that's a New Testament norm! A couple in ministry where the woman apparently had stronger gifts than the husband, and so became more prominent in the ministry they shared - this is a New Testament norm (Acts 18:18-26, Romans 16:3-4). No one should have a problem with that. Remember, we said that in the New Testament everything is for both men and women. Therefore, a couple working together in the ministry is not an exception. There is no evidence here that Priscilla was in covering ministry, and indeed there is no evidence that any woman in the Bible carried the responsibility of the covering.

Phillip's daughters, four women who prophesied, are another outstanding example of women in New Testament ministry who were successful, well-known and a blessing to the church (Acts 21:9). Again, this is a New Testament norm. Any woman may be called by God and raised to be a prophet to the church or the world. These four women identified as prophets are examples of that. This is normal New Testament church ministry.

Only in the area of the apostolate and the covering eldership do we have a grey area. God can make exceptions, but the grey area remains because of the special requirements for the apostolic covering.

Women Are Free to Dream

Meanwhile, there is no height to which a godly woman may not aspire. If God has put a dream in your heart, believe and pray for it to be fulfilled. If God has given you a promise, walk by faith and let Him raise you to it. Let God be God, and let no man resist the grace of God. We should encourage all women whose heart is to serve Christ in public ministry to believe God for anointing, grace and power for the ministry to which He would appoint them.

Apostolic Inheritance for Daughters

Just like sons, daughters receive inheritance from a father. Every woman in ministry, like her brothers, should be looking to an apostle for blessing and increase and help. When you are faithful to a father in the ministry, you qualify for the double portion of his spirit, as Elisha did. I know for myself as a father to others in the ministry, I want to give my daughters, as well as my sons, everything I have.

Whenever a woman is placed by God into prominent ministry and leadership, and walks in authority as a gift to the church, this may not necessarily be the average or 'normal' expression of the grace of these ministries, but if not, then it is *a special grace*. And we give thanks to God for that, who knows our needs and meets them faithfully and appropriately.

One Final Word

I feel compelled by the Spirit to add the following comments to what I thought was a finished chapter.

It is of the utmost importance to teach and confirm the spiritual validity and great value of all women who do not have a public ministry, and who are placed in the home.

I would say to all women who do not have a call to public ministry, you are very important. If you are in Christ, then you do have a ministry, and your ministry is of equal importance to that of any man or woman who has a *public* ministry. I would not like what I have written earlier to suggest that the only life or ministry of importance is that of leadership.

I would like to tell you Hazel's story. My wife Hazel knew a call to the ministry from her earliest teenage years. We met at 17, and married at 19, knowing we were both called to the ministry of Jesus Christ. At 21 years of age, we entered denominational training for the ministry. In a class of 31 ministry students, Hazel became the dux of the college.

In the years that followed, Hazel was regularly involved in public ministry and preaching, as I was. Because we had no children after five years of marriage, Hazel sought the Lord to understand His plan for our lives, so that by understanding His plan she would not be frustrated if she were to be childless. She returned from prayer with this word from God, *"...my words that I have put in your mouth will not depart from your mouth, or from the mouths of your children, or from the mouths of their descendants from this time on and forever,"* *says the LORD" (Isaiah 59:21).* She said to me, "We are going to have children," and she fell pregnant the same month.

Following that, each time we prayed, God gave us another child, and eventually we had four children. Both of us had always wanted to have four, so now in our minds our family was complete.

During this time we had been sent by the denomination to work in Papua New Guinea. There Hazel carried responsibilities, as I did, and like every place we have been, we were willing to invest the rest of our lives in that place. But after five years, we were obliged to tell the denomination whether we wanted to stay or return to Australia. We sought the Lord, willing to do whatever He said, and on this occasion, it was Hazel who received the response from the Lord. Inspired by Genesis 31:3, she heard the Lord say, "Return to the land of your birth, and the place of your forefathers."

It was very significant that this came to Hazel rather than myself. Several months later, the denomination appointed us to Rockhampton, which, of a number of vacancies in the ministry, was the one place in Australia to which we did not wish to go. The significance of God's word was this: even though Hazel had never really lived in Rockhampton, she was born there, and her very elderly grandparents lived there. Thus it was to the land of *her* birth and the place of *her* forefathers that we came in January 1986.

In those early years at 'Peace' in Rockhampton, Hazel was one of the worship leaders of the church. After some years, one day I heard the Lord say, "Six months from now, Hazel is to give up leading worship. I have another ministry for her." She was 37 years old at the time. We wondered, excitedly, as to what this new ministry for her would be. Would it be counselling, or deliverance and healing perhaps?

A prophet with a team from the Solomon Islands spent an evening in our home with all the worship leaders from the church. He prophesied over them one by one. When he came to me, he said, "You will be the father of many sons and daughters. I see them all around you, clinging to you." When he came to Hazel, he said, "...Oh... God has another ministry for you, actually."

At that time I spent two whole days in prayer, seeking God for a revelation of the church. I did receive a revelation with an amazing sense of glory on it, but I didn't realise it was about the church. In some kind of vision, I received strong impressions of how wonderful it is in God's sight to give birth to a baby for Christ, and I saw and felt the incredible glory of God on the raising of children. I went home to tell my wife what the Lord had shown me, but she was not pleased by what seemed to be suggested.

Soon after, the Lord provided supernaturally the airfare for Hazel to fly to Sydney for the 1990 John Wimber Conference on Spiritual Warfare. Surely the Lord was going to reveal to Hazel her new ministry call. As it turned out, He did. In every meeting of that great conference, the Spirit of God spoke to Hazel about "the importance of raising children for the glory of God". Furthermore, He gave her a word from scripture which applied to His call for her to be available to bear and raise more children for Christ. It was, *"present your bodies a living sacrifice, holy, acceptable unto God, which is your reasonable service" (Romans 12:1, KJV).*

Since then, God has given us four more children, Simeon Jeremiah, Joseph Isaiah, Ezekiel John, and Susanna Keren. They are the joy of our lives, and each is a story, but this is not about them, but about Hazel as a woman living for Christ.

For much of the 90's, we kept hearing prophecies from travelling apostles, prophets and teachers that Hazel had a remarkable prophetic gift, but we had never seen any sign of it. Then, a few years ago, that prophetic gift began to operate powerfully and consistently. Hazel is my secret weapon. She does not prophesy publicly, but has a wonderful gift which helps us obtain information and insight whenever we pray.

I was in India recently, and I and the team with me came under attack. I was very sick, and in the middle of important ministry. We knew it was a spiritual attack, but could not seem to discern the source. I rang Hazel to have her seek the Lord with some questions, and she rang back 20 minutes later with the answers, accurately naming the source of the oppression.

Hazel has on many occasions obtained answers, discerned the way of the Lord through difficulties, and supplied correction or gained understanding in our following the plans of God. For me as an apostle, she is the most important partner on my apostolic team.

Regularly I pray for Hazel, very often with laying on of hands and anointing with oil. A constant prayer is for the renewal of her youthfulness. Just a few weeks ago, we were in my office and I was pouring out my prayer for her. On this occasion, I anointed her with oil while praying for God to anoint her for the ministry. In that moment, she heard the Lord speak clearly, "I am keeping you in the home."

This does not mean she lacks freedom, or cannot travel with me, or participate in anything the church may be doing, or speak in a meeting. Rather, this is a revelation of God's anointed purpose in her. I can tell you in all honesty, I regard Hazel's call and place in the ministry to be at least the equal of anyone's in public ministry.

By extension, every woman, wife and mother is of the greatest value. If you are in Christ, you are in the ministry of Christ, and *"your inner self, the unfading beauty of a gentle and quiet spirit, ...is of great worth in God's sight "* (1 Peter 3:4).

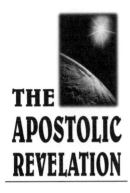

**THE
APOSTOLIC
REVELATION**

$\mathcal{C}hapter$ **7**

The Apostolic Covering

*"Then the LORD will create over all of Mount Zion and over those
who assemble there a cloud of smoke by day and a glow of flaming fire by
night; over all the glory will be a canopy. It will be a shelter and shade from
the heat of the day, and a refuge and hiding place from the storm and rain."*

(Isaiah 4:5-6)

*"Spread your protection over them, that those who love your name
may rejoice in you. For surely, O LORD, you bless the righteous;
you surround them with your favor as with a shield."*

(Psalm 5:11-12)

"...and he who sits on the throne will spread his tent over them."

(Revelation 7:15)

SECTION 1: Introduction to Spiritual Covering

From the beginning God has had but one method of providing a flow of
spiritual life, blessing and protection to His people as a whole — what we shall
call the covering of Christ — and that method was an *apostolic* method.

Other methods have come and gone, so there are now churches and
movements around the world functioning in other ways.

There are different systems and different patterns to leadership and government.
When that occurs, whilst they are Christian, and though they are preaching the
gospel, the covering they have established is a *partial* covering. It is a mixture of
Bible truth with man's wisdom, and is not an apostolic covering. Christ is present
and blesses, but the covering is not what we are calling the covering of Christ.

As we examine the pattern of spiritual covering in the Bible, we will discover that it always has an *apostolic* nature. When Christ provides a spiritual covering for the body of Christ, He provides *apostles*. This is a matter of great significance for the church today.

Illustrating the Power of Covering

Some time ago I flew to a city to meet a pastor who had written to me and phoned my office. I had never met him, but I made time to see him personally because the need to encourage him was a strong burden on my heart.

The story unfolded that he and the church had left their denomination (an evangelical institution) a few years before. They had struggled with many circumstances, and the church had become much smaller. At the same time, they were a really prophetic people, and were being blessed with great insight and some clear prophetic revelation of world events. Yet they had suffered a great deal, had taken a lot of bruising, and the church had dwindled to a much smaller group.

I asked if they had developed any relationships with apostles and prophets. No, they had no such relationships, and had never really known personally any apostles or prophets. I said, "You really must form such relationships. You need an apostle who is your spiritual father and mentor. You need the covering of an apostle. It is only when you put a relationship such as this in place that you will have the anointing and blessing flowing for the ministry."

That evening at dinner with the pastor, the 'elder' and their wives, the conversation centred around my explanation of how apostolic covering works, and how important it is for every work of God to be under this blessing. I mentioned that the apostolic anointing is gold, i.e., in the spirit, in visions, it appears as gold.

When I finished sharing the pastor said, "I need to tell you about 2 visions I have received." He went on, "While you were now talking, I was watching a vision unfold. In the vision I saw you as a very large man, much bigger than me. You were covered with gold, and your hand was outstretched. Coming off your hand was gold falling on to me. I was standing there being covered with gold, but my hand was also outstretched and gold was coming off my hand onto other people." Then he added, "But there is another vision - while I spoke to you on the telephone two days ago, I had a vision of you arriving at the airport, and your feet were gold."

Immediately he urged, "Let's sign this up right now. You be our apostle."

My response was more conservative. "I think we need to pray about it. Let's be sure of what God is saying to you. I am not here trying to sell myself. I never try to talk people into relationship with me. Let us test it and discuss it later." I am wary of building by the flesh, which we seem to do if we make assumptions, and make decisions on impulse. I am called to do this kind of work, but I avoid trying to enlist people to follow me in these formative days.

Two days later I was due to leave. While we were sitting at the table over morning tea, his need was on my conscience. I was thinking, "This brother has no covering. He needs protection. I am an apostle. I don't know whether I'm meant to mentor him in the Lord and be his apostle long term or not, but here he is, vulnerable, and my conscience is troubled." Even though there was no previous relationship, nor any plan to establish one, I was feeling in my heart that I was meant to pray some kind of covering over him. So I offered to pray such a prayer, which he eagerly accepted.

Up until this time I had always assumed that the power of apostolic covering flowed where there was an agreed, established relationship. Here I was exercising faith to release this grace purely on the basis of need.

I laid hands on him and prayed, "Lord I don't know whether the two of us have a ministry relationship for life or not, but I place on this man apostolic covering and I release your grace to him. I ask you to protect him." When I finished praying I said to him, "What did you see?" for I knew he had seen another vision. He said, "The moment you released that covering on me, I saw all these chains that had been wrapped around me go chink, chink, chink, chink, chink, and they all fell off." That is the power of apostolic covering!

'Traditional' Covering

The word '*covering*' is not new around the church. We have all heard references to spiritual covering, like: – "Who is your spiritual covering?", "What is your spiritual covering?", or "You should be under covering," etc.

Generally this expressed the need for everyone to be a member of a church. The pastor of that church (or the church itself) was seen as your spiritual covering. To say you were 'under covering' meant that you 'belonged' somewhere in the body of Christ, and by belonging to a specific church this provided you with your bona fides as a Christian. This meant you were not independent, you were submitted and accountable, you had a shepherd (someone who watched over your soul, someone who could presumably correct you if you were deceived or went wrong) and because of that you would be seen as a genuine Christian.

Thus you were under 'covering'.

The POWER Dynamic of Covering

Covering is in fact a *great deal more* than that, and largely occupies another dimension entirely. Spiritual covering is actually a *power* dimension. It is not only accountability; there is actually an objective spiritual protection in good spiritual covering. This is not just the protection of having a pastor who will correct you if you are wrong – although that is a protection. Neither is it just the protection of having relationships in the local church – although that too is a protection. Under true covering, spiritual power is flowing and at work, because something appointed by Christ is in place.

The Thesis

A spiritual covering is a **spiritual force field,** which helps bring in good things (blessings), and helps keep out bad things (protection). Every believer and all the church is meant to be under the blessing of this 'force field', which is the power of the life of Christ.

This life and power is provided by those anointings of Christ that flow through **apostles**, directly or indirectly.

My thesis is that the covering of Christ is vested in *certain* men (i.e. specific individuals). I am saying men, because these are the only examples we have of covering in the Bible. Even so, that doesn't necessarily exclude the possibility of God in grace using anyone, man or woman.

Godly women have stood in very important positions, and their lives are of critical importance to the work of God and his grace. Still, in speaking of key individuals whom God raises to be the spiritual covering for a movement or a nation, this is the role of an apostolic figure for which the biblical patterns show that these are, or should usually be, men.

God provides a spiritual covering through key apostolic individuals, and He has always done so. If we would have the *full measure* of the blessing of Christ (Romans 15:29), we need to have in place the relationships appointed by Christ that are a covering for us. These must be of a nature that relate us to the apostolic anointing from which flows the life of Christ for His body.

By this, I am saying that our lives are affected by other people. Yes, our lives are impacted by those who are over us in the Lord, whether we like this concept or not. An important key to obtaining and living in the fullness of the blessings and power of Christ is to be in proper relationship with the *apostolic leadership*, which He establishes in the world. This book seeks to clarify the *nature* of that apostolic leadership.

'Discovery' Of the Covering Anointing

When I first came to the church at Peace, like every minister of Christ I carried those anointings and gifts that God had given me. I held an anointing for five-fold ministry because I was called to be a leader in the gospel. Anointings to be an apostle and a teacher, and also the anointing to be the leader of the church at Peace, had been given me. In the ministry it is important to have each of the anointings you need.

In addition to anointings, there are also spiritual gifts. For example, I enjoyed a strong gift for healing. As I laid hands on anybody in need, many were healed.

These gifts and anointings I brought into the life of the church, and by the grace of God commenced building them into the 'fabric' (the life and belief systems) of the church. Then other people began to move in these things too. Healing became established widely as a gift in the church. Instead of me praying for everybody, others would pray. Every Sunday we would pray corporately for people who had very serious sickness or disease, and very frequently wonderful healings were the result. We witnessed many amazing miracles of healing, even of those great distances away.

After some time, I became conscious that *in Christ* I was providing a spiritual covering for the people. I discerned that a grace of blessing and protection was over the church, which seemed to come through my own life, as I walked with Christ and lived a holy life. This covering power flowed because the anointings of Christ were upon me for this purpose — I was the spiritual leader of the church and these were my people.

I understood this as a kind of 'umbrella' that went over the people, and it did two things. On the one hand it protected them from harmful things and helped keep out bad things, and on the other hand it brought to them good things, blessings. It seemed obvious that any Christian who was committed to the local church, and in this particular case, under my leadership or ministry anointing, was more blessed because of that, and more protected, than if they were not under that covering.

In time I felt led to develop an 'eldership' for the church (but see the current definition of eldership in chapter 8). By building a group of other leaders who were in harmony with me, we extended the covering and strengthened it - making it more effective and more powerful.

Thus we built over the local church, through the anointed leader and the 'elders', a spiritual covering that was a *power* dynamic. Consequently, for many years sickness was much diminished and healing was easily obtained. During that time we never had a divorce, nor a separation or marital strife, and if any of those things did occur it was because someone who already had these problems came for help to the church.

So we enjoyed a delightful season in which the power of Christ through this covering was at work. But the *key factors* were:

(1)   An anointed leader, and

(2)   Built around him were a group of men in unity, living godly, prayerful, and committed lives.

Sometime later this all changed for the worse when disunity amongst the 'elders' broke the covering. Out of this tragedy I was to learn the things I needed to know about spiritual covering. In the meantime, whilst things were still good and the work easy, the Lord began talking to me repeatedly about *another* covering. I came to see that every work of God actually needs a number of coverings:

·   One, the **local covering** which is provided through the local anointed leader and those who stand with him in that anointing.

·   Two, a second covering which is an *apostolic* **covering**. This covering is provided by being in relationship with apostles, specifically with one apostle who is your 'spiritual father', the primary apostle in covering over the senior minister and the church. That apostle also needs to have the spiritual covering of another apostle.

·   Later again I learned more about citywide covering through eldership — as I will explain in chapter 8.

This dynamic power of covering is meant to come to churches and the believers from three levels of ministry.

A Greater Covering – the Apostolic

For years the Lord was trying to communicate to me the need for apostolic covering. I had many dreams in which I would often discover that I was naked, or clothed inappropriately. In one particular dream I found myself naked, but out of my briefcase I was able to dress myself with really good quality clothes, except they were too *small*. I put them on because I had nothing else available.

What was the Lord telling me? In some dreams He was saying there was a missing covering, I was unclothed. Other dreams were saying that the clothing (covering) I did have was good quality, but it was no longer adequate to cover me. In all this, Jesus was trying to communicate that, aside from the covering I and other leaders were providing locally for the work, there needed to be *another kind* of covering — an apostolic covering.

I sensed the Lord directing me to find the apostle appointed for us. I came to know an American apostle, Chuck Clayton, but I continued getting more of those dreams. Eventually I heard the Lord tell me to go and stay in this man's house and spend time with him. I believed the Lord was saying I had to learn from the mistakes he had made in developing apostolic ministry, so that I did not unnecessarily make them as well.

He and his wife Karen welcomed me to share their lives. It so happened that, at the time of my visit, he was restructuring his approach to apostolic ministry after having built for some years on what he felt was one of his biggest mistakes. God sovereignly provided my apostolic covering, and this is one of the greatest blessings of my life. My relationship with Chuck as my apostle and spiritual father continues to grow in significance and power year after year.

As an apostle, I need an apostle whom I can regard as my covering and spiritual father. I am not 'dependent' on him, but there is a spiritual dynamic that makes it necessary, *essential*, that I have such a relationship.

Christ chooses to bless through these relationships. There are many blessings which are the inheritance of every Christian, but which do not come to us unless they are released through relationships. These relationships are the key to many of the things we need.

SECTION 2: Covering in Redemption History

From the creation of man we see the principle of apostolic covering at work, and it continues in all God's dealings with mankind. If you doubt whether the lives of other people affect us or not, that query should be settled the moment we consider the major characters of biblical history.

The Trouble with Adam

The first is Adam. When God made Adam, He made him the *father* of the human race and gave him dominion over the planet. Adam, the first apostle, your first spiritual father, was also the spiritual covering for the entire human race.

Whatever Adam chose to do with the dominion God had given him would affect the life of every single person ever born to the family of man. You know this to be true, because Scripture says, *"in Adam all die" (1 Corinthians 15:22).* Though you have never met Adam, like it or not, his life has affected you, and continues to affect you profoundly.

Adam chose disobedience and self-sufficiency, coveting after the knowledge of good and evil. This was a fall that plunged the whole human race into a darkness from which only Christ could rescue it. Born under Adam's sin, this sin is in you because he was your spiritual covering. This is why men must be *twice* born, because they need to be transferred to another covering.

So, the lives of *some* other human beings, even those you have never met, even those who lived thousands of years ago, do affect you today. Adam is but one example of many!

The covering for the human race had been vested in Adam, and when he fell the covering itself was destroyed. Nakedness was a sign that covering had been removed –now, not only personal righteousness, but corporate righteousness was missing. Adam had separated himself from his head, and stepped away from submission to authority, and both of these are requirements for apostolic authority. Sin entered the whole race, and evil in man grew increasingly worse to the point where God said, *"I am grieved that I have made them" (Genesis 6:7).* But God in his wisdom was looking for another man!

Abraham the 'Father of Faith'

Spiritual covering for the human race has to be vested in an individual. As you   come down the ages in the story of salvation history, you discover that the man of God's choosing would be *Christ.* However, Christ was not to come for a long time, so God who created all things had to provide another covering, and there are wonderful ways in which He has done that.

God was looking for the man to fulfill His purposes, and chose Abraham. Only in the context of the mystery of spiritual covering could we more fully understand what the Bible means when it says that Abraham *"is the father of us all"*, *"he is the father of all who believe"* and *"He is our father in the sight of God" (Romans 4:12,16-17).*

To the human mind that seems nonsensical, but believers are taught wisdom by the Spirit of God - a wisdom that is not of this age. Suppose you are a new Christian, and you come to Jesus. You learn that Christ your saviour is the Son of God, and you have a Father in heaven who is God. Then one day you read in the Bible that Abraham is your father. Does this make sense? In the context of spiritual covering, it does make sense! Fortunately the new Christian has the help of the Holy Spirit, and he or she will feel that a wonderful discovery has been made that adds to the richness of his or her spiritual life.

Abraham became, in the 'economy' of God's grace, the spiritual covering of that whole part of the human race that would turn in faith to God. So in this 'economy of grace', Abraham's life *continues* to affect you also. What Abraham, the father of faith, did by believing God in submission and obedience has meant that through the life of this one man, God could create something on planet earth that would enable Him to bring *"many sons to glory"* (Hebrews 2:10, Romans 4:16-17, Galatians 3:14, 16). In a sense, without Abraham you don't come to God.

Israel Baptised into Moses

In the story of Moses, important principles about spiritual covering are discovered. Moses was an apostle, *sent* to Egypt to deliver the people of God. Vested in Moses' own life was the power of God to father, lead, and protect these people. Protect? Yes, consider the power of Moses' intercession to save them from the imminent judgement of God (Exodus 32:9-14) and from the attack of the Amalakites (Exodus 17:12), but only when *Moses* prayed. Why? Because *"they were all baptised into Moses in the cloud and in the sea" (1 Corinthians 10:2)*. This is the ministry of spiritual covering at work, in the power of the anointing of Christ.

Are these not astounding things being said of ordinary men: Abraham is *'your father'*, and the people of Israel were *'baptised into Moses'*? Unfolding here is the 'mystery' that spiritual *covering* is a *power* dynamic enabling God to work in the world because, for whatever reason in the wisdom of God, He chooses to work through men. Though God is sovereign, still He has ordained the spiritual rule of this world in such a way that even He must work through man.

This is why the one who is worthy to take the scroll, to be seated upon the throne, and to break the seals which releases the judgements of God, is a man. The redeemer for the human race (the Son of God) became a man, because spiritual covering is ordained by God through men.

Therefore, because of this anointing, we find that the Israelites were baptised into Moses as well as Christ.

Now the task of caring for the people was too great for Moses. So the Lord instructed him to appoint the seventy elders. *"The LORD said to Moses: 'Bring me seventy of Israel's elders who are known to you as leaders and officials among the people. Have them come to the Tent of Meeting, that they may stand there with you. I will come down and speak with you there, and I will take of the Spirit that is on you and put the Spirit on them. They will help you carry the burden of the people so that you will not have to carry it alone' "*

"So Moses ...brought together seventy of their elders and had them stand around the Tent. Then the LORD came down in the cloud and spoke with him, and he took of the Spirit that was on him and put the Spirit on the seventy elders. When the Spirit rested on them, they prophesied, but they did not do so again" (Numbers 11: 16-17; 24-25).

Look closely at what He said to Moses, *"I will take of the Spirit that is on you and put the Spirit on them."* Why didn't the Lord say, "I will put My Spirit on them?" Why was it to be *"the Spirit that is on you"*? Because we are dealing here with the spiritual covering! Now for *'Spirit'* read *'anointing'*. Where it says *"I will take of the Spirit that is on you"* read *"I will take of the* **anointing** *that is on you and put the* **anointing** *on them"*.

It was essential in appointing elders over Israel that they did not have independent anointings at work in the camp. That would have been every man for himself, with each one's opinion as good as the next. The elders had to be subject to Moses as well as to God. There were not to be 70 new leaders with separate visions running in 70 different directions. They had to be a people of *one* spirit, *one* heart, *one* mind, and *one* vision. There had to be one common anointing upon them all, so that even though there were many leaders doing the work, there was unity of spirit and purpose under one leader.

Those in subordinate leadership must always function under the same anointing as the primary leader. This is the way it is meant to be in the local church, and in every ministry.

This important truth has applications not only at the apostolic level, but in every church and ministry. Anyone who is called into a leadership team must be prepared to submit to the anointing that God has placed on the senior leader He has raised for that work. That leader has the 'contract' (the commission) in the building of the house of God (Hebrews 3:2,5).

David the Shepherd of Israel

"He chose David his servant and took him from the sheep pens;
from tending the sheep he brought him to be the shepherd of his people
Jacob, of Israel his inheritance. And David shepherded them with
integrity of heart; with skillful hands he led them"

(Ps 78:70-72).

"I have found David my servant; with my sacred
oil I have anointed him"

(Ps 89:20).

Many amazing things are said of David, and promised to David, by the Lord, but the telling phrase for our subject here is that God made him the *"shepherd of his people"*, meaning the whole nation, the Lord's inheritance. We learn here that even though the nation is God's own inheritance, yet He entrusts the spiritual welfare of the whole land to one man, specifically because of his integrity of heart. This is everything that we are saying about apostolic covering — it is an anointing of grace and power to protect and bless the whole of God's work that is under the covering of the anointed man.

So significant is this that David, more than any other, is the type of Christ — and Christ is called the son of David, the one who will reign on the throne of David forever. David is also a type of the coming apostles, who will be together a corporate David, and who will likewise shepherd the people of God with integrity of heart. This is one fulfillment of Ezekiel 34: 23-24.

The prophet Amos prophesied that in the last days David's tent would be rebuilt (Amos 9:11). A tent is a covering, a shelter, a refuge, a protection, even a home — that tent is none other than the mighty apostolic covering which God is erecting over the whole world through the restoration of apostles, whose hearts will be knit together in the love of Christ.

So powerful is this apostolic anointing, that when the distressed, the discontented, and the indebted came to David in the desert (1 Samuel 22:2), these became his mighty men of valour. These men helped fulfil the promise God made David that He would subdue all his enemies, and every nation about Israel was made subject to David.

Elijah and Elisha: The Chariots and Horsemen of Israel

Elijah was the spiritual covering for Israel in his day. In 2nd Kings chapter 2, While journeying together, Elijah tried several times to release Elisha from following him. Elisha, devoted to his call and his master, would not be dissuaded. Suddenly the horses and chariot of fire separated them, and Elijah was taken up to heaven in the whirlwind. Elisha saw this and cried out, *"My father, my father. The chariots and horsemen of Israel" (2 Kings 2:12).*

Spiritual truth is hidden here. Elijah was the spiritual father of *Israel*, not just of Elisha, and the phrase *"the chariots and horsemen of Israel"* does not, I think, refer only to the fact that Elisha saw these horses and this chariot of fire. Spiritually, in terms of the dynamic of covering, Elijah *himself* was the horses and chariots of Israel. That was the anointing. By this grace, great spiritual power flowed through the life of this man so that God could do, through the anointing, what he needed to at that time in the life of Israel.

How can we be confident that the *"chariots and horsemen of Israel"* is a description or title for Elijah himself? The confirmation comes later, at a time when the city in which Elisha was staying was surrounded by a strong force of enemy troops, the Arameans. With his servant alarmed, Elisha made his famous statement, *"Don't be afraid. Those who are with us are more than those who are with them" (2 Kings 6:16).* The servant couldn't see it, so Elisha prayed, *"Lord open his eyes". "Then the Lord opened the servant's eyes and he looked and saw the hills full of horses and chariots of fire."* The assumption we usually make is that the horses and chariots of fire surrounded the *city,* because the account refers to the hills being full of them. However the text is specific that the hills were full of **"horses and chariots of fire all around Elisha"** *(2 Kings 6:17).* THIS WAS THE ANOINTING! Elisha had received Elijah's anointing in double portion, and the *manifestation* or *sign* of this anointing was the *horses and chariots of fire* — a sign common to both prophets!

Were you to meet Elisha in his day, you would see an ordinary man. But should your eyes be opened to see in the spirit realm, this particular man was surrounded by horses and chariots of fire. I think this was the permanent state of the covering, not just a one-off incident when enemy soldiers surrounded the city. This is what Elisha was in the anointing, except that it was not him, it was Christ! An *apostolic* anointing was upon him by the grace of God.

Chosen by Grace

Elisha was not necessarily better than any other person. This was grace at work. It was not that he deserved to be a prophet. It was that God chose him. This principle is made plain in the New Testament examples of apostolic grace. Paul says, *"For I am the least of the apostles and do not even deserve to be called an apostle, because I persecuted the church of God. But by the grace of God I am what I am," (1 Corinthians 15:9-10a).*

By grace, someone was going to be such a prophet. God laid His hand on Elisha and by grace he became the 'horsemen and chariots of Israel'. There have been key figures all through history who affected for good the whole or part of the human race, just by being who they were in Christ. This enabled God to put on them what He wanted, even though they may never have understood it. This will be seen more clearly when we consider Paul as the apostle to the Gentiles.

Earlier we saw that the lives of both Adam and Abraham still affect us today. Adam's life affects the whole human race. Abraham's life blesses everyone who comes to Christ. I believe that in every generation, and in many places, there are always contemporary, living people upon whom rests this kind of grace. As they faithfully hold on to what God calls them to be, it opens the spirit realm for God to do what He needs to do on earth with humanity.

The Initial New Covenant Coverings

Coming to the New Testament we discover a curious thing. Though there were many apostles that went to the Jews, Peter was called *"the apostle to the Jews"*. Furthermore, though many apostles worked amongst the Gentiles, Paul makes a very significant statement about himself that his contemporaries agreed was true. he was *"the apostle to the Gentiles"*.

Peter himself was the spiritual covering for all the work of grace to be done among the Jews. Paul carried a separate anointing to be the spiritual covering for the work of grace to be done amongst the Gentiles.

The Apostle Paul: Covering for the Gentiles

Many apostles were at work amongst the Gentiles, but only one brother, Paul, could lay claim to the title *'The Apostle to the Gentiles'*. There were places Paul never went, and there were places where Paul did not have direct authority, such as Rome. He was nevertheless, *the* apostle to the Gentiles.

Most of Paul's letters were written to churches over which he exercised direct authority. He had planted the church, appointed the elders, and would go back to visit. We find in those letters (for example, the letters to the Corinthians, the Galatians and the Thessalonians) that Paul is plainly expressing a direct and accepted authority, and giving explicit commands and instructions, as we have already seen.

Yet in Paul's epistle to Rome we find he writes with a totally different tone. This was a church to which he had never been, a church over which he had no direct authority as an apostle. You don't find in the letter to the Romans the strong language of most of his other epistles. Rather you find a more winsome speech, explaining his doctrine, saying he is longing to meet them, and hoping to impart some spiritual gift and be a blessing to them. Yet it is in this letter to the Romans that he says, *"I am talking to you Gentiles. Inasmuch as I am the apostle to the Gentiles" (Romans 11:13).*

Even though he held this important office, Paul spent years of his life in prison. Surely at times he must have wondered what his life was amounting to. Can you imagine Paul restricted to these few things; sharing Christ with his guard, praying night and day with tears, and writing occasional letters? He could not go and teach in the cities, or visit and strengthen the churches, or care for the elders. However, embodied in Paul was a grace. While he remained faithful, and bore up under the suffering with thanksgiving, not yielding to pressure but looking to Christ, that grace and his faith opened the Spirit realm over all the Gentiles for the gospel.

In these periods in which Paul was out of action, there were many other apostles working amongst the churches. Even false apostles were getting around some of his churches and he could do nothing about it except write the letters. Regarding Paul's call, Christ had said to Ananias, *"Go! This man is my chosen instrument to carry my name before the Gentiles and their kings and before the people of Israel. I will show him how much he must suffer for my name" (Acts 9:15-16).* The suffering of Paul is directly related to God's need to provide a spiritual covering for the Gentiles. Paul would suffer, because his life was the channel for a certain grace, and the enemy, knowing what he represented, would target him again and again, in an attempt to break him.

Paul had to stand in the place of his calling **no matter what**. No matter what the opposition, or the undermining of false brethren, or what harm or persecution arose against him, it was essential that Paul *stand*.

Paul's life represented something at another level. He was the gate or the 'door' for the blessings of Abraham to come to the Gentiles (Galatians 3:14). By means of his faith, obedience and perseverance, he was the door through which God would bless all the Gentiles, including those churches over which he had no particular working authority.

Based on these Old and New Testament examples, I surmise there are a variety of highly strategic positions of apostolic covering. So far as I know, some apostle is going to be the spiritual covering for every nation on earth. His name might even be unknown to most of the church, but in the economy of grace his fight of faith is somehow going to be used to hold together the battle, as did the prayers of Daniel and Moses.

SECTION 3: Spiritual Covering in Practice

The Critical Importance of the Covering

When God raises a man or woman to spiritual significance in the body of Christ, it is greatly destructive if they fall. There are far greater consequences if a leader falls than if another believer falls — and the further the Lord raises them the 'higher the stakes'. If God raises someone to critical significance in the covering, much is riding on their shoulders. If they fall into sin this is a great tragedy. The Kingdom of God is greatly harmed — not only because someone's sin has given the church a bad name, but because a fallen and broken covering allows the entrance of demonic, destructive powers into the realm of men and the church.

On the other hand, if this person, despite what they may have to endure, what opposition they have to face, or how dark things may appear, will hold on to God, the covering is in place for the sake of others. Even if they are never again free to minister publicly, or write another book, their life has a tremendous value in the economy of grace, even if they are not fully aware of it. As a result, there are multitudes of people who are under some greater measure of blessing, and the Kingdom of God continues to advance, because the one person who carried this anointing stood firm by faith in Christ, and did not yield.

It is not death that harms the door, it is sin. Imagine if the same apostle Paul, late in life after he had done so much, was taken in a fault –that would be very destructive for the work of God. If the apostle to the Gentiles had fallen into sin it would have destroyed and ruined so much of the work of God, so many people's lives. But if the same man is taken by his enemies, persecuted and made a martyr, he mightily blesses the work of God and multiplies it, as if planting a great deal more seed.

A graphic story, but not possible to verify, was reported in recent years by a mission newsletter. A pastor, somewhere in Asia, was arrested by the authorities. They put a horse trough in the street, rounded up his congregation, and made them urinate into it. Then they drowned him in it. Within two weeks his church had doubled in size, and continued growing.

This does illustrate the point that, if persecution comes against someone who is a spiritual covering for some work, but they stand in faith to the end, then even if they are cut down in martyrdom, it mightily empowers the work of God. If the same person is brought down by sin, it greatly harms the work of God. That is why God very carefully chooses whom He raises to these positions of covering.

A Personal Note

When it comes down to you and me, each one of us is a door for something or somebody. It is essential that we stand, that we remain holy, that we walk with Christ.

Sometimes difficult and strange things happen to us, and we don't understand why. We are at war, and do not always understand the significance of our 'holding on' at times. Now be faithful! It is a fundamental New Testament truth that the perseverance of the saints is of great importance and great value in God's eyes. *"You need to persevere so that when you have done the will of God, you will receive what he has promised" (Hebrews 10:36), "being strengthened with all power according to his glorious might so that you may have great endurance and patience, and joyfully giving thanks to the Father, who has qualified you to share in the inheritance of the saints in the kingdom of light" (Colossians 1:11-12). "Brothers, as an example of patience in the face of suffering, take the prophets who spoke in the name of the Lord. As you know, we consider blessed those who have persevered. You have heard of Job's perseverance and have seen what the Lord finally brought about. The Lord is full of compassion and mercy" (James 5:10-11).*

In service to Christ, some measure of responsibility or authority is given to you, and though you cannot see the anointing resting on you, you must stand firm. In some way, the lives of other people are affected by you. An open heaven over the town in which you live may depend on whether you walk by faith or fall into self-pity and despair.

The Broken Covering

Earlier I began the story of our journey of discovery of the covering, and mentioned that disunity arising in the leadership broke the covering at Peace.

The question might be asked, "If spiritual covering is vested primarily in the one man who has the anointing for the leadership, how can subordinate leaders who have a difference with him or others break the protection and power of the covering?" One must understand that when hands are laid on someone to share the leadership, an authority is given to share in the work of the leadership, and with that comes an access to the anointing. It means that the person so trusted to stand with the leader has access to spiritual power, for good or ill. That authority can be used well, or abused. Paul referred to this authority as *"...the authority the Lord gave me for building you up, not for tearing you down"* (2 Corinthians 13:10). The Holy Spirit has said, *"The spirits of prophets are subject to the control of prophets" (1 Corinthians 14:32).* These scriptures indicate clearly that everyone with anointing or power must make a choice to serve God and His people with a right spirit. And some people do get it wrong.

In spiritual covering, the actions of individual leaders will be determined by their own belief systems. Their world-view and mindsets, their ideas of what is right and wrong, and their ability or willingness to act ethically in relationship to others during difficult and testing times, will all be factors affecting their decisions and actions. It requires understanding, strength of character, emotional self-control, a pure heart, a genuine submission to God and a spirit of submission to those over them in the Lord. Then, with no secret agenda in the heart, they are to act ethically and honestly when testing times come. Those testing times do come when in leadership.

Subordinate leaders, (i.e. members of a leadership team) are brought into a position of great influence. They have the right to speak, and their words have power. They are respected by those around them, and by those over them in the Lord. How important it is then, that they act and speak in an ethical manner at all times, and are worthy of that respect, for their words and actions will either build up or tear down the church. I have discovered that two things are of the utmost importance: All leaders must have a clear view of how leadership is meant to function under the anointing and leading of the Holy Spirit (rather than having a traditional or denominational view), including an understanding of spiritual authority and submission. As well, they must have a holiness of heart and fear of God that will allow them, indeed constrain them, to act spiritually and ethically on every occasion.

We were to be sorely tested because we had a 'mixture'. I appointed leaders thinking they understood these things, only to discover when difficult times came that they were operating out of old denominational mindsets about what the 'eldership' was. To some degree it was my own fault, because I assumed that, since they had sat under my ministry and I had raised them to share the leadership with me, and we were happy and prayed much together, they shared my values. It turned out that they shared my values when things went well, but when tests came some had other values, secret fears and hidden agendas.

One Sunday morning I was away ministering at a nearby church when the wives of three of the 'elders' acted, without my knowledge or the permission of the 'eldership', to distribute a letter to the church taking issue over some things. They did this with the knowing consent of their husbands, but without the knowledge of the other 'elders'. This was not only inappropriate and unethical, but very destructive. This act, in conjunction with the words and attitudes associated with it, immediately broke the covering of the church, because it represented the destruction of the unity of the leadership. As a result, a flood of destroying spirits entered the church causing marital discord and health problems. The result was a difficult struggle over several years, as we were burdened with attacks on health, marriage, leadership, and church vision, while we worked to rebuild, heal, deliver, and pray people through.

Such a complete contrast to what we had known! One clear example of the contrast is that in 1994, twenty-two healthy babies were born in our fellowship –but in the midst of our trouble, five miscarriages occurred in a few months. When I speak of the covering and its effects, I know from firsthand experience the blessings of the good, and the sorrow of the struggle in times of defeat.

Apostolic Covering Comes to Peace

It is not my intention to go into the detail of these events, as that would be a distraction from our purpose. But we were faced with the task of a major rebuilding of the local covering, and it took two years to work through all the complex issues. We did rebuild a godly, prayerful and effective leadership team, but it did not give us all that we needed in spiritual covering. Something was lacking, and there was a reason.

Over the years something had changed. In the 10 years that elapsed from the building of the first local covering to this re-establishment of it, the anointing on the church had shifted. During those years we had been praying, crying out to God for Him to bring us into the apostolic and prophetic purposes of God for this day. We had prayed for new things, and God had given them. Consequently He had removed old anointings and released new ones.

Previously we had built under the old anointings with a denominational mindset. This had been effective, up to a point. Now under new anointings we had to build differently, because we had moved into a different season of the work of God in the world. This I will explain in a later chapter. The old methods were no longer effective, because the anointing had changed, and God was doing new things. In this new territory, we needed the apostolic covering.

I puzzled for a short time about what was lacking, until one day I heard the Lord say that for apostolic covering to be really effective, I had to make it 'official'.

Up to this point I had been cultivating relationships with apostles for some years, and with Apostle Chuck Clayton in particular. Our relationship had been of the heart, loyal and trusting, but it was an informal relationship. He would visit us occasionally; I would support him financially, and we felt the relationship was a blessing. Now I realised that to obtain the benefit of apostolic covering over the church, we needed covenant relationship with a covering apostle. We needed to have a clear agreement about the meaning of the relationship. God had given us someone to trust as an apostle, and to submit ourselves to in an accountable relationship. I had plenty of good brothers, but here was one who was meant to be a spiritual father to me personally, and to the church.

I felt the Lord saying, "You have to make it official. Write down what the relationship means, "this is how we serve you, this is how you serve us," speak to him, agree to enter into dynamic relationship, stand before the church and announce it to all the people, pray and ask God to 'put this covering in place'."

So I did! And on that very day, in the moment that I prayed asking the Lord to put the apostolic covering in place, the Spirit of God touched our people, and something was 'sheeted home' in the spirit realm over our church. We found that when we entered into agreement with the apostle, something immediately changed. And as evidence, healings were taking place.

Christ the Source

Jesus is the actual covering of the church, but the nature of covering is that the anointing flows by grace through His apostles who are living on the earth. Of this God speaks to Paul, *"My grace is sufficient for you, for* **my power is made perfect in weakness"** *(2 Corinthians 12:9).* God's power always flows through a weak vessel that is surrendered to Him.

All life and every blessing you will ever receive is going to come from Christ - but He has specific ways of divesting this to you. Normally, the grace of God will flow more fully, more completely, through a covering which is *apostolic.*

"New" Truth Resisted by the Powers

Keep in mind that our understanding of apostolic grace is still developing. This is an unfolding truth. We haven't seen the apostolic gifts and graces fully re-established in the church yet.

Every truth that has been restored to the church through reformation and renewal has been initially resisted and opposed by spirits and powers, working through both circumstances and people including other believers. This we need to understand for a good reason. Though the truth of the power and grace of Christ in apostolic covering will bring life and blessing to the church, and will increase the protection, blessing and power of the church, *nevertheless,* the powers fight any attempt to establish the Kingdom of God, so the short-term effect will often be that the 'pioneers' struggle. For a while, they can look worse off than before.

This is not different to what has occurred in the restoration of all other truth. At the time of the Reformation, armies marched, and blood flowed, because of the preaching of the Gospel. In many cases believers were killing each other; Catholics were killing Protestants, Protestants were killing Catholics, and they were both killing Anabaptists. Apparently the most contentious and divisive issue in church history, resulting in large numbers of martyrs, was the question of baptism. Baptism is a life giving sacrament, yet its message brought struggle, suffering, persecution and bloodshed in the day of its restoration.

It was the same in those exciting days of the 'charismatic movement' in the 1970's. Many churches experienced division and acrimony over the gifts of the Spirit that were meant to help and unify us. In the short term, (along with a thrilling adventure of discovery of the Holy Spirit), came trouble, suspicion and opposition from the 'religious' establishment - and vile accusations from self-appointed heresy hunters. In the long term, a great battle for freedom was won, and the church has been greatly blessed by the restoration of the gifts of the Spirit, by more personal and passionate worship, and with many other benefits. That movement also prepared the church for the restoration of her apostolic nature.

In every age God has looked to raise apostles who would be a spiritual covering for His people. For many of these apostles it did not mean success in outward ministry and the building of churches. Rather, it meant suffering, so that an opening could be created in the spiritual life of this planet for God by His Spirit to work. Luther didn't arise as a result of his own effort. Luther succeeded amazingly, but a price was paid by the saints that went before. John

Huss of Bohemia was burned at the stake, great saints like Savonarola, Wycliffe and others were also persecuted or martyred, so that a Luther could arise who, despite all the opposition and persecution of his own day, could walk through it all and bring the church into better things. There could never have been a Luther without those other spiritual coverings that preceded him.

Gratitude for Those Gone Before

We must be grateful for the many things that have prepared the way for us – including some of the things we are tempted to despise. We look at some of the history of the church, and think we would never have done it that way. We look at denominationalism and the institutional church and if we are not careful we despise some of what we see. But, through it all, we could not be today what we are if they did not pay a price. And they did pay a price! So we should keep a grateful heart, even though we are not to build according to the old denominational view of the wineskin. We are going to build the way God shows us today.

Greater Grace for A New Day

It is not as if there have not been apostles in every age. In every generation God has raised apostles, but in many generations and in most of the centuries of church history, the church did not know or understand this aspect of God's work. Today it is very different. As a result of the work that the Spirit has done through people who have suffered yet believed, we have come to the time in salvation history where He can raise apostles, prophets and saints who will finally be able to do what He was working towards all along.

We now see a great company of apostles being prepared by God all over the world. We are going to see old systems left behind, old wineskins crumble, and some of the old leadership of the church set aside. Apostles are raised specifically to be the leaders of the body of Christ in the coming day. Every believer, every evangelist, every Christian school, every local church, every pastor, all eldership and all ministry, will need to find apostolic covering (i.e. relational covering) instead of denominational covering in the days ahead.

Apostolic Example in Church History

In the history of the church there have been some outstanding examples of leaders that seem to have been apostles. John Wesley had to be a great apostle. I think also of Carey, Hudson Taylor and Watchman Nee to name a few. William

Booth, the founder of the Salvation Army, was a strong and gifted apostle. His story is a significant illustration of power through apostolic covering being recognised, positioned and accepted.

Booth was a minister of the Methodist New Connection in England, and was having amazing results in evangelism when travelling to other parishes. At a conference of the denomination a motion was passed forbidding him to preach outside his own parish, because of the jealousy of other ministers. He and his wife Catherine refused to be controlled by religious prejudice and left immediately, but there followed years of financial struggle and diminished opportunity, until he found his destiny.

One day he walked down Mile End Road, a terrible slum in the East of London. These were putrid places of awful poverty. An evangelistic open-air meeting was taking place, and he stepped into the circle of believers to stand with these brothers and sisters. One of them asked him if he would like to 'have a word', so he stepped forward and preached. They truly appreciated the power of grace upon him, and invited him back to their mission to preach in the crusade meetings being conducted in a tent on an old Quaker burial ground.

So effective was his ministry, they requested that he stay as their regular evangelist, and later elected him the General Superintendent of the "East London Christian Mission". The anointing was great, and many alcoholics, prostitutes, and the poor and downtrodden, began to come to Christ. The mission workers were busy — they felt they needed to attend to the work of evangelism and pastoral care, but the democratic process of the mission (decision making and planning through committees and meetings) was slowing and harming the work. A proposal was made that their gifted Superintendent, William Booth, take total authority over the mission. So they voted out democracy, and voted in the equivalent of apostolic leadership.

Then William Booth and the mission experienced an explosion of the power of grace. With rapid growth, the East London Christian Mission had to be renamed the London Christian Mission, and renamed again The Christian Mission. Finally, in a stroke of genius under Holy Spirit intervention, the mission was named "The Salvation Army". William Booth was no longer the General Superintendent, but the General. The work exploded from one place to over 80 nations in just 25 years – and from one evangelist to 10,000 evangelists. Ultimately millions came to Christ, especially the poor and downtrodden.

And the anointing transfers to others. The one with the apostolic anointing doesn't have to be present for the anointing to be effective. William Booth sent two young men to New Zealand. One was 20 and the other only 19, and both were single. He had commissioned them as Salvation Army officers, and sent them to 'invade' New Zealand. They arrived via Australia, from where they had conscripted three helpers. They landed at Port Chalmers in March, 1883, and agreed on an audacious plan of attack. One would take an assistant, go to Auckland in the north, and preach their way south to Wellington. The other with two supporters would go to Dunedin in the south, and work their way north to Wellington, where they would meet. After only nine months, they held a congress, with a vast army marching, and five brass bands. Many were unable to gain admission to the great meetings. They had established 11 Corps and numerous missions, 30 evangelists were working, and over 5,000 converts had knelt at their penitent-forms and drums. That was the story of The Salvation Army repeated in many places, at least partly because a small group of people touched the power of the apostolic anointing.

It is imperative that we do the same.

Freedom and Power through Apostolic Grace

In this true story about William Booth, we have an example of what is meant to happen under apostolic grace. When apostles are in place and the authority they are meant to have is *recognised*, the power of Christ can appropriately flow as it should. This is not an argument in favour of control, because in fact it works the other way around. Apostles are not going to bring in 'control', but *freedom*. Apostles will release believers and give the consecrated a lot more responsibility. Only apostles can do that. Committees and hierarchies and synods are not successful in giving people more power, authority, and responsibility, but that is what the Lord desires to do for His people, through apostles.

Elijah's Cloak: Sign of the Covering

In response to Elisha's plea for a double-portion of Elijah's anointing, two signs were given to him. One sign was, *"if you see me when I am taken from you, it will be yours" (2 Kings 2:10)*. The other was that Elijah's cloak was left behind for him. Elisha picked up the garment, went back to the river, struck the river with Elijah's coat and cried, *"where now is the Lord, the God of Elijah?"* and the river opened for him. The watching company of the prophets from Jericho observed, *"The spirit of Elijah is resting on Elisha" (2 Kings 2:14-15)*.

These two signs were the initial confirmation that the anointing was passed to Elisha in double portion. Then Elisha stood as God's anointed, the spiritual covering of Israel.

Now the Bible is consistent in carrying forward the meaning of these types and symbols. In the New Testament we have another garment that is singled out for mention and description. It is the tunic of Christ, the principal and expensive clothing of Jesus, literally the covering of Christ.

The Robe of Jesus: Symbol of the Covering

We know from the Old Testament that the cloak or the covering is a symbol of the anointing. In the New Testament, it is *Christ's* clothing that is spoken of, and about His clothing we are given some detail.

> *"When the soldiers crucified Jesus, they took his clothes, dividing them into four shares, one for each of them, with the undergarment* (the tunic) *remaining. This garment was seamless, woven in one piece from top to bottom. 'Let's not tear it,' they said to one another"*
>
> *(John 19:23-24).*

Most Bible commentators point out that this is the description of a high priestly garment. Aaron's tunic was to be woven in one piece, fitted close to the person, and made in such a way that it was not to be torn (Exodus 28:4,31-32, 39:22-23,27-29). Jesus went to the cross as our great High Priest, appointed by God.

In the epistle to the Hebrews which contains an extensive exposition of Jesus as High Priest, He is referred to as *"Jesus, the apostle and high priest whom we confess" (Hebrews 3:1)*. These two titles relate to each other — it was as the apostle of the Father that He became High Priest. It was the purpose of His apostolic commission, the reason for which He was *sent*, that He became the sacrifice being offered, and also the priest offering the sacrifice, for our sins.

So the priestly garment is the symbol of apostolic covering, the 'clothing' of the body of Christ, and we are to note three important details. *Firstly*, we are told that His garment was *seamless*. In other words, it had no joins. It is not separate pieces sewn together. It is one piece, it is whole, a complete unity. *Secondly*, it was *woven from top to bottom*. This is an indication of God at work, just as when the veil of the temple was torn from top to bottom by the hand of God in the moment that Christ died. And *thirdly*, concerning this particular garment, the soldiers who crucified Him said, *"Let's not tear it"*.

Detail is not given in Scripture without purpose, and in these details God is speaking. The clothing Jesus wore in the days of His earthly ministry was literally the covering of His body. It is the symbol of the covering that should be upon His body now. This covering should be *seamless, woven from top to bottom,* and *without division.* That is the nature of the apostolic covering as against other forms of covering that we have seen in the church.

Our Old Denominational Covering

Our understanding of the covering emerged over many years. Just when we thought our covering was now in order, the Lord began speaking through dreams and prophetic gifts to many of our people about the *denominational* covering. I had not realised there really was one, or that it had any effect on us, but as it turned out, we had to address it as a real issue.

We had by now rebuilt the *local* leadership and put in place the *apostolic* covering. Apostolic covering was 'official', we prepared a new apostolic constitution, and had informed the denomination. But now all the prophetic indications from many of our sensitive and discerning people were agreeing, 'the Spirit is saying we must remove the denominational covering.' As we sought the Lord, several compelling reasons for doing so were made plain to us, but it came down to these few things. The denominational covering was for us both inappropriate and infectious. God had an apostolic purpose for us, for which we needed to be non-sectarian, outside the denominational system, and looking to relate personally and sincerely to the whole church, especially the believers of our own city.

Our old denominational covering was *inappropriate* for us because, whilst we had the call of God to build in a certain way, the denomination had no vision for what we were doing. They would not support us, did not encourage us, were opposed to what we were doing, and were 'speaking' about us. They also came to dispute with us because we were actively pursuing certain biblical graces. We felt the mind of the Lord was, "because they claim authority over you, when they speak it has power, and thus they are hindering you from doing what I am asking you to do."

Then it appeared there was *infection* in the denominational covering. There are often things in the history of denominations that are contrary to the Spirit of Christ. When such an institution claims authority over you, these things can continue to infect and contaminate the spiritual life of the church.

Basically, we were unequally yoked. Now a yoke is a wonderful thing if you are equally yoked, because a good yoke is meant to be a blessing. In that yoke you share the burden. That is why Jesus says, *"Take my yoke upon you and learn from me, for I am gentle and humble in heart, and you will find rest for your souls. For my yoke is easy and my burden is light"* *(Matthew 11:29-30)*. But when you are not equally yoked it makes life more difficult, because someone is pulling against you, and you are being pulled in different directions.

It was necessary to release ourselves from an unequal yoke. After working through the issues in all good grace with our brothers, the denominational leaders, we resigned and were released from the denomination. As a church, we decided to take our freedom whatever the financial cost may be.

The Covering of Pure Gold

When the Lord first told me that I was to have the covering of Christ over my life, I thought this meant that Christ *Himself* was to be my covering; that, as an apostle, I would not need any other kind of organisation or relationship to provide covering, but Christ alone. I kept thinking this through, weighing it up, evaluating the ideas, to get to the truth of the matter. I knew there were reasonable objections to the apparent dangers of that position.

Then one night I experienced a revealing of truth – a 'vision' into the realm of the Spirit — and saw things that one cannot really 'see', nor explain. The covering of Christ is *gold,* and when you place the covering of Christ over any ministry, the results it produces are gold. Spiritually, you build with gold under the apostolic anointing. But the covering of men is a *mixture.* There is some gold, *and* some silver and precious stones. But there are other things, some not so worthy materials – wood and hay and stubble – all mixed in together. When you place a covering of men over any ministry (and they are good men, *Christian* men) it is a different covering from the apostolic covering of Christ, and the result is *mixture.*

This is precisely what we find in 1st Corinthians 3:10-15.

> *"By the grace God has given me, I laid a foundation as an expert builder, and someone else is building on it. But each one should be careful how he builds. For no one can lay any foundation other than the one already laid, which is Jesus Christ. If any man builds on this foundation using gold, silver, costly stones, wood, hay or straw, his work will be shown for what it is, because the Day will bring it to light. It will be revealed with fire, and the fire will test the quality of each man's work. If what he has built survives, he will receive his*

reward. If it is burned up, he will suffer loss; he himself will be saved, but only as one escaping through the flames."

Here St. Paul confirms it. We must build under apostolic covering, and on apostolic foundations.

At last I saw clearly that when Christ spoke about me being under His covering, He was speaking about the need for me to relate to an apostle of Christ. This did not mean I was not to be under anyone but Him, but that I was to be in a covering relationship with an *apostle*. The covering of apostles *is* the covering of *Christ,* because a specific anointing is on apostles for that purpose.

The Covering of 'Men'

All denominations claim to provide covering. Indeed, they do provide some kind of covering — some form of accountability, relationship, accreditation, and some protection, etc. This is provided by Christians - but is not *apostolic* because it is an institutional covering rather than that of a personal relationship with an apostle. It is therefore not, technically, the covering of Christ. What you have in these organisations where Christian brothers and sisters establish some kind of covering through an *institution* is the covering of *men. Christian* men, but still the covering of men.

However, we should remind ourselves that a denomination, any denomination, is not the church. A denomination is merely an organisation, an institution, which is supposed to help believers be effective as Christ's church. A denomination is meant to serve the church, not pretend that it is the church. The church is never an institution, although the believers may build institutions to serve their callings and the need around them, as Christ leads. More about this later.

'Patched' Coverings

Covering which is made up through management systems and committees, or by officials appointed, whether by a hierarchy or committees or general meetings, is a 'patched' covering. It is made up of pieces. Most denominations and movements have in them some of this and a bit of that. If we examine the denominations and movements of Christianity, none have all the truth, none have all the understanding, and none have all the gifts or the power of the anointings. Certainly, some seem to have more than others. Look at certain pentecostal or contemporary movements and your opinion might be, "Well, they have more gifts and more power, more anointing." Yes, they may have more, but they don't have it all. Alternatively, you can go to some of the historic denominations and find in them a rich, rich vein of truth, a rich expression of Jesus, but again it is not the whole.

So the 'covering of men', or denominational covering, is a patched covering. They have simply pieced together whatever they had and called it a covering. Some are strong in pastoral care, and some in evangelism. Some are strong in the healing of the heart, some strong in missions, or welfare, or social justice, or leadership, or academic defense of the faith, or something else, but it is all bits and pieces, with seams. The true apostolic covering, when it is fully built, will be a seamless anointing woven from top to bottom by Christ through apostles - without join, without tear and without division - complete. All the anointings and wisdom of Christ are meant to be in *that* covering.

A Further Symbol - the Ark of the Covenant

Amongst the Old Testament types and symbols of Christ, we find a beautiful illustration of the covering of Christ in the Ark of the Covenant. The Ark of the Covenant was a box built of wood and covered with gold. The lid of the Ark was called the Mercy Seat, but this was made of *pure* gold. That lid is called the *covering* for the Ark of the Covenant. The covering is pure gold thus the wooden box is covered with gold. The lid is called the Mercy Seat, and this is Christ. The Ark, covered above by a lid of pure gold and covered below by gold also, is the church.

The church is the Ark of Salvation. When the covering of Christ is in place the gold is on the Ark. We must have the covering of Christ, not just the covering of men, because we need the apostolic anointing that can only flow through the right covering. All other systems of church, mission and ministry government – whether democratic, presbyterian, or authoritarian, whether boards of elected or appointed officials, whether gifted administrators or teachers are in charge – it is *man's* system of trying to do God's work if the covering is not specifically apostolic.

They are Christian men or women teaching Christian doctrine, they have a Christian goal, they may be building a Christian organisation. But as *Christian* as all that may be, it is not under the covering of Christ but the covering of 'men', if they have not looked to Christ to provide covering that comes from Christ's appointed apostles.

When we say 'the covering of Christ' and 'the covering of apostles' we are speaking of the same thing, not two different things. When I finally took the step to 'formalise' a covenant relationship with another apostle that I could recognise as a spiritual father, and made myself accountable to him, I came under the blessing of an apostolic covering. Then I was positioned to receive more fully the flow of Christ's life and protection. I can receive increase, and be a more effective covering for others

Fill the Apostolate

When the early church met for prayer after Jesus' ascension, one of the 'twelve' was missing because he had fallen. Under inspiration, Peter brought to the meeting this word from Holy Scripture, *"For,"* said Peter, *"it is written... 'May another take his place of leadership.'" (Acts 1:20).* We could say in other words, "let the office of the apostle be filled." Peter at that time instructed the church *"it is necessary" (Acts 1:21).* The apostolate (the office of the apostle) must be filled!

Before the day of Pentecost, *before* the church could go on to receive the Holy Spirit who was to be poured out into the world, the apostolate had to be complete. They were about to carry the responsibility of the Great Commission to the nations, but not without the twelve apostles of the Lamb in place.

Some in the church have judged this event inaccurately. Over the years we have heard many people say things like, "Oh, you know Matthias, that was man's idea, but Paul was God's idea." That is not right. Matthias *was* God's idea. This is placed in Scripture to teach us something! – that the church should always fill the office of the apostle. Let there never be a church or any Christian ministry that has not put in place apostolic relationships. This is how the work of God is to be furthered in the world.

Where does Paul fit? When James was put to death with the sword, Paul was raised as an apostle. Note the proximity *in the texts of Scripture* of Paul's visit to Jerusalem at the time of James' martyrdom (Acts 11:29-30 & Acts 12:1-2), and Paul's return from Jerusalem immediately followed by his ordination as an apostle (Acts 12:25 & Acts 13:1-3), as evidence that Paul was an immediate replacement for James. Note also that in the gospels the three primary apostles were Peter, James and John, but in the history of the early church, and the writing of the epistles, it is Peter, Paul and John.

Paul was not an apostle of the Lamb, however. He did not qualify according to Acts 1:21-22, and in any case others already held this honour. Rather, the time had come for the Lord to appoint *the apostle to the Gentiles*. When James died, an apostolic office was vacated, and God filled it. The church should always look to God to fill the apostolic office.

We also need wisdom and discernment, because today the apostolic office is drawing attention, and some are finding it attractive to think of themselves as apostles when they are not. It is the 'flavour of the month'. Up to a point, we can accept this for a season because there is a natural process of discovery to go through. When prophecy was the current renewal, everyone wanted to be a prophet. I think it is natural for us to want to be in on what God is doing, and it takes time to evaluate these things and see where everybody fits.

Of special concern is the tendency of some believers who have been in prophetic ministry to now want to be apostles. I have heard a few anecdotal but credible reports from both Australia and U.S.A , of prophets who have been in public ministry as prophets, who are now thinking of themselves as apostles. Certainly, apostles are usually raised out of the place of an existing teaching or prophetic ministry, as Barnabas and Saul were (Acts 13:1-3). Yet still we must clearly understand that, where someone has been established as a recognised prophet with a public ministry to the wider body of Christ (rather than to the *local church* of their own city), generally their purpose is to point the people to the leadership of the apostles, not usurp the apostles. In this, prophets today must be very careful.

We have been through a period of time over the last two decades or so where the prophet was the centre of attention. Theirs was the ministry being restored, the greatest expression of what God was doing and saying at that time, and with a special authority for that period. Part of the message of those prophets was to say, "The apostles are coming!" These prophets should not then presume to be those apostles, when the attention shifts for a season to the restoration of another ministry, and apostles start receiving some of the attention previously given to the prophets.

One of the main functions of the prophetic office today is to partner with and support the ministry of apostles. Like John the Baptist, prophets today are meant to point the people to those who come after them, those whose task it is to provide the leadership and government of the church. They will need to find the grace to say, *"A man can receive only what is given him from heaven. ...He must become greater; I must become less" (John 3:27,30).*

Whilst there may be some exceptions, there should generally be a clear distinction between the prophetic office and the apostolic, and the New Testament consistently maintains this clarity. Prophets have an entirely different purpose than apostles in the body of Christ, and we must not confuse them. We need both.

But Get it Right

I shared lunch one day with a businessman who had been one of Australia's most successful ministers, but had left the ministry. This brother had often taught at conferences about apostles, describing them as the coming leaders, mentors and spiritual fathers of the body of Christ. Talking over lunch, I said to him, "There's something else – apostles are not just spiritual fathers and mentors." I stated, "There is the whole issue of covering here – blessing, power, protection and anointing that flows through apostles from Christ," and I explained how it worked.

He said to me, "That explains a lot!" and told me this story. Years ago in the ministry, he had linked himself, quite appropriately, to another man who was senior to him in the Lord. This man became his mentor, and my friend made himself accountable to him. One day, this senior mentor, a godly man, prayed for him and cut off the denominational anointing he had been under, and put his own anointing over him as a covering. However, he was not an apostle, he was a prophet. My friend said to me, "from that time, I struggled." So it is important to get it right.

In Conclusion

The church is meant to come into the exercise of a very great authority, so that every believer can minister with power, healing, miracles, signs and wonders. Every believer can help take the gospel to all nations. Every believer must have authority, but authority does not flow to anyone who is not under authority. For the authority of Christ to flow to every believer, apostles must be in place in the church. For authority to flow to you personally, you yourself must be committed to the dynamic relationships which God ordains for you, and which must be related in some way to the apostles of Christ.

Those apostles, who have been tested and have faced more 'death', are clothed with a grace they can release to people who are serving under them, and to others. It will be for them like it was for Jesus, who was able to 'speak and it was done', because as the centurion observed, Jesus was also *"a man under authority"* (Matthew 8:9). There will be an authority structure in the church, but it will function through relationships and not committees, through dynamic works of God that are now being prepared, rather than through old wineskins.

Can just any leader provide covering? Not if you want the gold. Not if you want the apostolic anointing. It must be the person of God's choosing. It must be one who has the anointing for the task. It must be an apostle. Not just anyone can take the place of an apostle. If someone else takes the place of authority or covering leadership that should be an apostle's, you will have the covering of a Christian, rather than Christ's covering through the anointing.

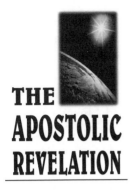

THE APOSTOLIC REVELATION

Chapter 8

Apostles and Elders, with the Church as One Body

In the year 2000, the 'elders' of Peace International Christian Church met for the last time. We had called a special meeting to discuss the leadership needs of Peace Christian Community, and to evaluate what we felt the Lord was telling us about the future of the church generally.

The 'eldership' was comprised of eight men, and on this occasion we were meeting with our wives. These were good people, great Christians and loyal friends. Change was in the air, and I wanted the wives of the men to share and be very much a part of what we were doing. The atmosphere of change had been with us for some years, and it had become obvious that New Testament eldership was quite different from what we had known of local churches all our lives. We had come to believe that simply electing a group of good people as leaders within a local fellowship, and calling them elders, did not equate with biblical eldership. Even though many churches had done things that way for a long time, we felt God was now about to work differently, and restore biblical eldership.

Surely the eldership of the future would be a leadership over the whole church of the whole city, made up from qualified fivefold ministers. We needed to stop calling people elders who were not elders, and instead build a leadership team appropriate for our fellowship, while at the same time opening the way in our hearts for a future eldership to be built in the city by the Spirit of God.

Having a small leadership group in the church called 'elders' seemed more like a 'bottleneck' than an effective means to equip and release the saints in ministry. We even discussed the nature of bottles in the meeting — some bottles are made with long, thin necks and small openings, whereas others are wide, open jars with openings as big as the body. Some bottle shapes are suited for one purpose, but not for another. The Bible likens the work of God to a wineskin, which was a container for wine. These have now been replaced by a slightly more modern technology — glass wine bottles — so we had a living analogy. We felt we were being urged by the Spirit of God to change from being one kind of 'bottle' (or wineskin) to another. We needed the kind of leadership that would open up the bottle, and give more freedom to all the believers to be involved in leadership and ministry. Of course, ministry for all had always been our ideal, but really, the old-fashioned leadership structure was a hindrance to pursuing that ideal.

And we made a decision. From that night, no one but the fivefold ministers of the church would be considered elders in the New Testament sense, and the eldership group would be disbanded immediately in favour of building a broad-based leadership team which would involve many people, under the leadership of those fivefold ministers. We have never regretted this decision, and in the period since have made very good progress in the things of the Spirit, as well as in our ministry goals.

The reformation of the church calls for a clear understanding and activation of some very basic biblical concepts. In any given locality (i.e. in any city, town or region), the church should be recognisably *one body*, with a *common leadership* recognised as the *apostles and elders*, every ministry and church fellowship self-governing, and every leader in accountable relationships. The elders and every ministry should be under apostolic covering. Apostles and prophets should be functioning as foundational ministries of the church.

The implications of these concepts are very far reaching. If we believe these biblical truths, this does call for a major overhaul of church structure, a complete reformation of the wineskin of the church.

The Church is One Body

There is not a church or denomination anywhere in the world that does not teach the unity of the church, i.e. that the church is one body, and we all belong to the whole body of Christ. Unfortunately, for much of the church, this is only a theory. The way we live, and the way most of the church actually functions, is quite different.

The body of Christ as we have known it is a far cry from being one body in any practical, recognisable way, although we see that progress is being made — reform is under way. Some might argue that the unity of the body of Christ is spiritual, mystical and eternal; that the truth of unity is not necessarily measured outwardly. Whilst there is some truth in that, and on earth there will always be tares amongst the wheat and challenges to the unity of the church, nevertheless an outward unity is required by Holy Scripture. We are to make every effort, to work hard in fact, to keep the unity of the spirit in the church (Ephesians 4:3). Divisive 'believers', whether false or foolish, are to be removed and ostracized by all believers if they do not heed suitable warnings (Titus 3:10, 1:10-11,13). The right spirit by which this is to be done is covered by Paul in 1 Thessalonians 3:14-15.

It is obvious from the prayers of Jesus that the unity of the church is meant to be <u>outward, visible, practical, recognisable and effective</u>. Jesus prayed for us, His future disciples, *"that all of them may be one, father, just as you are in me and I am in you... so that the world may believe that you have sent me"*. He further prayed, *"that they may be one as we are one: I in them and you in me. May they be brought to complete unity to let the world know that you sent me and have loved them..." (John 17:21-23).* The unity called for is equivalent to the unity of the Father and the Son, described by Jesus as a 'complete unity' — one which is so visible and recognisable that the world sees it, and so effective the world believes the word of God.

You know very well that we do not have this unity, except perhaps in a few rare places. Something must change, and the Spirit of God is calling for this change. But it begins with us, in a change of our hearts, and a change of our values. For this, we must develop understanding. We must take seriously what Scripture tells us about the nature of the body of Christ. We must be prepared to obey. We must be prepared to put aside some things we have previously clung to, and yield in submission to doing things God's way.

This unity is meant to be a *real* and *practical* unity, no more just a theory. We must be a people belonging to each other from the heart (Romans 12:10. 1 Peter 1:22), sharing a true love and acceptance of one another (Romans 15:7), and enjoying a true common unity which is 'community' (Acts 2:44). We are meant to stand together as one man (Philippians 1:27), and to think with one mind and speak with one voice (Acts 4:32, Romans 15:5-6). In any given community the church is meant to have a solidarity of witness which is in total unity and harmony.

When I read the following scripture I hear the cry of the Holy Spirit. *"There*

---

is one body and one Spirit — just as you were called to one hope when you were called — one Lord, one faith, one baptism; one God and Father of all, who is over all and through all and in all" (Ephesians 4:4-6). What I hear the Spirit cry is, "One body! — *One body!* — ***One body!*** — ***ONE BODY!"*** This is because there is only one Jesus, there is but one Holy Spirit, there is just one baptism, there is one God alone, and the household of God is the **one and only** household of God.

We must have our eyes opened, and allow the truth of God's word to actually grip our hearts. We can no longer live for ourselves, self-serving in our own spiritual 'worlds' where our own influence and our own way rules supreme. Rather, we must recognise the clear implications of these scriptures. The body of Jesus is one household, one family, and over this family God has ordained a method of leadership whereby all believers can look to a common leadership — that of the apostles and elders. This form of leadership does not require an institution, so there is no talk here of amalgamated denominations. Rather, we are trying to escape from institutionalised Christianity.

For years I have noticed something very, very strange. In towns, cities and rural communities right across the nation, there are Christian believers who never, or rarely, speak to each other, who never attend the same meetings or worship, who never pray together, and who never share their vision, their goals or their faith with each other. Yet they live in the same community, and in some cases they live in the same street, or at least nearby. What is more strange, is that very often they will have exactly the same prayer goals and vision for their community. What keeps them apart is institutionalised Christianity — they happen to belong to a different denomination, or a different movement, from each other. They act as total strangers, they are virtually foreigners, and they have been alienated from each other – by 'religion'.

We find the same strange phenomena occurring with ministers of the gospel. Even in small towns there are ministers who know of each other, but do not communicate or share in any meaningful way, yet they claim to have the same call to follow the same Christ, and to believe the same Bible. When you get to know them they will often have the same goals for the community. They will be praying for the lost to be saved, and for the Spirit of revival to come upon their town or city. There will be several others in town leading their own small flock in prayers for the community to be saved and for the Spirit to be poured out, yet they will never meet with them, and they never actively seek a way for the body to be whole.

Does this not seem strange to you? Born-again, spirit-filled believers who have the same beliefs, pray the same prayers, and believe in the unity of the church, are never given the opportunity to be one in any meaningful way. And this is despite what the Bible says, even though they live within the same locality.

Is there an explanation for this strange and grotesque peculiarity of much of the Christian world? There are two observations that could be made, both of which I believe to be true.

One is that there is upon the leaders of the church a mindset, a denominational and institutional paradigm. It is the leaders and the denominational structure that is at fault — the shepherds have erected fences that keep the sheep apart. In my experience the problem is never that the sheep are unwilling to mix. The leaders of the church will need to see things differently, or God will raise other leaders before too long.

The second observation is that a spirit not of God is blinding much of Christianity. A spiritual veil has been over our hearts, hindering us. A deceiving spirit of division has taken advantage of the many denominations and movements that have been effective in the past, and has worked to use these to create separation contrary to the will of God. And the hearts of men have allowed this in the course of the church's history.

However, today is a new day, and here is the scripture for today!

"Consequently, you are no longer foreigners and aliens, but fellow citizens with God's people and members of God's household, built on the foundation of the apostles and prophets, with Christ Jesus himself as the chief cornerstone. In him the whole building is joined together and rises to become a holy temple in the Lord. And in him you too are being built together to become a dwelling in which God lives by his Spirit" (Ephesians 2:19-22).

No longer foreigners! No longer strangers or aliens! Why? Because you are fellow citizens and members of one household! What is the key here? Apostles and prophets! — as you can see from the text.

The word *'built'* is here used twice. To obtain the desired result described in verses 21-22, these believers are firstly *'built on'* the foundation that is provided by apostles and prophets, and then they can be *'built together'*. This brings the most dramatic result of all — they become a dwelling (a house) in which God lives by His Spirit.

If we are not careful, we will miss the amazing significance of this last verse, because we are already familiar with the idea of verse 21. For years and years we have all been taught that the unity of the church is eternal and mystical, and we were not encouraged to have great hope for anything in this world beyond perhaps unity in the local congregation or the denomination. We were told, correctly, that all the believers of all ages who were in relationship with Jesus were God's household, and that God was building an eternal temple, and we were each the living stones of that temple. That part is true — this is precisely what we are to believe, and Ephesians 2:21 (above) describes this for our faith.

But the following verse (22) is not speaking of the same thing. Verses 21 and 22 sound similar, but they are not saying the same thing in different ways. First Paul speaks of the whole building, and then he speaks of a *local* building. Every one of us is meant to be *'built'* into a body which will be a house for God to come and live in by His Spirit, *in our city*. This *'dwelling'* is meant to be built as part of our present, local experience of Christ, in every place where there is a church.

Here we must make an all-important, climactic decision. In any given geographical locality, there can be only one church. There is only one body, and it is *the* church. We must allow this truth to change our attitudes, our values, our prayers and our goals.

I am not proposing that there should be a merger of denominations so that we have just one denomination — this is not the church unity we are speaking of. To do that is to assume that the church is an institution. The church is not this kind of institution, and an institution is never a church. Rather we are talking of the restoration of the apostolic church, where unity is based on actual relationships, values, love and devotion under the authority of apostles and the leadership of elders. Of this the church fathers confessed this creed, "We believe in one holy catholic (universal) and apostolic church" (The Nicene Creed).

One day in prayer it was as if, suddenly, I could see through the wall into the auditorium where all the people on Sundays worshipped. I could see them singing and praying, when I heard the Lord speak, "The reason many believers experience sickness, and often struggle to receive answers to prayer, is because they do not pray for the unity of the church."

Could this statement really be true? As I weighed it up, I realised this was indeed a profound truth. Every believer is a dynamic part of the whole body of Christ. We are each connected to all other believers, not in theory but with actual spiritual power, and the health and well-being of the whole body affects us personally. If we are careless and neglectful in our hearts toward the body of

Christ, that carelessness and neglect affects us. If we have no care for the health of the body of Christ, our prayers for our own selves and families, and our own congregations, have been rendered powerless by our attitude. This is the same spiritual dynamic at work as that concerning a man's prayers if he does not honour his wife (1 Peter 3:7).

Not only that, but if we are critical or disparaging of other parts of the body, we are cursing ourselves. You cannot curse a part without cursing the whole. You who curse are a living part of what you have cursed. This is why Paul wrote to the Corinthians, struggling as they were with a problem of division, these startling words, *"For anyone who eats and drinks without recognizing the body of the Lord eats and drinks judgment on himself. That is why many among you are weak and sick, and a number of you have fallen asleep. But if we judged ourselves, we would not come under judgment"* (1 Corinthians 11:29-32).

The weakness referred to here is spiritual weakness, the sickness is physical, and some of them had died prematurely. This is a genuine judgement of sin in the church (the sin was wrong attitude to the body of Christ) and as a result both spiritual and physical weaknesses and sicknesses abound. Yet Paul had said that the Corinthian church came behind in no gift (1 Corinthians 1:7). Here was a church that had the gifts of the Spirit in abundance (gifts such as discerning of spirits, prophecy, and words of knowledge), yet could not see the answers to their own problems, because they were under judgement. And the root cause of that judgement? Their attitude to one another — they did not recognise others as Christ!

This is no different to what many believers do today. Very few recognise the need to pray for the unity of the body of Christ as a pressing priority for prayer. No wonder weakness abounds. When we pray great blessings upon the body of Christ, such as health, vigour, wisdom, progress in the faith, revelation of Christ, possessing inheritance, etc., we are able to receive these blessings for ourselves. The unity of the body must be the great goal of our prayers, our faith, and our active obedience.

These conclusions about unity raise the question of leadership. If the body is whole, one, a unit, and if it is to be so in some honest, practical and visible way, then there must *also* be unity of leadership. The Bible does indeed provide such a model for the leadership of the church, and it is an apostolic model, as we shall see.

A Common Leadership for the One Church

The first thing we notice about the church in the New Testament is something starkly different to the church as we know it today; in any given city or locality there was only one church. Paul's epistles were written to churches at Corinth or Ephesus, for example, which were cities; or to Galatia, which was a region. The point is that wherever there were Christians, there was but one church – and these churches all accepted each other as *the* church.

The seven letters of Jesus recorded in The Book of Revelation chapters two and three are each written to a single church, and each was the church of a whole city. Nowhere in the New Testament revelation do we find anything that allows for any other option but one church in one locality. Anything else is division of the body.

The second thing we notice about the church of the New Testament apostolic revelation is that it had an amazingly diverse leadership, yet one that remained bound together in love as part of one whole. This remained so despite difficult issues that had to be worked through by the early church. Even when there were personal differences, there is no sense that this produced a divergent leadership (compare Acts 15:39 with Colossians 4:10, and Galatians 2:11 with 2 Peter 3:15).

The apostolic church had a single, identifiable, authoritative, relational leadership structure. It was not every man for himself; each knew they belonged to each other in the fear of the Lord, and there was an ultimate accountability to the apostles, as well as a submission to the words of those apostles.

In the biblical revelation, the leadership of the apostolic church recognised one another, walked in mutual submission and respect toward one another, and worked together knowing they shared a covenant relationship for the work of God. There was a spiritual 'fabric' that linked the fivefold ministry of the church in the anointings of Christ. This is what must again be found amongst us, and we will, because in these days God is giving His people a new heart. The anointing for leadership in these days is to give to Jesus the church that He wants. I will later make further comment on 'the fabric' of the fivefold ministry.

New Testament Eldership

Where the 'Acts of the Apostles' begins its narrative, the only recognisable ministry and the only position of any official status in the church is that of the apostles. But before long there were deacons (literally servants, but meaning officials in charge of work), evangelists, prophets and teachers. Then, at the end of Chapter 11, we find the first reference to an <u>eldership</u> in the church: *"During this time some prophets came down from Jerusalem to Antioch. One of them, named Agabus, stood up and through the Spirit predicted that a severe famine would spread over the entire Roman world. (This happened during the reign of Claudius.) The disciples, each according to his ability, decided to provide help for the brothers living in Judea. This they did, sending their gift to the elders by Barnabas and Saul" (Acts 11:27-30).*

From this we understand that the church in Jerusalem had been under the leadership of an eldership from an early time. As we read on, we learn that *"Paul and Barnabas appointed elders for them in each church and, with prayer and fasting, committed them to the Lord" (Acts 14:23).* Wherever apostles established churches, sooner or later they appointed elders. But in keeping with what we learned above about the nature of the apostolic church (i.e. one church in one locality), the elders appointed were the spiritual leaders for the whole city or the whole region. This Paul confirms when he wrote to Titus; *"The reason I left you in Crete was that you might straighten out what was left unfinished and appoint elders in every town, as I directed you" (Titus 1:5-6).*

Chapter 15 of Acts records the fascinating account of the events surrounding the 'Jerusalem Council', a special meeting of the senior leadership of the church, called to make an authoritative decision concerning what was to be required of Gentiles who became believers. In that chapter there is a recurring phrase, shown in the following quotations:

- *"So Paul and Barnabas were appointed, along with some other believers, to go up to Jerusalem to see **the apostles and elders** about this question" (Acts 15:2).*

- *"When they came to Jerusalem, they were welcomed by the church and **the apostles and elders**" (Acts 15:4).*

- *"**The apostles and elders** met to consider this question" (Acts 15:6).*

- *"Then **the apostles and elders**, with the whole church, decided to choose some of their own men and send them to Antioch with Paul and Barnabas"* (Acts 15:22).

- *"With them they sent the following letter: **The apostles and elders**, your brothers, To the Gentile believers in Antioch, Syria and Cilicia: Greetings. We have heard that some went out from us without our authorization and disturbed you" (Acts 15:23-24).*

Here we see that the apostles were a part of the eldership of the church, yet at the same time distinct from it. These apostles worked as one with the other elders, but nevertheless held an authority as apostles that was not dissipated within the workings of this body of other leaders. This is even more pronounced when we observe that whilst everyone present had much to contribute in debate (Acts 15:7), and Peter made a final authoritative appeal, in the end the leader of the Jerusalem church, James, made a final judgement on the matter (Acts 15:13,19). This was not democracy at work, but community.

It seems that genuine city eldership is always drawn from amongst those called by Christ to the fivefold ministry. How do we know that the elders were each fivefold ministers, as is now suggested. Let's examine the evidence:

*"And in the church God has appointed **first of all apostles, second prophets, third teachers**, then workers of miracles, also those having gifts of healing, those able to help others, those with gifts of administration, and those speaking in different kinds of tongues" (1 Corinthians 12:28-29).* (Emphasis mine)

Here we are informed that, following apostles, God has appointed in second place in the church, prophets. Scripture says that apostles and prophets comprise the foundation of the church (Ephesians 2:20). We have, then, a clear authority in these 'two witnesses' for recognising that prophets are among the body of elders. They must be, since they stand next to apostles.

Then, God has appointed in the church *"third teachers"*. As it turns out, the ability to teach and to understand the doctrines of the faith was a requirement of anyone appointed as an elder. Paul instructed Timothy that anyone considered for the eldership must be *"able to teach" (1 Tim 3:2)*. Then he expanded instruction on this requirement when writing to Titus, *"He must hold firmly to the trustworthy message as it has been taught, so that he can encourage others by sound doctrine and refute those who oppose it" (Titus 1:9)*. Teaching as part of a ministry is, then, a requirement for qualification to the eldership. This alone invalidates most of what has been considered 'eldership' in the past.

So we see that the elders are made up of apostles, prophets and teachers. These teachers are the *"pastors and teachers"* of Ephesians 4:11. This was a combination role, rather than separate offices. The church of Antioch provides a model of an eldership at work. Luke describes it: *"In the church at Antioch there were prophets and teachers: Barnabas, Simeon called Niger, Lucius of Cyrene, Manaen (who had been brought up with Herod the tetrarch) and Saul. While they were worshiping the Lord and fasting, the Holy Spirit said, "Set apart for me Barnabas and Saul for the work to which I have called them." So*

---

after they had fasted and prayed, they placed their hands on them and sent them off" (Acts 13:1-3). Here the eldership is specifically comprised of prophets and teachers, who have been working together in the leadership of this city for some considerable time. It is evident from other Scripture that Barnabas was a prophet and Paul a teacher. Revelation comes that shows them called to other work, and they are released into their apostolic mission.

We do not have evidence to show that evangelists are normally in the eldership, but this does not necessarily exclude them, since they are ministers of Christ with a 'fivefold' ascension anointing. The practicality of the matter is that the ministry of an evangelist is not for the purpose of the pastoral care of the church, which is the primary purpose of the eldership. The eldership appointment is especially one for watching over the flock of a particular locality (Acts 20:28, 1 Peter 5:1-4). Rarely would an evangelist be gifted for or called to this role.

In summary then, the eldership is always a team of anointed, fivefold ascension ministers, drawn from the apostles, prophets, and pastor/teachers of the church of that region.

Of special note is that not every fivefold minister of a given city is in the eldership. If this were so, there would be no need for Paul's list of qualifications for such leaders, as sent to Timothy and Titus. It so happens that there are believers who are called to the ministry, and who are spiritually gifted and functioning in ministry, but who are totally unsuitable for the eldership and the covering because of their character. They may carry anointings in accordance with their faith and their call, and have built or are attempting to build ministries, but simply do not qualify for the eldership. Others are unsuitable because they are still maturing, or for other practical reasons. So, not every fivefold minister is an elder.

If we would build an apostolic church, following the principles of the apostolic revelation of the New Testament, then the leadership teams of individual local churches, fellowships, ministries or house churches are not elders in their own right. Rather, elders are drawn from amongst those who are the ascension ministry gifts of Christ, and, under the apostles, are appointed to watch over the whole church of the whole city.

The RIGHT Eldership

Many so-called elders in churches are not really elders at all. When we lay hands on men from the congregation who are not, by calling and anointing, five-fold ministers and declare them to be 'elders', we place on them an authority and responsibility which is not theirs. This is very often why the leader, the pastor of the local church, is so often inhibited, or hindered, sometimes opposed - his way made more difficult one way or another. We have confused 'eldership', which is the 5-fold ministry over the whole body of Christ in a given city or region, for leadership which God raises and anoints at every level in every ministry.

This mistake is not without consequences. We have seen some unqualified men given the place of eldership only to slowly become a great hindrance to the work of the Spirit. It is also possible that others, good, sincere and believing men, sicken and die because they came under attack after they were promoted to the eldership without the anointing to cover and protect them from the power of the enemy.

Leaders in today's local churches, cells and house churches are not elders in the New Testament sense unless they are qualified as follows. They must be called and appointed by Christ with ascension ministry gifts, have suitable character and homelife as required by scripture to be a blessing and protection for the church in covering, and be recognised by apostles and the other elders.

Elders in the New Testament were appointed by the apostles, and whilst necessity may require other methods at times, this is the only biblical model we have. For example: *"Paul and Barnabas appointed elders for them in each church and, with prayer and fasting, committed them to the Lord"* (Acts 14:23), and *"The reason I left you in Crete was that you might straighten out what was left unfinished and appoint elders in every town, as I directed you"* (Titus 1:5).

People with 'five-fold' ascension ministry gifts have an understanding and perspective of the body of Christ because of specific 'Christ' anointings upon their lives, giving them that which is essential for elders to *be* elders. Whilst every believer is a priest, and every member of the body a minister of Christ, only *some* are anointed to represent Christ *as head* to the body. There is therefore a distinction between body ministry and Headship ministry. The 'headship ministry' anointing, or 'five-fold' ministry gift, brings with it a specific love for the church, an urge to build-up the body, and a perspective on the direction the Spirit wants to take, in a way which goes hand in hand with genuinely anointed leadership.

Many have been appointed to the so-called eldership of churches without the heart understanding of the work of God that this anointing is meant to give, because they don't have the anointing. Without the spirit of understanding, they will hinder the leader of the work, because they have been given a false authority over the work by being declared to be 'elders'.

City Eldership: How Do We Get There?

City eldership can only be built as a work of the Spirit of God. Christ said He would build the church (Matthew 16:18). But the Holy Spirit does give us wisdom, revealing His plans and purpose so that we may cooperate with Him, because we are co-labourers in building the house of God (Psalm 127:1, 1 Corinthians 3:10).

There are certain things essential to achieving this purpose. We must build *relationships*, change *values*, *pray earnestly* for God to build the city eldership and unity of the body, and *yield,* i.e. *allow* the Holy Spirit to make changes and bring about these results.

Firstly, Build Relationships

No one is going to create unity by amalgamating denominations. Who would want a bigger, more centralised, institutional religion anyway? In any case, there are too many differences and institutionalised errors to overcome. The pentecostals are not going to submit to the practices and 'errors' of the traditional denominations, and neither are those of the older traditions about to suddenly accept 'shortcomings' of the teaching and methods of the newer. The future is not found in this direction, and it would be a waste of time contemplating it.

The only way forward is with what comes from heart relationship. In every place, real men and women of God must find each other, and begin to walk and talk together. They are personally the ministry of Christ, not the institution to which they belong. They must begin to accept each other personally, despite any initial differences. The body will be built by leaders in relationship, whose hearts will be knit together like David and Jonathon (1 Samuel 18:1-4), and who will bring the people of the whole church into a one-heart, one-mind, one-spirit relationship (Acts 4:32). Only leaders of genuine spiritual integrity are capable of these personal covenant relationships.

The entire new wineskin of the church will be based on relationships that are personal rather than formal and institutional. Until now, very little genuine relationship of a personal nature has existed between most pastors in any given area. Despite a doctrine that said they were brothers, in practice they were competitors, and well outside each other's circle of friends. Though ministers of the gospel to the same place, they were strangers to one another.

Relationship has to be built, but cannot be built using meetings that have a business agenda. We've all tried it and it doesn't work. Relationship has to be based on friendship and covenant love. The only way to build friendship is to spend time together with no other purpose than that. When we get to know others well as friends, we come to love them. And when we love them, we come to trust them. This is the only basis for partnership in ministry.

If you think my emphasis on personal, loving friendship is inaccurate, consider what may be the most common form of address and endearment we find in the New Testament epistles. Paul, Peter, John, Jude, and the writer to the Hebrews all address their people as *'agapetos'*, which is, beloved. This is the same form of address the Father uses for Jesus. It is translated in various versions as *'dearly beloved'*, *'dear brothers'*, and in the NIV as *'friends'* or *'dear friends'*. Jude in his short letter uses this expression three times, the apostle John uses it six times in his first epistle, Peter uses it twice in his first epistle and four times in his second, and Paul uses it in three epistles. This surely is a significant, not a casual, use of language.'

Some Experiences in Relationship Building

I have lived in Rockhampton since 1986. Historically, this has been a spiritually divided city. Not divided in the obvious sense, of opposition and bitterness, or criticism, between churches and denominations — not in living memory, anyway, except in some individual cases perhaps. Instead, in this city the churches have, generally, simply gone their own way. They have focused on their own good work, their own needs, and seen no need for anything more. It has always been difficult to bring the church together in Rockhampton to any effective degree.

In 1988 I became the pastor of Peace, one of the well-established churches in the city. Peace had been amalgamated from four Baptist churches that had a history in North Rockhampton and Mount Morgan going back about 100 years. After a year I noticed a curiosity — in the course of that whole year there had been no occasion to meet with other ministers. I had not become familiar with even one other pastor in the city, and none had contacted me. I made enquiries, and was informed that there had not been a meeting of any minister's fraternal in Rockhampton for over 20 years. No trouble was evident, simply apathy. This was a yawning chasm of division, which outwardly appeared simply as indifference.

Early in my second year I wrote to all the pastors and the bishops. I proposed that every month we have lunch together — no agenda, no chairman, no secretary, no minutes, no treasurer, no business except having lunch and talking. This continued for six years with mixed results. The ministers of the older historic traditional churches were generally regular attenders, but the pastors of evangelical and pentecostal denominations were almost all conspicuous by their absence. Most of the ones who claimed to believe and obey the Bible more, and love Christ the most passionately, were the least moved by any appeal to develop relationship with others. The main reason given was that it was a waste of time, because nothing would change.

This did not become a great unity movement in the city, although I was glad to develop acquaintance and cooperation with others whom I came to love. The very institutional and structural nature of the churches represented, combined with the underlying curses and spiritual strongholds of the city, prevented anything exceptional developing at that point.

There was one shaft of light that appeared for a time, however, just like the tabernacle of David that appeared in Israel sandwiched between the tabernacle of Moses and the temple of Solomon. In the neighbourhood where Peace was located were four other churches, namely Anglican, Catholic, Lutheran, and Uniting churches. These four were traditional, while Peace was, call us what you will, contemporary/ charismatic/ pentecostal/ prophetic etc., but something very interesting eventuated amongst us.

Because of those monthly lunch meetings, the Catholic priest felt close enough to us, his neighbours, to invite us to his house on Friday afternoons, where we would share coffee and cake, and talk personally. At the time the Catholic Church was working through a group programme called 'Renew', and he invited us to participate in some of those exercises. All of this helped develop an acceptance, and some trust. Soon we began having regular combined church services. Some of the special experiences of God we had at that time were actually when we met with these others. Unfortunately, as always in the way of the institutional church, three of these pastors were relocated, and the fellowship ceased to exist.

From this experience I discovered a power dynamic. When leaders enjoy personal relationship with one another, with affection and acceptance, then there is power and divine presence when their people meet. This was vastly different from the usual 'ecumenical' services I had experienced previously. Those had brought together various parts of the body but, by comparison, lacked power and anointing, because there was not any sense of personal relationship between the leaders.

Entering Dynamic Relationship

Years went by when suddenly, after what appeared a void of relationships, came something sovereign, wonderful, and fruitful — real relationship with other ministry leaders. God brought three men, each of different movements or denominations, together for friendship and intimacy and trust. We had not previously had any relationship, and very little contact with each other.

I cannot remember what changed, or how it happened, or who initiated it. But Brian, John and I began finding ourselves meeting every week. It was quickly apparent that this was the most important event of our week, and we devoted fully half a day — just to talk. We talked for hours, about anything and everything, but especially about Christ, and grace, and our expectations and hopes. We shared about our families, our experiences and our sorrows. Our acceptance of each other grew into love and trust. Our lives became enriched and our hearts enjoined, and we cared about each other's success. All the while we talked, we were, without planning anything, sharing and exploring our values, until we discovered how much we held in common. We were of one heart, and had a remarkably similar vision for the work of God.

Then our wives began to get together, and their love and acceptance of each other was even greater than our own. Fellows are slow — it was through our women that we discovered more about how the men saw each other, and how we saw the future of the relationship and the church of the city. Here was a deep desire for God to do with the church whatever He wanted, and to not hold back from giving God whatever He planned for us.

One day in April 2001, in a 5.30 am prayer session, there was a great breakthrough in defeating a certain principality, a spirit of division that had been in the city for a very long time. This opened the way for a number of wonderful developments. Within two months we began having combined church services, and something amazing was happening in the hearts of our people. Now the people of one church would think of the members of the other as belonging to them. They were all our people. I visited an elderly woman who had attended my church for years and loved me, but who was now having difficulty travelling to our meetings. She lived opposite John's church. I said to her, "These are good people, and they are our family. If you worship with them, you are worshipping with us." She has been there ever since.

Gone is the distance that was between us, and gone is the spirit of competition. Recently John was going to be away from the city. He instructed his youth leader, "if you have any problems while I am away, go and see Brian or John and talk to them about it." That is trust.

In that trust is the inner peace that comes from knowing there is but one church in the city, and that your brothers will guard your place and your work in it.

These are still very early days for us, and there is much yet to be built by the Holy Spirit for our city. In the city are many others, good people, ministers of Christ like ourselves. Somehow the Holy Spirit will build a more extensive fellowship and trust in the coming days. John, Brian and I each know that the Holy Spirit will build an eldership over the city. We are not trying to build it, but our hearts are ready to grow in relationship with the leadership of the body of Christ. And our people are actively praying, crying out to God to build the unity of the body and establish the eldership of the city.

I should comment here that the views expressed in this book are my own. It should not be assumed by the reader that John and Brian have automatically endorsed all the viewpoints I have presented. The healthy relationship we share does not need to be based on identical viewpoint.

There will be no true eldership, there *cannot be* eldership, without the elders being in personal, committed, trusting, covenant relationship with each other. Those who believe they are called to serve as elders should look for such relationships, and the people of God should pray for them to be established. There is great authority and power in the covering through such relationships.

Secondly, Change Values

William Beckham, author of *"The Second Reformation"* (Touch Publications, 1995), travels the world instructing pastors and cell leaders on how to transition to the cell church. He constantly says, "We do what we value, and we value what we do." Part of the instruction on transitioning from a traditional programme based church to a cell group church is this — "don't change structures until you change values". In other words, we must give understanding to people before asking them to do things differently. Even when it is the will of God for change to take place, we will get more cooperation when people understand through having a proper set of values.

We always function according to what we really believe, whether we are conscious of it or not. While ever pastors and leaders hold only the traditional values, or concepts, of either their denominational or their 'independent' background, there will be little change. We must insist that church leaders have an open believing heart to embrace what scripture tells us about the body of Christ, not what is demanded by church traditions, denominational vested interests, or the stronghold of the way things have simply been in their experience.

As more and more Christian leaders are motivated by Christ's passion for His church in accordance with biblical apostolic values, we will see a transformation take place in the church in community after community. This is a current work of the Holy Spirit being carried forward all over the world.

Thirdly, Earnest Prayer

Hand-in-hand with the apostolic reformation worldwide has been a partnership with prophetic intercession. There are many strongholds to be brought down, and there are many underlying curses, not only in the communities but in the churches. Satan has taken advantage on many past occasions to entrench traditions, divisions, and cultural attitudes, to resist and prevent the future unity of the church. Warfare prayer and supplication with tears is needed, not in an occasional manner, but as a devoted way of life by the many saints who have understanding. For many, intercession and sacrifice in vigilant spiritual warfare is to be a long-term lifestyle, until the church becomes mature (Isaiah 62: 6-7, Ephesians 4: 13-16).

Most of the things God has promised, and which are in the ministry visions of leaders, cannot be achieved without intercession. The greatest need of all, and our greatest opportunity, is to pray for the unity of the body of Christ, and the restoration of apostles and New Testament eldership. More than anything, this will have a direct bearing on the health, well-being and success of all Christians, their families and their businesses, as well as the life and ministry of the church.

Fourthly, Allow the Holy Spirit to Have His Way

God wants to bring change, and He is asking for our cooperation. This will mean surrender in some areas where we thought we owned the ground. We must make room for others. Pastors who were the leaders in their domain will need to submit their vision to the greater vision of the city. All local ministry will need to become of one spirit with the leaders of the city, and there will need to be an active searching after the experience of being one in heart and mind with others in the ministry. There will be an overall anointing for the spiritual leadership of the city, and all who have ministry in the city will need to be in harmony and submission with that anointing.

Every pastor will have to address in their own hearts the issue of independence, and of their 'rights', no matter how large their church. Leaders will have to give each other their hearts. We are not called to be independent, we are called to be one. And the Holy Spirit is well able to make us one if we will love and trust with a pure heart that does not carry a 'private' agenda. This calls for the heart of integrity that is to be in the true shepherd (Psalm 78:72, Ezekiel 7-10, 22-24).

If the leaders of a city have right values, and clear understanding of what God wants and where He is taking the church, then with perseverance, prayer, and surrendered hearts, Christ will build an apostolic city eldership for the church. There are a few cities that have already made some very significant progress in this journey.

Autonomy of Ministry

What has been said implies that the pastors and the ministries are autonomous, which as you know is mostly not so. Most pastors have a 'career' in a denomination, and most churches are part of a national or international institutional religious system. This does not leave a lot of freedom of movement for change in the direction I am speaking of.

Most congregations are constitutionally or legally tied to some specific religious organisation which operates from another place, i.e. from outside the local area. This means that the allegiance of the pastor and the church is to an institution other than the spiritual leadership of the city. Spiritually, they are tied to people and systems that have no effective spiritual authority in the local city. This is in fact a bondage, because it prevents the one thing essential for the body of Christ — that the body be *whole*, that the body be one, in its local setting.

Following are some possibly controversial statements of propositional truth. It is more important for a pastor to have relationship with the fivefold ministry of his own city, than it is to have relationship with any other leader in the body of Christ outside the city. It is more important to relate to the overall church leadership of your own city, than to relate to the leadership of a denomination. A minister in a given place should be in submission to the spiritual leadership of his or her city, rather than under the authority of a religious institution based elsewhere.

Every local church should be autonomous, under apostolic covering, and in fruitful relationship with the city elders. Autonomy is the right of self-government or self-determination. A local church is not meant to be owned and controlled by a multi-national institution, *which is never a church* anyway, as we shall discuss in a moment. I would remind you that when apostles provide covering, this is a personal and relational authority functioning in the anointings of the Holy Spirit, not an institutional, denominational authority. Apostles, not institutions, are meant to be the overall relational government of every church, and all anointed ministry.

It is essential that pastors and congregations give their loyalty to the city leaders, rather than to absent denominational hierarchies. It is also essential that the pastors have authority to lead the local church over which they have been appointed as a shepherd, and build the body of Christ in cooperation with the other shepherds of the city. The apostles and elders will be held dear by such a church, and the church itself will be greatly blessed because of the fruitfulness of such relationships.

Pastors and the elders relate to apostles as sons to a father. The pastor of a church is not meant to relate to some official in a religious institution, but rather to walk in love with the spiritual father whom Christ will provide. In denominational Christianity, the leadership positions of bishops and general superintendents etc. are changed from time to time. There is a regular process of electing or appointing new officials. Spiritual fathers cannot be appointed in this way. If you are in the ministry, no hierarchy or selection committee can appoint your spiritual father for you. Nor should they, after a few years, appoint a new one for you. When this occurs, this is institutional Christianity, not apostolic Christianity.

Denominations: Spiritual Colonialism

Denominationalism is a kind of spiritual 'colonialism'. Historically, each of the denominations has considered every town, city or region its own target for expansion. No matter what work was being done by others, that place was not reached unless they themselves were established there. For the Baptists, for example, every town had to have a "Baptist witness". In the past, when it was decided to plant a new church in a given area, no discussion was entered into with the believers who lived there. No consideration was given to the fact there may be people who had the authority of Christ in that area. So the work of the great commission has been fragmented, and disempowered.

Each denomination would enter a community and establish its own 'colony'. Today our cities and towns are full of these spiritual colonies, who give scant heed to one another. They fail miserably at relating to one another because it is not seen as a real need, and is not a priority. But they spend a lot of time and effort relating to their colonial masters. We have, then, a strange and irrational form of Christianity, where lots of little groups ignore each other almost completely, and give their allegiance to leaders of religious institutions who do not live in the area, have no vision for their city, and can give no real leadership. And they offer no real power through their anointing to the city or the local churches.

These kinds of churches are like spiritual islands. Our towns and cities are full of them, and they keep largely to themselves. This is not biblical Christianity.

We must prayerfully look forward to the day when this will no longer be the structure of Christianity. We should no longer want the faith to appear as spiritual islands, or colonies of old denominations headquartered in far off cities, but rather as ONE church in the city under the leadership of the apostles and elders appointed by Christ.

The Right and Wrong of Institutions

An institution is never a church, even though there are many institutions that call themselves churches. To help understand this, I will explain the right place of institutions in the ministry of the church, but first, let's go back to a basic lesson we have all learned, which is, "*A building is not a church*".

Preachers have worked hard for years to convince the believers that the word 'church' is not referring to the building we meet in, but is referring to people. It is a gathering of believers which is a church. Jesus said that where two or three of us met in His name, He would be in the midst. That is basic church, a gathering of believers with Christ in the midst. Most of us are clear on the truth that *a building is never a church*. Now we must take a step forward in our thinking, and understand that *an institution is never a church*. An institution is only another kind of building.

In the same way that we need the use of buildings for the ministry, we also do need institutions in the ministry. But the ministry itself is a grace entrusted to individuals, and when those individuals meet with Christ they are the church.

It is essential that we have institutions. If a few of us get together because the call of God is upon us to minister in His name, the ministry is ours. But we may need to form an institution to be our tool, a vehicle for the ministry.

Suppose you are an evangelist, and you form a partnership with two others who want to work in the ministry with you, and you enlist supporters. You will need a bank account, you will draw up some guidelines for the ministry, and before long you have formed an evangelistic association. You now have an institution, but this institution is your servant, a tool for the ministry. The ministry itself is yours. The ministry is actually you, the anointed minister of Christ. The two who joined you are also in the ministry. The institution is not the ministry, but is a vehicle for the ministry. It is a means by which you are helped in the ministry.

Unfortunately, institutions have tended to become more important than the ministers over time, and eventually we are fooled into thinking that the institution is the ministry. In this way we have been fooled into thinking that churches are institutions, and institutions are churches.

An institution is meant to be our servant, but never our master. When I incorporated an apostolic ministry in the Philippines in the early '90s, I spoke very clearly to the other ministers who were involved with me in that ministry. I said to them that the incorporated body, Peace International Ministries, Inc., was a servant of the apostolic ministry. The apostles and ministers of Christ must always have control of the ministry. If ever the incorporated body controlled the ministry rather than serving it, we were to close it down.

Many spiritual movements, begun under great Christian leaders of the past, have become institutionalised, and many of these have become denominations. The problem is that often they become a master instead of a servant. Ministers of Christ end up being controlled by institutions, employed on the payroll, bound by tradition, locked in by mindsets and majority opinion, and finding it impossible to do anything easily except maintain the status quo. If and when an institution becomes a controlling master, it is technically Babylon, which traded in the bodies and souls of men (Revelation 18:13), rather than the City of God. I don't mean to be offensive in saying this, and I apologise if I have offended, my intention is simply to make an objective comment, warning of the potential danger of the situation.

Wherever believers gather to meet Christ, to seek intimacy with God and with each other, and to pursue the purposes of Christ, this is a church. I am not referring to people who occasionally meet, but who are committed to meeting with each other for this purpose — this is a church, if they desire to relate to the apostles and elders, and to the rest of the church. (If they are independent of spirit and reject relationship with headship ministries and other Christians, they are a cult).

On the other hand, we have institutions that organise property, insurance and finance, supervise churches, collect funds for missions, and train candidates for the ministry, etc. This kind of institution often calls itself a church but, even though it may be attending to the needs of churches, and the people working in it are part of the body, it is not a church.

Let's take a simple example, not for the purpose of drawing attention to any one more than another, but to illustrate. Recently a number of Anglican church leaders were being interviewed on a current affairs programme. Their comments reflected denominational values, rather than apostolic biblical values. Chief amongst these was a statement to the effect that their desire was for the Anglican Church to be one of the truly great churches in the world. Another comment referred to the people of the 'Anglican communion'.

Without meaning to break fellowship with the beloved brethren of Anglican churches everywhere, there is no such thing as 'the Anglican Church', and no such thing as the 'Anglican communion', unless they want to claim something that is outside of Christ. But if it is in Christ, then there is only one — One Christ, One Church & One Communion. If an Anglican sister eats of Christ, and I a non-Anglican eat of Christ, we have eaten at the same table. The Anglican institution, as such, is not in itself a church. At the same time, though, many local groups meet who call themselves 'Anglican', and these are churches.

These kinds of false perceptions, held for a long time by good people of all denominations, are deceptions brought about by the institutionalisation of Christianity. These are examples of some of the hidden denominational values that need to be cleaned out of our hearts.

The anointed ministry of Christ is always *personal*, never institutional. Christ places His call and anointings for ministry on individuals. The Holy Spirit then builds the power of the ministry and anointing as others come into *relationship* with each other in ministry. It is individuals who are pastors, teachers, and evangelists, etc. Because the ministry of Christ is *personal*, the structure of the ministry should always be *relational*. It is as anointed ministers relate to each other, and agree to work together under the leading of the Holy Spirit, that we have the true ministry of the church. Because the true ministry is personal and relational, it cannot become institutional and remain anointed.

No one should ever build an institutionalised hierarchy and call it the Christian ministry. When the church has such a hierarchy, where a professional priesthood is a separate class to the rest of the believers, we have created a terrible problem. The call of the gospel is for every believer to find intimacy with God, but the search for intimacy is hindered when a believer's worldview of the faith has in it a professional priesthood and a hierarchical religion.

The Fabric of the Fivefold

There is a spiritual 'fabric' that causes the fivefold ministers, those of the headship ministry of Jesus, to be linked together in the Spirit. Even when there is no harmony or agreement, they are still joined by an anointing. Even while they are opposed to one another, or one secretly despises or rejects another, they are spiritually connected, because each one represents Christ — something of Christ is upon them and, whether they are aware of it or not, they are connected.

There is one Christ, and His own personal anointings are on the ministers who have the ascension graces for leadership of the church. When these stand together as one, there is great power for the Kingdom of Christ in that city. Alternatively, if one pastor despises another, or preaches against him, his actions are harmful to the whole body, including himself, and the church is weakened.

Sometimes, the attacks of darkness which come against a church or a minister and his family have actually been released unknowingly by someone in the fivefold ministry, who is effectively, if ignorantly, cursing the other minister or church by words and attitudes. (As an aside, let me advise that every believer in ministry must learn how to recognise and cut off these attacks of witchcraft which have been unleashed through division occurring in the heart of other members of the body of Christ).

The following passage of scripture is largely ignored, yet still applies to us all.

"I appeal to you, brothers, in the name of our Lord Jesus Christ, that all of you agree with one another so that there may be no divisions among you and that you may be perfectly united in mind and thought. My brothers, some from Chloe's household have informed me that there are quarrels among you. What I mean is this: One of you says, "I follow Paul"; another, "I follow Apollos"; another, "I follow Cephas"; still another, "I follow Christ." Is Christ divided? Was Paul crucified for you? Were you baptized into the name of Paul?"

(1 Corinthians 1:10-13).

Paul reacted with alarm and sent this strong appeal to the Corinthian believers when he heard of them dividing into separate spiritual camps over senior ministry leaders. *"I follow Paul"* or *"I follow Apollos"* or *"I follow Cephas"* was totally inappropriate in a context of comparison, superiority and disharmony. Even *"I follow Christ"* was equally suspect when motivated by division or party spirit.

A climactic moment in Paul's corrective appeal here was the question, *"Is*

Christ divided?" And the immediate response that should be forthcoming from every believing heart is, "This must never be!" Yet we have tolerated such division for a long time, and mostly we do very little to bring about change, mainly because *unbelief* helps to maintain the status quo of a divided body. In the main, we do not believe, and we have not taught our people to believe, that things can ever be any different.

Worse yet, we have institutionalised it. We don't say *"I follow Paul",* instead we say, "I'm a Baptist", or "I'm a Pentocostal", or "I'm an Anglican", or "I'm Church of Christ". We have done precisely what Holy Scripture has told us not to do, and unbelief has allowed this institutionalised division to remain a stronghold on the church. At least the passage above does clearly prove that the ministry of the early church was personal, as has been asserted.

The nature of the anointings that are on this headship ministry mean that it <u>must not be divided</u>. Hence Paul's question, *"is Christ divided?"* Because of the fabric of the fivefold ministry, the elders must stand together as one. Any other attitude or value system comes from either spiritual ignorance, or else because we are in the flesh. In the case of the Corinthians, Paul said they were carnal i.e. worldly or fleshly. *"Brothers, I could not address you as spiritual but as worldly... Are you not acting like mere men? For when one says, "I follow Paul," and another, "I follow Apollos," are you not mere men? What, after all, is Apollos? And what is Paul? " (1 Corinthians 3:1,3-5).*

Paul had opened his appeal with *"...agree with one another so that there may be no divisions among you and that you may be perfectly united in mind and thought" (1 Corinthians 1:10).* This is the apostolic position in response to those who think that we must stay apart from others because we see things differently to them. Argue your case as you might, you are still *"acting like mere men".* By the Holy Spirit, and with the leadership of apostles and the input of prophets, both the eldership and the whole church will be brought to the place of being *"perfectly united in mind and thought".*

And guess what? That is precisely the fulfillment of Ephesians 4:11-16 we have all been looking for.

It is not necessary to divide camps when the ministry is personal instead of institutional, for a very good reason. You don't need to listen to only one man, or benefit from the anointing or wisdom of only one minister of grace. You can have, and enjoy, them all. *"So then, no more boasting about men! All things are yours, whether Paul or Apollos or Cephas or the world or life or death or the present or the future-all are yours, and you are of Christ, and Christ is of God" (1 Corinthians 3:21-23).*

The Door of the Sheepfold

We will turn our attention briefly from the *eldership* covering, to the *local* covering over each fellowship (local church) or ministry.

The many fellowships and ministries which we today call 'local churches' are only part of the whole; alone they are not the body of Christ for their area. In the past, many of these local churches would have a group of upstanding 'laymen' elected to be the 'elders' of that local church, serving alongside the pastor. But we have discovered that these are not elders at all, since New Testament elders are those who have an anointing to provide spiritual covering for the whole body of Christ over the city, town or region. Nevertheless, leadership teams for these local churches are needed, and these also are a spiritual covering for their people. Though they are not the 'eldership' spoken of by the apostles, New Testament elders may well be amongst them.

The minister of Christ is the door to the sheepfold - he *himself* is the door. The old middle-eastern sheepfolds had a wall around with just an opening for the door. The sheep would be herded in and the shepherd himself would lie in the doorway. The body of the shepherd was the door that provided security and protection for the sheep.

This is the same in the church. The senior leader is the door, and the other leaders with him are also each doors and windows to the church. It is very important that we build leadership aright - the right leadership in the right place.

Leadership Anointing and The Local Covering

When God raises a minister to be the leader of a local church, he must build a leadership team. That leader and his leadership team become a spiritual covering for their people and their work. But the covering is founded in the **one** man. Therefore, when a leadership team is built around that senior leader, the anointing that God has given *him* must come to rest on those other leaders.

There has often been division in churches where a leadership team is *elected*, because then you have a leadership that is representative of the people. Consequently they represent different interests, there may be different anointings upon them, and there is no true spiritual unity. Biblically, a leadership team should be representative of the senior leader and of Christ. Leadership is not an elected body to represent the people and to demand that the pastor do their will — it is a ministry that is to represent God to the people.

We must build leadership teams that are of one heart, one mind, and one spirit. The leader's primary anointing must rest on them. When someone is raised to leadership, they must submit to their leader's anointing, and receive it.

When I visit churches, I will often have the leaders stand before the people. I lay my hands on the senior pastor, take of his anointing and then lay my hands on the other leaders, placing on them their leader's anointing. Alone this would be a wonderful object lesson for the church and the leaders, but it is more than that - the power of Christ is present, and the anointings are real. This is an important part in building a spiritual covering for the local church.

Building the Local Covering

To build effective covering over a local church or any ministry, it is very important that the senior leader lives a holy life, and personally walks with Christ with a prayerful and humble heart. Guided by the Holy Spirit he will build up a leadership team, not based on the gifts and abilities of the individuals, but their character and spiritual life. Over that church will be established a spiritual covering.

Notice that in the lists of qualifications for elders set out in Paul's letters to both Timothy and Titus (1 Tim 3:1-7, Titus1:6-9), spiritual gifts are not mentioned as requirements at all. Rather the requirements listed are to do with holy living and Godly character, quality of home life including relationship with wife and children, hospitality, and maturity in faith and doctrine.

Obviously these appointments are being made in the context of providing *leadership* for the ministry, so the question of suitability *will also* include consideration of a person's ability for the work involved. But do not fall into the old trap of thinking that if someone has the gifts, they must be right for the job. If you do this, you can get yourself very badly burned! If someone has good character, it is not hard to see them advance in spiritual giftedness - but if someone has giftedness yet are of questionable or unknown character, DO NOT promote them in ministry. This is very dangerous.

We have found it necessary, and biblical, to place several other determining factors well ahead of either *spiritual giftedness* or *ability* when considering leadership appointments. In addition to the character qualifications Paul gives us, we look for at least three other things. These touch on prayer, finance and relationships.

Firstly, we will not raise anyone to leadership who does not have good relationships with the existing leaders, especially the senior leader. The leaders are a team, to be of one mind and one heart. No one with a contentious spirit should ever be raised to leadership. There must be harmony and unity. Here is the New Testament position: *"I appeal to you, brothers, in the name of our Lord Jesus Christ, that all of you agree with one another so that there may be no divisions among you and that you may be perfectly united in mind and thought."* (1 Corinthians 1:10) Therefore, not only is proven character a pre-requisite for leadership, so also are sound relationships.

We are not in the business of promoting into leadership the 'devil's advocate' just to represent other points of view. The leadership does not exist to promote or give equal time to every shade of human opinion, but to seek and do God's will. It is true that good leadership is not made up of "YES men"; each will pray to seek God's will, and they should have the mind of Christ. They will each help the senior leader and each other find God's way for their people and the work He has given them. But the "NO men" should NEVER have any part in the work. Yet that is what many churches have ended up with - an 'eldership' that thinks their job is to protect the church, but they spend their time 'protecting' the church against the things the pastor wants to do in case he is deceived. They resist the anointing, because spiritually they are out of order.

Secondly, we would not promote anyone to leadership who does not have a commitment to prayer. The *first* responsibility of every leader in the body of Christ is to walk with Christ personally, and to pray for their people and the health and direction of the work. Their first work, the work of prayer, is to seek and to know the Lord, to know God's will, to obtain the blessing and power of God for the work, to believe for the moving of the Spirit of God, and to see the release of His provision. We have specific times when this work of prayer by the leaders is to be done corporately. Every leader needs to make themselves available to be one with the others in the spirit of prayer, and, however inadequate one may feel, at least the desire of the heart should be appropriate. The example of the prophets and teachers at Antioch (Acts 13:1-3) is the New Testament model of the praying leadership team.

Thirdly, but not less important than any other qualification, a leader must lead in the matter of giving to God, and in his or her financial commitment to the work of God. This includes tithing to the church, and a life of sowing, reaping and generosity in the Kingdom of God. Anyone in a leadership position whose finances are not submitted to Christ is in bondage, whether to fear, or love of the world, or whatever. One of the greatest and most important freedoms for *every* believer is to walk in the grace of obeying God in financial matters, usually beginning with tithing. Jesus said, *"Where your treasure is, there your heart will be also."* Leaders who are not committed financially to the work are not real leaders, certainly not spiritual leaders. To think so is deception, and they will need to take this bondage to the cross of Jesus.

Of course the local covering can be *strong* or *weak* depending on the nature of the spiritual leadership that is given. I do not mean it is made weaker or stronger according to the nature of the gifts and abilities of the leaders. Rather it is the nature of their spirituality - their prayer, love, unity, obedience and holiness. This is the very important reason why the leaders must live holy lives, and why only those qualified should be raised to stand in the covering of a work of God.

Honour and Protect the Covering

The following eldership principles apply to those who are in covering ministry at all levels.

There are good reasons why the New Testament gives certain commands to apostles, and to the whole church, regarding elders (1 Tim 5:17-20). We are to honour the elders who direct the affairs of the church well and reward them; we are not to consider any accusation against an elder unless it is substantiated by at least two material witnesses, but if an elder sins he is to be publicly rebuked. All these instructions are concerned with maintaining the covering, in two important respects.

One, if you want the blessing of covering, you must *honour* the covering. This is akin to the commandment to honour your father and mother, a commandment which had the promise of long life and good things for you. These are the blessings of covering. Your father and mother are also a part of your spiritual covering. Just as honouring them is essential for life to flow to you from God, so also is it essential to honour those in authority over you in the Lord. You cannot receive from any source you do not honour - disrespect will drive its blessings away from you - this is spiritual law. *"The elders who direct the affairs of the church well are worthy of double honor"* (1 Tim 5:17).

Two, if an elder falls into sin, it is to be dealt with openly and quickly. It is not to be covered up. The elder is to be placed under public correction and the discipline of the church. This is very, very important! This is the way to *heal* the covering and *protect* the people and the work of God from further damage. If an elder sins and is not made publicly accountable, something is opened up in the spirit realm that will greatly damage the church. This would become an open door to large numbers of deceiving and lying spirits to enter into the life of the church. It is not only the elder sinning which gives rise to this vulnerability, but the failure of the senior minister, or the other elders, or the covering apostle, to deal with it appropriately according to this command which is designed to protect the church. Every elder and leadership team member should be informed that this is a requirement that goes hand in hand with the responsibility of leadership.

In Paul's lists of qualifications for elders, his instructions to consider the wives and especially the children of prospective elders are of great importance. The blessing on his home and the attitude and behaviour of his children will reveal whether the covering he provides is good enough for church leadership. The nature and quality of his spiritual life will be reflected in the wellbeing, the attitudes and values, and the spiritual life of his wife and children. Are they spiritually protected, from lies and deception for instance? Is there a sense of blessing over them each and their home? Is faith in their hearts? If not, this man is hardly qualified to stand in the covering of the church.

The character qualifications for elders were requirements for anyone to be part of this spiritual covering. Only those of the right character, not necessarily the greatest abilities, were spiritually able to be appropriately placed in the covering at all, or else the church was in danger.

To ensure that only suitable persons were placed in the covering, Paul gave an earnest command to the Apostle Timothy, *"Do not be hasty in the laying on of hands, and do not share in the sins of others"* (1 Tim 5:22).

Adjust for Weaknesses in Covering

When the dynamic of spiritual covering is in place over your life, you receive of the good things (the strengths and the blessings) that have been established in your covering by the anointings. But there may also be in you a vulnerability to their weaknesses. This is why leaders especially must have a witness of the Spirit that the people you relate to are the ones appointed for you by the Lord.

If you examine various Christian movements you will find that their strengths and powers very often strongly reflect the strengths and power of their leaders, especially their founders. But also, anything that was missing in their leadership with respect to a gift or an anointing is often missing through the whole movement. Later on others will have to work to fill those gaps.

If you see in those over you in the Lord something missing, or some kind of weakness, you don't reject the person or reject the covering, any more than you would reject your own parents. Instead, you make that a matter of prayer. You recognise that in your covering are many good things that God has provided for you, and you give honour, but you also wisely see where something is lacking that you need. You pray and build yourself up in the Holy Spirit with respect to those things, and then it is never a problem for you, or a weakness in you. In Christ we need lack no good thing (1 Corinthians 1:5-8, James 1:4-5). Any potential to weakness in covering is greatly diminished when we have a strong, extensive eldership over the city.

The Changing Model of Church/Apostle Relationship

It is difficult to write with a greater clarity, at this time, about the structure of the relationship between pastor/elders and apostles, because so much rapid change is taking place at the present time in our understanding of the structure of the local church itself. The Spirit of God is bringing an unfolding revelation of God's purpose. As the process continues over time, understanding brings better values, and changed values become changed structure, or new wineskin. This gives us something of a problem with communication, since terms which are common, such as 'local church' and 'eldership' are undergoing a change of meaning even while we are using them.

I have begun to use the term 'local church' more exclusively for the whole body of a given locality, and use the terms 'local ministry' or 'fellowship' or 'congregation', or similar, for the entities we used to call churches, so as to simplify communication and clarify values. I know there is an argument that can be made for every group being considered a church, but this is never true if they do not endeavour to relate to the whole body of Christ anyway. Independence is cultic. Recently I ministered to a small gathering of pastors and church leaders from a small town. The town had seven 'churches' (institutional congregations). During discussion someone referred to the town as having seven candlesticks, a reference to the golden lampstands of Revelation 1:20. Kindly, I pointed out that there is only one candlestick in the town.

In the past and up to the present day, each congregation was, in our thinking, a local church, with any number of congregations in each town or city. Each had a pastor, each was considered a church, each developed their own 'elders' or the equivalent. Under this concept of the church, we have been teaching that each of these pastors, leadership teams and churches should pray for God to bring them into relationship with an apostle.

In this model, by extension there would ultimately be any number of different apostles relating to various 'churches' in the city. Apostolic covering would be effective for individual congregations, but very piecemeal in the life of the city.

Christ would have not a bride, but a harem. Nevertheless, it was, and remains, the way ahead for those wanting to move with the things of God, since the body as a whole is still so divided and institutionalised.

But the Spirit is now moving the body of Christ everywhere towards the concepts outlined in this chapter, i.e. one church in each locality with a city eldership. This surely brings with it some changes to the way apostles will relate to congregations and ministry leaders. The city eldership will need to relate to apostles, who will represent an apostolic covering for the whole city. Sometimes, apostles will be resident as part of the eldership (as was the case of the original church in Jerusalem, Acts 15:2,4), and sometimes the city eldership will be comprised of prophets and teachers, as was the case with Antioch (Acts 13:1), who related to apostolic covering provided by the apostles of Jerusalem (Acts 11:22,27). I imagine the city church of the future will have both resident apostles in the eldership, and relationship with external covering apostles.

Obviously, there will need to be a transition from one form of apostle/church relationship to the other, since a 'local ministry' could hardly relate to separate spiritual authorities (i.e. apostolic covering through the eldership of the city, and independent outside apostolic covering). These will need to be harmonised. This will take time, and will require not only the building of the unity of the local church and the true eldership, which we discussed in this chapter, but something else. Apostles will need to come into fruitful unity, as one before Christ. In the past we have seen relational networks of churches built. Now is the time for relational networks of *apostles*. But not as an institution! It must be a *personal* network, by means of healthy, loving, committed, covenant, 'willing to lay down your life for your brother', 'not building your own kingdom' type *personal relationships*. It is our hearts that must be knit together. Christ alone we must serve. And we must hold each other dear.

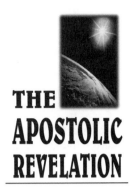

THE APOSTOLIC REVELATION

Chapter 9

Fathering and Sonship in the Ministry

From the beginning God had revealed Himself to be a *personal* God, but more amazing is this; when Christ came in the flesh as the great revelation of God, He revealed God to be *God in Father and Son.*

God as Father and Son

A Father/Son God! And the Son was of the very essence and nature of the Father, was One in being with the Father. Furthermore, He taught us, the Son does nothing except in submission and agreement with the Father, and the Father does nothing except through the Son. The Son loves the Father, and the Father loves the Son!

> Jesus speaks: *"I tell you the truth, the Son can do nothing by himself; he can do only what he sees his Father doing, because whatever the Father does the Son also does. For the Father loves the Son and shows him all he does. Yes, to your amazement he will show him even greater things than these. For just as the Father raises the dead and gives them life, even so the Son gives life to whom he is pleased to give it. Moreover, the Father judges no one, but has entrusted all judgment to the Son, that all may honor the Son just as they honor the Father. He who does not honor the Son does not honor the Father, who sent him. By myself I can do nothing; I judge only as I hear, and my judgment is just, for I seek not to please myself but him who sent me" (John 5:19-23,30).*

This is astounding. God is, at the same time, a father to a son and a son to a father. Now that revelation must become typical of the life of the church, or we fail to know Him as we could, we fail to fully share His nature as we could, and we do not bear His image in the world.

The 'Nature' of Church and Ministry

If we would show God to others, revealing the light of Christ, the nature of the church must reflect the nature of God. The church must be a *relational* people, or else we are *not able* to impart to others the life and love of God. The heart relationships of God's people are the key to power for taking the gospel to our world.

Jesus clearly meant us to understand this. Consider the words of His prayer, *"I pray... that all of them may be one, Father, just as you are in me and I am in you. May they also be in us so that the world may believe that you have sent me. ...that they may be one as we are one: I in them and you in me. May they be brought to complete unity to let the world know that you sent me and have loved them even as you have loved me" (John 17:20-23).*

Over the years, it has been said by many authors and teachers that the leadership, ministry, and life of the church is to be relational, and that all authority in the church is meant to be a relational authority. Going further, I believe the Lord has said that the father/son relationships that will be established amongst leaders and believers is the new wineskin of the church.

The 'Spirit of sonship' is about to be newly understood by God's people. We shall grasp greater meaning in such scriptures as, *"you received the Spirit of sonship" (Romans 8:15).* This will change the church, and ultimately the nations.

Father/Son Ministry Model

When we consider the Father/Son nature of God, we can begin to understand why fatherhood is so important to God in His dealings with humanity.

To begin with, the first man, made in God's image, was to be the father of the human race. Subsequently Abraham, the friend of God, was chosen to be the father of faith, and the father of many nations — and he was so chosen because, as the Lord said, *"he will direct his children and his household after him to keep the way of the LORD" (Genesis 18:19).*

It is greatly significant that the word of God to Abraham was centred around his *fatherhood*. For much of his lifetime, Abraham's faith was focused on a single promise that God gave him — that he would have a *son*. Just as he was chosen to be a father, a certain kind of father, so every ministry leader today is called to be a father in the faith, and to exercise faith to raise 'sons' for the ministry, since Abraham is our model for faith according to the scriptures.

Later, a greater test of Abraham's faith came again over that son, as to whether he was willing to sacrifice him for the purposes of God. This was to bring Abraham's heart to maturity in the faith he held, showing the evidence that his heart belonged to and trusted the living God. Further, this effectively put him spiritually into the same position as the One who would later sacrifice His own son on the mountain where Abraham was tested.

Throughout the Old and New Testaments we see a repeated emphasis on the importance of 'father and son' type relationships in the ministry. The outstanding examples in the Old Testament are Moses with Joshua, and Elijah with Elisha. Both Moses and Elijah are ministry 'fathers', mature experienced men who carry great anointings and responsibilities, the outstanding leaders of their day. Joshua and Elisha are younger men who served faithfully as sons, waiting as servants upon their fathers, honouring and obeying them, walking with them in complete devotion. When it came time for Moses to die, the Lord instructed him to lay his hands upon Joshua as the new leader. *"Now Joshua son of Nun was filled with the spirit of wisdom because Moses had laid his hands on him. So the Israelites listened to him and did what the LORD had commanded Moses"* *(Deuteronomy 34:9)*. When Elijah was taken, the anointing fell upon Elisha in double portion.

Moses and Elijah happen to be the two prophets chosen from amongst numerous outstanding and highly esteemed prophets of the Old Testament (such as Samuel, Isaiah, and Daniel) to appear with Jesus on the Mount of Transfiguration. This is very significant. They were the two outstanding 'fathers' of the Old Testament, the two who most obviously and successfully raised a 'son' to succeed them in the ministry. These two were symbolic of the nature of the ministry to come, which was to bring *"many sons to glory" (Hebrews 2:10)*.

Spiritual Fathers

As we move into these coming days, every church, and every pastor or minister, will need to relate to apostles and prophets, but in particular to an apostle who will be to them a father. Remember how Paul wrote to the Corinthian church and clarified matters, *"Though you have ten thousand instructors, tutors, guides, though you have ten thousand others in Christ all eager to teach you, you have only one father. I became your father through the gospel" (1 Corinthians 4:15, paraphrased)*.

Many of the pastors and churches in the world today do not have such a spiritual father. In reality, denominational Christianity has a terrible record with respect to providing true spiritual fathering. Some institutional systems just 'ship in' and 'ship out' ministers all the time without reference to relationships. The allegiance required is to the institution, not to specific people.

And many churches don't really have a pastor. They might have someone there who is called to be a pastor, but he's not allowed to work as a pastor — if he was, he'd be serving as a representative of Christ. In representing the Head to the body, he would have authority, the right to say, "I believe this is what God requires of us." Then, ideally, the people should have an inner witness that what he was saying was true, and rise up with one heart to work together with understanding to do the will of God.

Instead of a pastor, many institutional churches have a chaplain. A 'chaplain' is someone hired to say nice things, conduct the ceremonies, and visit. We do not call him or her a hireling, for the term 'hireling' has negative connotations and is actually a comment on the heart of that person, and their motivation. That is not what we are discussing here. Many of the people working as 'chaplains' to our churches really want to serve God and their people. They are not hirelings, unless someone is only there to get paid, in the sense that "It's a job". But the system, the corporate culture of many denominations, has established parameters in much of Christianity that has forced them to be chaplains rather than pastors. Much has to change.

Now not just anyone can be your father. There may be many that will be valuable instructors and teachers, but there are few who can be your father. Nor will it be the church members who vote on who the 'spiritual father', or apostle, will be.

It is the senior minister of any given ministry or fellowship (whether that leader is a pastor, prophet, apostle, teacher, or whatever his primary gift may be) who will need to enter into meaningful relationship with an apostle as spiritual father. The one called of God to lead a company of people on a journey, travelling with Christ in the things of the Spirit to the City of God, will need to identify the spiritual father who has the love, anointing, and heart of God for them. Naturally, that leader will not be alone in this process, for each will be in co-operative covenant partnership with those around him or her in the Lord, but at every point this must represent a meaningful and personal relationship, of anointed covering, accountability, and fatherly care, for that leader.

The whole ministry of the Church ought to be built, must be built, on wholesome father-son relationships. We are not leaving mothers and daughters out of the 'equation'. Please take that as implied here. Fathers and mothers, sons and daughters — that is what the Church is meant to be. Go to most churches, however, and you won't recognise father-son relationships. Mostly they do not exist, since they are outside our mindset of what the church is, because we have been raised with an institutional Christianity that has a professional priesthood.

But when God the Father anointed and released His Son into ministry, to launch with power the ministry of the New Covenant based on better promises (Hebrews 8:6), He made this pronouncement with *"a voice from heaven"*. He declared, *"This is my beloved Son, whom I love; with him I am well pleased" (Matthew 3:17)*.

We have been raised with an institutional form of Christianity that has denied the real nature of the church, the father-son type relationships that should develop amongst God's people. Why is this critical? Why is this issue so central to what the church should be? Because, just as Christ was in a personal way the spiritual father of His twelve apostles, so are relationships such as these the vital manifestation of the apostolic nature of the church in every age.

In both the Old and New Testaments, central to the meaning and purpose of the covenants is that Abraham is a father to a son. Everything you know about the gospel goes back to that. Abraham was to be the father of nations, of multitudes, but in the first instance he was to be the father of a son. Everything God has done for you and me through Christ, has come from God challenging a childless man to believe that he would be given a son who was called the son of promise.

It didn't end there. When Moses came as the lawgiver, the anointed leader of the first covenant, we find Moses had a 'son' in the ministry, Joshua. Everything that Moses knew and learned, all that was in his heart, he taught to this young man, and — Joshua became the great warrior leader of the people of God.

God gave the great prophet Elijah a 'son' also. And with Elijah's passing, not via death but alive into heaven, the anointing and power to be the father of Israel transferred in double portion from Elijah to Elisha. It is all there in the pattern God has given us, and that is why, when we come to the last verse of the Old Testament, we discover that it closes with a statement that holds a promise, a prophecy, and a curse. *"I will send you the prophet Elijah before that great and dreadful day of the LORD comes. He will turn the hearts of the fathers to their children, and the hearts of the children to their fathers; or else I will come and strike the land with a curse" (Malachi 4:5-6).*

This is a tremendously significant statement, as we shall see.

But why *Elijah*? Because he successfully passed a father's anointing in double portion to a son in the ministry. This is the only example we have in the scriptures of a double-portion of anointing for ministry being actually received. Yet it is the rightful inheritance of every first-born son, and biblically, every believer is a first-born son. The church is *"the church of the first-born"* (Hebrews 12:23), which is a reference not to Christ but to every saint *"whose names are written in heaven"*.

The Power of the 'Fathers' Anointing

"But the angel said to him: 'Do not be afraid, Zechariah; your prayer has been heard. Your wife Elizabeth will bear you a son, and you are to give him the name John. And he will go on before the Lord, in the spirit and power of Elijah, to turn the hearts of the fathers to their children and the disobedient to the wisdom of the righteous - to make ready a people prepared for the Lord'" (Luke 1:13,17).

The angel foretold, and Jesus confirmed, that John the Baptist was the promised Elijah, who would go ahead of Christ with the specific purpose of turning the hearts of fathers and children to each other, and to prepare a people for the coming of the Lord.

In Matthew 17 Jesus replied to His disciples' questions concerning the prophesied coming of Elijah, and made the following comment. *"To be sure, Elijah comes and will restore all things"*. This is clearly a reference to a yet future outworking of the prophecy, but to this He added, *"But I tell you, Elijah has already come, and they did not recognize him, ... the disciples understood that he was talking to them about John the Baptist" (Matthew 17:10-13, also 11:13-14)*. Thus, Jesus Himself has made it very clear that this prophecy will be fulfilled twice.

Whilst John the Baptist was the specific fulfillment of the prophecy in relation to Christ's first coming, Christ is coming again. And it is the second coming of Jesus which is more specifically referred to in the words of Malachi 4:5.

Both Elijah and John are types of the apostolic ministry, as we can see from these words in Luke's gospel, *"But what did you go out to see? A prophet? Yes, I tell you, and more than a prophet. This is the one about whom it is written: 'I* will send my messenger ahead of you, who will prepare your way before you.' " *(Luke 7:26-27).* The coming apostles are the ones who *"will restore all things"* and *"make ready a people"* for the Lord, as we have discussed earlier. These apostles do come in *"the spirit and power of Elijah",* and several similarities immediately occur to us when the ministries of Elijah and John the Baptist are compared with that of modern apostles. They were reformers, they spoke with a powerful authority, and were *'sent'* to prepare a people for the Lord by changing their hearts and turning them back to God. Furthermore, they were spiritual fathers who pointed the people to another.

Elijah pointed Israel back to the true God, the God who could answer by fire, whilst confronting the false religion and idolatry of his day. John the Baptist also turned Israel back to righteousness, preparing them *for* Jesus, and pointing them *to* Jesus whilst, again, aggressively and forthrightly confronting the false religion and idolatry of the nation. Both Elijah and John were dealing with, not the idolatry of the pagans, but the idolatry of the people of God. Apostles today who come in the spirit and power of Elijah are likewise, 'fathers' who bring reform, pointing the believers to Christ, and challenging the idolatry and false religion that is in the *church.*

The *'spirit and power of Elijah'* is actually an anointing — the anointing of a father. Elijah was not only a father to a son in the ministry, and to Israel, but one who successfully passed his 'spirit', that is, his *anointing* (the spiritual power and gift that God had given him) to another. Moreover, his son received it in double portion. This is the way the ministry of Jesus Christ is meant to function.

The *'spirit of Elijah'* is not something that guarantees miracles. John the Baptist did not work miracles, and it was never God's intention that he should. The degree to which the miraculous is a part of the apostle's ministry will depend upon the purposes of God. According to Luke 1:17, the purpose of the spirit of Elijah i.e. the 'fathers' anointing, is to turn the hearts of God's people to each other and to God. Specifically, it is to turn *"the hearts of the fathers to their children, and the hearts of the children to their fathers",* and as well, the *"disobedient to the wisdom of the righteous",* in preparation of God's people for the coming of Christ.

This is a powerful and essential work that must be done, and for which God sends apostles. It takes great power to achieve these results, and that power is given to apostles. Note again, however, that the nature of that power is that it is a *fathering* anointing. It cannot be said that someone ministers in the power of

Elijah to turn the hearts of the fathers to the children, unless they have the heart of the father. This is a grace, an anointing, and a wisdom in the heart given by the Spirit. The genuine apostle has a heart for his children, and creates in others also this love of relationship, of personal covenant commitment from the heart to one another, as the true nature of the family of God.

Paul and Timothy as Father and Son

In the New Testament, the revelation of fathering and sonship in ministry is made quite plain by Paul's words concerning both Timothy and Titus. Of the former he wrote, *"Therefore I urge you to imitate me. For this reason I am sending to you Timothy, my son whom I love, who is faithful in the Lord. He will remind you of my way of life in Christ Jesus, which agrees with what I teach everywhere in every church" (1 Corinthians 4:16-17).*

He wrote similarly to others, *"I hope in the Lord Jesus to send Timothy to you soon, that I also may be cheered when I receive news about you. I have no one else like him, who takes a genuine interest in your welfare. For everyone looks out for his own interests, not those of Jesus Christ. But you know that Timothy has proved himself, because as a son with his father he has served with me in the work of the gospel" (Philippians 2:19-22).*

The relationship was real, not contrived, as seen in his personal manner of address to Timothy, *"To Timothy my true son in the faith" (1 Timothy 1:2),* and also to Titus (Titus 1:4).

Paul exhorted the Corinthians to imitate his ways in Christ, which he had taught them previously. He could not go to be with them at that time of need, so to help them imitate his example, he sent Timothy. As Paul's son in the ministry, Timothy would guide the Corinthians in living for Christ according to Paul's example. The situation needed Paul's personal attention, so in response to the need he was not going to send just anyone, not just any teacher. He could only send one kind of person, one who had the heart of the father. He sent his son.

Of him he said, *"my son whom I love ...is faithful in the Lord. He will remind you of my way of life in Christ" (1 Timothy 4:17).* Here is our model for the relationships that are the essence of true Christianity. The apostolic church is to reflect the nature of a Father/Son God, a relationship in which the son is of the same essence and nature as the father, is one with the father. A relationship in which the son does what the father's heart desires, and the father expresses himself through the son. This has to be the spirit of us all. The heart for this has to be restored to the church. This is apostolic Christianity.

The Relational Ministry

The ministry of the church must function through its ministers being in relationships of this kind. We also, not just the Corinthians, are urged to *"imitate"* Paul. The exhortation to *"imitate ...my way of life in Christ Jesus, which agrees with what I teach everywhere"* is now a scriptural command, and one which instructs us to imitate his relationships, values and lifestyle. Paul's 'way of life' meant total commitment to these covenant relationships, which were very heartfelt, and personal, and permanent, as in any real family.

Each of us is to be a son to a father, and to become a father to sons. The pastor of every church or fellowship should be a son to an apostle. Every such pastor or church should have an apostle as a father, and these relationships should be personal and wholesomely intimate. They require openness, honesty, transparency, and accountability. Their purpose is oneness and unity, as well as strengthening and encouragement. Further, the nature of these relationships of the heart must extend to everyone in the fellowship. Every believer will be helped into appropriate oneness in the body, and have supporting and accountable relationships, as they see the example of their leaders and are helped to understand the relationship dynamics of following Christ. The subordinate leaders, or the leadership team, must be fathers, sons and true brothers to each other. Ultimately, each believer should be a Timothy to a Paul, and a Paul to a Timothy; and each of us should be a Barnabas to our Paul's, or a Paul to Barnabas', as well. This is the simple New Testament model for every believer to follow in being a father, a son, and a brother, in the ministry.

Need for Relational Ministry Training

Unfortunately, something else has been happening in much of institutional Christianity. Young people in the church would feel the 'call to the ministry' (i.e. the call to become pastors or missionaries), but the local church would say goodbye, and the denominational institution would take them over. No longer did the local church speak into the lives of those young people. The very womb that had born and nurtured them often had no further relationship with them. When they did come back to visit, a year or two later, or five or ten, it was never the same. The relationship had changed.

Institutionalism swallows up the candidates for the ministry. When they leave their local church, they are on fire for God, but after the years of being put through the 'sausage machine' of institutional training, they are cold and formal.

They have often been trained in scepticism, and almost never in faith. For too many of these young people, the fire has been 'educated' out of them, and now the denominational parameters are locked in place, even more than before. It will take them years at the front lines of spiritual struggle in ministry to throw off those shackles, if they ever do, or else for the rest of their lives they are prisoners of traditional mindsets. Am I making it seem worse than it is? I don't think I am in much of the case. I know there will be many exceptions, but I am here realistically comparing and contrasting institutional Christianity and its traditions, with apostolic Christianity, which is the life of Christ.

This is not to denounce education as such, or the many godly people called of God who are working earnestly to equip church leaders. There are a variety of effective ministries that provide a sound spiritual and biblical education for believers wanting to equip themselves for a life of service to Christ. The instruction and discipline of everyone for the ministry of Jesus Christ is vital. My comments are directed to the manner, or the spirit, in which this takes place, especially concerning the relational and personal nature of what that equipping should be.

It is critical that the pursuit of someone's call to serve Christ should not be removed from accountable covenant relationships, wherein we walk with others in our pursuit of the Christ. Christian ministry education should not be academic for its own sake, and institutions should not provide an education with an institutional mindset for the purpose of creating bondservants of the institution.

Where should those 'called' be trained for the ministry? Allowing for exceptions, and the freedom and variety which the Spirit gives, generally they should be equipped under those who have the anointings for the ministry, that is, apostles, prophets, evangelists, and pastor/teachers, in the very the life of the church. They should be trained in the community of faith, during the thrust of the battle, and under the immediate authority of those over them in the Lord, *as were all the ministers of grace who appear in Holy Scripture, who are our very inspiration.*

The Need to Restore Fatherhood

The danger of the earth being struck with a curse if the hearts of the fathers and their children were not turned back to each other was prophesied in Malachi 4. In many ways, fatherlessness is the curse, and fatherhood cancels the curse. This is true in both the natural and the spiritual world. It is true in the society around us, and in the church.

        The Apostolic Revelation

For decades now, fatherlessness has been a growing curse in many nations, especially affluent nations. The number of boys and girls growing up without fathers is enormous, and the impact on our society is horrendous. The world and the church has been largely ignorant of the full ramifications of this tragedy because we are uninformed about the purpose and the value of fatherhood. And for years, dads have been despised, denigrated in the media and suffering injustice in the courts. It has been considered that a mother's role was more important than a father's role. Only now are we beginning to understand the tragic consequences of this foolishness.

I sometimes wonder whether the curse of fatherlessness upon society has not resulted because the institutional church has emasculated spiritual fathering. Has the church's failure to honour leaders, and to listen to the voice of fathers, been a primary cause of the dishonouring of fathers in the world? The maxim remains true, "As goes the church, so goes the world".

Fathers in family life have a very important role in their children's lives. Of course, it is best when children have both parents, for both a mother and a father have something of great importance to impart to their children. But here, I am addressing specifically the importance of the father's role, as it gives insight into our present spiritual need in the church.

Identity and Impartation from Fathers

Briefly, fathers impart courage, security, discipline, identity and blessing to their children. Concerning courage, it is the encouragement of a father that releases a child from fear. It is the strength and comfort of a father that keeps a child from insecurity, enabling a child to grow up secure. A father's discipline deals with the child's lack of motivation, and urges them to live worthy lives. It is a father that gives a sense of identity, purpose and destiny to a child. Furthermore, with a father's blessing there is placed within a child a clear sense of having permission to succeed.

Without the ministry and impartation of a father's strengths and love, children can grow up not knowing who they are, why they are here, or where they are going. They grow up at risk to fear, insecurity, lack of discipline, lack of motivation and without a sense of either personal or corporate destiny. That is the curse of the one parent family.

With this in mind, we can all the more fully understand the importance of the words which God the Father spoke over His Son on the day that Jesus was baptised and anointed for ministry. He said, *"This is my Son, whom I love:*

with him I am well pleased" (Matthew 3:17). Here was an affirmation of identity, love, acceptance, blessing, honour and, indirectly, permission to succeed. The key elements here are: the father gives identity, expresses His love, and declares the delight He has in His son. Everything flows from this, both in natural families and in the spiritual life of the family of God.

In the ministry of the church, there are important things that can only come to us through the ministry of fathers. Every young man and woman growing into spiritual maturity, and hearing the call of God to the ministry, is greatly helped if there is for them the voice of a father, who communicates to their hearts love, acceptance, identity, and permission to be a success.

The following biblical description of the apostolic ministry comes alive for us when we are more informed of the importance of a father's role. *"As apostles of Christ we could have been a burden to you, but we were gentle among you, like a mother caring for her little children... For you know that we dealt with each of you as a father deals with his own children, encouraging, comforting and urging you to live lives worthy of God..." (1 Thessalonians 2:6-7,11-12).*

Honouring Fathers

"A son honors his father, and a servant his master. If I am a father, where is the honor due me?" (Malachi 1:6)

The church must honour the fathers. The giving of honour is a key principle if we would obtain life. Not only do the Scriptures call us to honour God (1 Timothy 1:17), we are also called to honour every person in authority over us (Romans 13:7, 1 Peter 2:17). This is especially true of our parents and the leaders of the church.

The command to honour your father and mother was the only commandment that had attached to it a promise — and it is a very specific kind of promise. *"Honor your father and your mother, as the LORD your God has commanded you, so that you may live long and that it may go well with you in the land the LORD your God is giving you" (Deuteronomy 5:16).* This is the promise of a *longer* life, and a *better* life, to those who give honour. The New Testament renews the promise which was given under the old covenant (Ephesians 6:1-3), and shows that the giving of honour is a life-giving principle. When we fail to give honour, we curse ourselves, and effectively cut ourselves off from the springs of life, which are for our blessing.

The elders who govern the church, in particular those responsible for teaching, are to be especially honoured. They are worthy of double honour, says Paul. *"The elders who direct the affairs of the church well are worthy of double honor, especially those whose work is preaching and teaching" (1 Timothy 5:17).*

When the church fails to honour its leadership, we fail to walk in the fullness of the blessing of God. If the church does not honour its fathers, the promises and great blessings that attach themselves to the giving of honour are not appropriated. When we fail to honour, the command to bless is not given. This is, unfortunately, the very reverse of the process which brings such abundant blessing described in Psalm 133, for there can be no unity in the church of Jesus Christ without the leaders being held in high honour, loved from the heart, and imitated as role models. Scripture commands these things.

In the apostolic church, which is established by the power of Christ through relationships, the giving of honour is central to Christ's purpose. If we lack in the giving of honour, we lack grace. When our hearts are pure, so that we love to give honour, we are Christlike.

Sonship in the Ministry

"In bringing many sons to glory" was a phrase we quoted earlier as we outlined God's purpose. The text of Hebrews continues, *"Both the one who makes men holy and those who are made holy are of the same family. So Jesus is not ashamed to call them brothers" (Hebrews 2:11).* Here we see again the repeated emphasis of the importance of family relationship in the household of God. In this house, there is but one family.

Many believers, including anointed ministers, do not understand the grace and relationship dynamic of their adoption as sons (Romans 15:17). They know *in theory* they are *sons,* but do not think and relate to God that way in practice. Like the prodigal son in Jesus' parable, they are forever coming to God hoping to be treated as one of the servants. The prodigal said to himself, *"I will...go back to my father and say...'I am no longer worthy to be called your son; make me like one of your hired men' "(Luke 15:18-19).* Most Christians relate to God as a disciple to a teacher, or a servant to a master, rather than as a son to a father.

Of course we are all disciples and servants, as well as sons. Our problem is that we relate to God out of a servant's mentality, which He never intended. We still subconsciously think of ourselves as unworthy to be sons. It is a tremendous breakthrough when we discover the true nature of grace and relationship with

God, and learn to come to Him with the confidence of a first-born son. Then do we walk in the grace of God, and find it has great power.

God's purpose is that we would not only relate to Him as sons to a father, but that we would also relate to those over us *in the church* as sons to a father. Our relationship with those over us in the Lord is not meant to be distant, formal, religious, hierarchical, mechanical, or institutional. Neither is it meant to be untrusting or impersonal. It is meant to be *very* personal. It should be the trusting, relaxed, intimate, caring, gracious, non-legalistic, warm, selfless, giving, honouring, committed and 'without private agenda' relationships of a good family.

In a good family we care about others, and we live for each other. In a good family, despite what ups and downs there may be, the most important thing is other people, and maintaining healthy, appropriate, personal relationships with them.

No one is suggesting that we submit ourselves to leaders who are tyrants. We have all heard stories of manipulative, controlling leaders, and of problems caused by deceptive and inappropriate religious leaders. We are free to obey Christ and not men, when men have a wrong spirit or a personal agenda, just as the apostles have told us, *"We must obey God rather than men!" (Acts 5:29).* These words, however, must never be used with an arrogant independence, contrary to the spirit of the Word of God that calls us into community. Paul made it clear that God uses leadership authority to bring about obedience to God, as in these words, *"I will not venture to speak of anything except what Christ has accomplished through me in leading the Gentiles to obey God by what I have said and done" (Romans 15:18).*

What we are speaking about is the giving of allegiance from the heart to true apostolic fathers, who are not controlling, and never motivated by greed or personal ambition, but who have the heart of God to care for you and all the saints. Here, from the heart of the apostle John, is an example of fatherly care. *"I have no greater joy than to hear that my children are walking in the truth" (3 John 4).* Here is one from Paul. *"My dear children, for whom I am again in the pains of childbirth until Christ is formed in you, how I wish I could be with you now and change my tone, because I am perplexed about you!" (Galatians 4:19-20).*

Spiritual fathers love their sons, and spiritual sons serve and honour their fathers. The relationship is mutually beneficial, and involves mutual giving. The son gives, and the father gives. They honour one another, and each wants the other to succeed. These are life-giving and freedom-giving relationships, for an apostle loves to see other people set free. There is accountability and authority, but not control, and a true father does not create dependency. Like a Dad with his family, the way in which fatherly authority is exercised varies greatly with the maturity of the child. As sons become mature, they also become more 'independent', yet all the while remaining strongly bonded in love to their spiritual father. **This kind of life *is* the life of the church, and these values are central to the ministry of Jesus Christ.** If we misunderstand this, we miss the substance of what the faith and the gospel is all about.

We return again to the example of Jesus, upon whom we are told, as brothers, to fix our thoughts. *"Therefore, holy brothers, who share in the heavenly calling, fix your thoughts on Jesus, the apostle and high priest whom we confess. He was faithful to the one who appointed him, just as Moses was faithful in all God's house" (Hebrews 3:1-3).* There is in this text a fascinating phrase, which is definitive of both the relationships and the nature of the apostolic church. Following the instruction to focus our full attention upon Him, we are told that Christ, as an apostle, was *"faithful to the one who appointed him"*. This is therefore a piece of information of the utmost importance.

Notice that the appointment is personal in every respect. The appointment is not only given to Jesus as an individual person, but the authority of the appointment is conferred upon Him by an individual, God the father. Christ was not called to be faithful to an organisation, or to an office in an institution, but to a person. He was faithful to *"the one"* who appointed Him. Sons in the ministry are also called to be faithful to those apostles who confer authority upon them. The future effectiveness of the church will come from sons who will be faithful to those who appoint them.

Read the New Testament again, and tell me it is not all about how we relate *to each other* as well as to God. Christ and the apostles spent as much time instructing us on how to love and relate to others, as they did on how to respond to God and pursue Christ. Holiness and obedience to God is defined as much by your fellowship with, attitude to, and treatment of others, as it is by what goes on in your heart and mind, or your service to Christ.

There is much that could be said concerning this, but in the end I desire to make one main point. Each of us is meant to find the 'Spirit of sonship' in our relationships in the church, as well as in our relationship with God. If we miss this, we will miss the way of God, and the purposes of God. But when we relate to those over us in the Lord as sons to a father, we will have effectively discovered and entered into the real life that God intended for the body of

Christ. This is church reformation, and it will result in community transformation.

Sonship and Inheritance

Sonship is the secret to spiritual inheritance. Wherever the Bible speaks of sonship, we discover that in close proximity it speaks of inheritance also. For example, *"But when the time had fully come, God sent his Son, born of a woman, born under law, to redeem those under law, that we might receive the full rights of sons. Because you are sons, God sent the Spirit of his Son into our hearts, the Spirit who calls out, "Abba, Father." So you are no longer a slave, but a son; and since you are a son, God has made you also an heir"* *(Galatians 4:4-7).*

The Bible makes extensive reference to our inheritance, and there are two stages in receiving inheritance. Ultimately we obtain the amazing provisions of God, things that really cannot be described (1 Corinthians 2:9), which comes to us after the Day of the Lord, and which is the day of our redemption. *"Having believed, you were marked in him with a seal, the promised Holy Spirit, who is a deposit guaranteeing our inheritance until the redemption of those who are God's possession...And do not grieve the Holy Spirit of God, with whom you were sealed for the day of redemption"* *(Ephesians 1:13-14, 4:30-31).*

This vast future inheritance, jointly sharing everything Christ inherits, is spoken of by many biblical authors. It is preserved for us by the power of God, *"...an inheritance that can never perish, spoil or fade - kept in heaven for you"* *(1 Peter 1:4-5).*

In addition to future inheritance, there is also much that we are meant to receive whilst in the body on the earth. We are told to *"...imitate those who through faith and patience inherit what has been promised"* *(Hebrews 6:12)* and, in the case of Abraham who is in this text referred to as one we should imitate, it is made plain that there is also an inheritance for here and now, since *"...after waiting patiently, Abraham received what was promised"* *(Hebrews 6:15).*

As believers, there are a number of ways that we receive the things we need, and which God has promised. We exercise faith to receive answers to prayer, we walk in the principles of sowing and reaping, we believe the promises and receive their outcomes just as sons would receive an inheritance, and over and above all these, there is abundant and merciful grace.

Here I want to make a distinction between receiving from God on the basis of sowing and reaping, and receiving from God what is promised as inheritance given to sons.

The laws of sowing and reaping are universal, and everyone may benefit by this provision. Many scriptures attest to this, such as 2 Corinthians 9: 6-11, and Luke 6:38. Every believer should participate in sowing and reaping, or giving and receiving as Paul called it in Philippians 4:15. Then we are blessed and benefitted by the laws of harvest. It is God's will that all of us should work and believe for a great harvest. God promised He would enlarge the harvest of your righteousness, and that you would be made rich in every way so that you could always be generous, to the glory of God (2 Corinthians 9: 10-11). These laws of harvest are to benefit you and the Kingdom of Christ, both spiritually and materially.

However, the harvest field requires your labour, in the form of good stewardship of your wealth, your regular generosity, and your exercise of faith. You must learn how to sow by faith, and you must also learn how to reap your harvest by faith. Therefore, you work for a harvest.

Obtaining Inheritance

But inheritance is obtained differently. You do not work for your inheritance, instead you simply *receive* it. Inheritance comes to you because of relationship. You are a member of the family, and specifically, a first-born son. Sons do not work for their inheritance, although as a member of the family a good son will certainly work hard for his father. For a son, both the motivation for service and the manner in which reward or provision is received, is entirely different to that of an employee.

Consider the following scripture: *"For it is written that Abraham had two sons, one by the slave woman and the other by the free woman. His son by the slave woman was born in the ordinary way; but his son by the free woman was born as the result of a promise. These things may be taken figuratively, for the women represent two covenants. One covenant is from Mount Sinai and bears children who are to be slaves: This is Hagar. Now Hagar stands for Mount Sinai in Arabia and corresponds to the present city of Jerusalem, because she is in slavery with her children. But the Jerusalem that is above is free, and she is our mother. ...But what does the Scripture say? 'Get rid of the slave woman and her son, for the slave woman's son will never share in the inheritance with the free woman's son' "(Galatians 4:22-26, 30).*

The two sons of Abraham represent people in the church today. There are those that have, albeit unknowingly, a slave mentality, and there are those who live as sons of a promise. We mentioned earlier the tendency for many to continue coming to the Father as the prodigal did, hoping to be treated as one of the servants. The prodigal in Jesus' story was not received as a servant, but as an honoured son, yet many in the church, even though God has received them as sons, continue to function as if they were slaves.

A slave, servant, or hired hand does not receive inheritance. Likewise, any Christian with this mentality will find it difficult to receive through *inheritance*, because to receive anything from God requires faith, and faith for inheritance is effectively absent in a slave mentality. Remember there is a spiritual principle that says, *"the slave woman's son will never share in the inheritance with the free woman's son" (Galatians 4: 30)*. To walk in the abundant provisions of inheritance made by God for His children in this life, one must walk in the freedom of the Spirit of sonship. This must be, by faith, our experience of God, not just a theory.

The things that we obtain by inheritance are all those things that are *promised*. Abraham's son by the free woman was born as *"the result of a promise"*, and all sons that walk in the inheritance provisions of God look to the promises so as to receive them. This does include anointing for ministry, and the power to do what God has called us to in the Kingdom.

As an aside, I do not wish to imply that *inheritance* replaces *harvest,* or that believing the promises displaces the need for generosity, and sowing and reaping. Actually, both are needed for you to be complete in faith and righteousness (James 1:4, 2: 22).

Relationship, The Key to Inheritance

Having explained a little about the principle of inheritance, we now proceed to a climactic discovery. God intends that we shall inherit the promises and anointings, not only by relating to the Father in heaven as a son, but also by relating as a son to a spiritual father on earth. This is precisely why Elisha received a double portion of Elijah's 'spirit' — it was his inheritance as a first born son who had served a father in the ministry. Double-portion inheritance is, therefore, an inheritance received from God via relationship with a spiritual father who is in Christ. We gain, not only what our faith is able to obtain from our Father in heaven, but also what our spiritual fathers themselves have obtained by their faith, and which is passed to us through the power of faithful, submitted, accountable relationships, with God's blessing.

On the other hand, a spirit of independence robs us of our inheritance. There are many in the ministry who have failed to obtain inheritance, that which could have been theirs, that which was available to them, because they have failed to understand and walk in the call of God to relate to fathers in the faith. We must have the spirit of submission in our hearts (Ephesians 5:21) or we miss much of the grace and miraculous provision that God our Father has made for us.

To illustrate, Elijah found great power with God, but he came forth out of years of rejection, wilderness experience, and testing. This is one way in which men and women of faith grow in the power of God. However, Elisha did not obtain grace for ministry in that way, but rather by walking with Elijah and serving him. For Elisha, years of submission and service to a spiritual father was the key to the anointing and the prophetic office. For this faithful service he was given the *double portion,* as the right of a *first born son,* and an easier, more sociable life. Elijah had been a prophet of the wilderness, but Elisha of the towns and cities. This represents a great advance for the work, an acceptance of the prophetic ministry, and an honouring of the prophet. Elisha obtained the greater anointing and the advance of the ministry through being a son to a father.

On the other hand, Elisha did not successfully pass on his prophetic authority. He died, and his corpse went to the grave still carrying the anointing, as we learn from 2 Kings 13: 20-21. It seems that he was training his servant Gehazi to be his successor (2 Kings 4: 29), but Gehazi was not submitted or faithful as a son. Because he did not have the heart of a son, he fell through greed, and was judged (2 Kings 5: 19-27).

We can understand now more clearly why the New Covenant was prefaced with these words, *"I will send you the prophet Elijah before that great and dreadful day of the LORD comes. He will turn the hearts of the fathers to their children, and the hearts of the children to their fathers; or else I will come and strike the land with a curse" (Malachi 4:5-6).*

A Coming Judgement

There are numerous witnesses in Holy Scripture that point to a coming judgement upon, not the world, but the church, specifically the shepherds and leaders.

Earlier I referred to Psalm 78: 9-12, 65-72 as a precedent now being used by the Holy Spirit to communicate an imminent leadership change in the body of

Christ. In addition we have the prophecies of Ezekiel and Jeremiah. In Ezekiel 34: 7-10 God declares that He is against the shepherds who do not care for His flock, and predicts that He will remove them from attending the flock. Jeremiah 25: 29, 34-38 contains some of the most fearful words in all the Scripture, and we must not assume that fulfilment of these words is complete. Like all prophecy, this passage will have both a 'near' and a 'far' outworking. The witness of the Spirit seems to be that these words will have yet another fulfilment, and what is so fearful is that the *"city that bears my Name"*, with its *"shepherds"* and *"leaders of the flock"*, is the church.

To clarify matters, and to confirm the prophetic interpretation of Psalm 78 and Ezekiel 34, both of which refer to David as the shepherd of integrity that God will appoint to replace the rejected shepherds, I feel the Lord has drawn my attention to the following passage. Here in the prophecies of Isaiah, Shebna is ousted from his position, and the Lord appoints another, Eliakim, to whom He will give the authority of David, for he is to become a father to God's people. This is very much in the spirit of the prophecy of Malachi 4:6, and the restoration of apostles and spiritual fathers of great integrity for the people of God.

> *"This is what the Lord, the LORD Almighty, says: 'Go, say to this steward, to Shebna, who is in charge of the palace: "...I will depose you from your office, and you will be ousted from your position. In that day I will summon my servant, Eliakim son of Hilkiah. I will clothe him with your robe and fasten your sash around him and hand your authority over to him. He will be a father to those who live in Jerusalem and to the house of Judah. I will place on his shoulder the key to the house of David; what he opens no one can shut, and what he shuts no one can open. I will drive him like a peg into a firm place; he will be a seat of honor for the house of his father. All the glory of his family will hang on him: its offspring and offshoots — all its lesser vessels, from the bowls to all the jars" (Isaiah 22:15,19-24).*

THE APOSTOLIC REVELATION

Chapter 10

The Humanity of Apostles

The biblical picture of the true apostle would not be complete without including reference to the natural and obvious fact that apostles are human, and must live and work with the faults and weaknesses of their own humanity. This is not an excuse for sin, for that must be repented of by every believer. But every apostle, like all believers, has the ongoing need to watch over the heart, guard against false motives, and maintain a vital experience of God. Each must continually choose the way of the Spirit, and continue in submission and obedience to Christ.

This brings us to a vital question.

Do Genuine Apostles Make Mistakes?

Ask yourself, do *fathers* make mistakes? Of course, even the best dads do, but this does not disqualify them from being dads, nor from being considered *good* dads. It certainly does not change a family's need to have such a father, and to continue to receive the love and leadership of such a father. Neither does it remove the love of all the members of the family for dad. Not in a good family!

Usually mistakes, honestly and openly dealt with, draw a family closer together, increasing the love and support given to one another, and can result in an increased sense of closeness in the family. In a good family, this is what should happen.

Apply this lesson then to the family of God. Furthermore, very often it is the wisdom of God that allows mistakes to occur, for in this way we all learn, and we maintain our love and dependence upon one another. It is not always a bad thing that mistakes occur, if we deal with them and each other with a right spirit. This helps to bring the believers, indeed the whole church, to maturity.

I always tell the members of our fellowship, "It's O.K. for you to make a mistake." Otherwise, no one will feel the freedom to step out in faith in the things of God. We must create an atmosphere for all where it is acceptable to try, even with the risk of failure.

Now concerning apostles, let's ask the question again. Do genuine apostles make mistakes?

Peter's mistakes are written large in the pages of the New Testament, but he was still 'the apostle to the Jews'. I refer not just to the well known stories in the gospels, but to Paul's exhortations to the Galatians, using Peter's mistake, and Barnabas', to help them understand their own error. *"When Peter came to Antioch, I opposed him to his face, because he was clearly in the wrong. Before certain men came from James, he used to eat with the Gentiles. But when they arrived, he began to draw back and separate himself from the Gentiles because he was afraid of those who belonged to the circumcision group. The other Jews joined him in his hypocrisy, so that by their hypocrisy even Barnabas was led astray. When I saw that they were not acting in line with the truth of the gospel, I said to Peter in front of them all, "You are a Jew, yet you live like a Gentile and not like a Jew. How is it, then, that you force Gentiles to follow Jewish customs?" (Galatians 2:11-14).*

These are very strong words used here by Paul. *"He was clearly in the wrong", "he was afraid", "his hypocrisy", "Barnabas was led astray", "not acting in line with the truth of the gospel"* and *"force gentiles"* are phrases that indicate a serious friction between the apostles, and not a small error on the part of Peter and Barnabas.

Did Paul himself ever make a mistake? Well, he admits it. *"How were you inferior to the other churches, except that I was never a burden to you? Forgive me this wrong!" (2 Corinthians 12:13).* This is not a doctrinal error, nor any real fault on the part of the apostle. He has done them no real wrong, but had followed the unfruitful policy of not requiring the church to support him while he was ministering to them. It is a big mistake to fail to teach the believers to support and honour their leaders through financial commitment. This truth is fundamental to a healthy church, and Paul had taught the principle of it in 1 Corinthians 9:7-15. Despite the principle, still he continued to make the mistake, as you can see by his comment in verses 12b and 15.

Up until the time of Christ, Moses was the one man revered above all. God's witness concerning him is, *"Moses was faithful as a servant in all God's house"* *(Hebrews 3:5).* Yet Moses also made great mistakes, from trying to do it all himself, as many of us have done, and needing Jethro's advice, to his big mistake of striking the rock in anger, whereby he was forbidden to enter the promised land.

These facts do not lessen our great respect and love for Moses, Peter, Barnabas and Paul. Neither do they indicate that these men were anything less than God's chosen apostles. In the ultimate outcome of their words and their lives, they were everything we have said about apostles.

Do Apostles Ever Speak Their Own Thoughts, Rather Than Purely the Mind of the Lord?

Paul gives advice in areas where angels might fear to tread — that of whether to marry or not. These are examples of those passages where Paul speaks his own mind, and yet clearly specifies that he is not speaking for God, but out of his own trustworthy heart. *"Now about virgins: I have no command from the Lord, but I give a judgment as one who by the Lord's mercy is trustworthy. Because of the present crisis, I think that it is good for you to remain as you are. Are you married? Do not seek a divorce. Are you unmarried? Do not look for a wife"* *(1 Corinthians 7:25-28).*

"In my judgment, she is happier if she stays as she is - and I think that I too have the Spirit of God" *(1 Corinthians 7:40).* Note in these two passages the use of *"I think"* and *"in my judgment"*.

Do Apostles Pursue Dead Ends?

Do they ever set out on a course of action they think is according to their call, pursuing what they believe is the right vision, only to find it isn't? Do they mistakenly pursue a course, but need to be redirected?

The answer is yes to both of these questions, and the biblical illustrations show the simple humanity of even the greatest apostles.

> *"When they came to the border of Mysia, they tried to enter Bithynia, but the Spirit of Jesus would not allow them to. So they passed by Mysia and went down to Troas. During the night Paul had a vision of a man of Macedonia standing and begging him, "Come over to Macedonia and help us." After Paul had seen the vision, we got ready at once to leave for Macedonia, concluding that God had called us to preach the gospel to them"* *(Acts 16:7-10).*

We see that the apostles pursued their goals pretty much as we do today — prayerfully and sincerely, but with a little trial and error, and making conclusions based on the presenting evidence and the inner witness of the Spirit, as much as on more obvious direct revelation. God is pleased to guide us step-by-step, and often uses very ordinary looking processes to do so.

Quite often Paul would have strong desires to pursue a course of action which he felt was right, but which the Lord never enabled. *"But, brothers, when we were torn away from you for a short time (in person, not in thought), out of our intense longing we made every effort to see you. For we wanted to come to you - certainly I, Paul, did, again and again - but Satan stopped us" (1 Thessalonians 2:17-19).*

I often wonder in what sense it could be that Satan could stop the great apostle from doing what he believed was the will of God. In the end it could only be that the Lord had other plans for Paul, that Paul had many goals as an apostle that he could never follow-through on, whilst at the same time he fulfilled God's purposes in many other ways without knowing it. Surely this reveals how human is the apostle, and yet how sovereign is God working through the apostle.

Can Other People Take an Apostle 'Off Course'?

Is it possible for others to adversely affect an apostle's time and ministry, or cause events to turn out contrary to the apostle's knowledge of the will of God? Yes again!

At least one of the shipwrecks Paul endured, it seems, was not intended by the will of God. *"Paul warned them, 'Men, I can see that our voyage is going to be disastrous and bring great loss to ship and cargo, and to our own lives also.' But the centurion, instead of listening to what Paul said, followed the advice of the pilot and of the owner of the ship" (Acts 27:9-12).*

Nevertheless, a sovereign God has His hand upon His apostles, as He does with all who walk in the covenant of Christ. Despite many small things that might seem to work contrary to God's purpose, even at odds with His revealed will, grace continually intervenes to bring about God's ultimate purpose. This is particularly true with the servant of God who continually submits his life and circumstances to God in prayer. The record of God's dealing with His called, chosen and faithful servants (Revelation 17:14) shows that He always knows the way ahead, no matter what the circumstances.

The shipwreck story continues, *"After the men had gone a long time without food, Paul stood up before them and said: "Men, you should have taken my advice not to sail from Crete; then you would have spared yourselves this damage and loss. But now I urge you to keep up your courage, because not one of you will be lost; only the ship will be destroyed. Last night an angel of the God whose I am and whom I serve stood beside me and said, 'Do not be afraid, Paul. You must stand trial before Caesar; and God has graciously given you the lives of all who sail with you.' So keep up your courage, men, for I have faith in God that it will happen just as he told me. Nevertheless, we must run aground on some island" " (Acts 27:21-26).*

God's hand held the apostle safely, to bring him to his ultimate purpose (*"You must stand trial before Caesar"*). The grace of God was such, however, that extended to Paul was an additional gift — the deliverance of all those with him (*"God has graciously given you the lives of all who sail with you"*). It is usual that, when God's grace and power is on an anointed servant, such as an apostle, the grace and power of that anointing carries the favour of God, causing blessing and miraculous outcomes for people and circumstances nearby. Notice that the text said that *"God has graciously **given you**"*. Both the grace and the gift was because of the apostle, not because of the lives or the circumstances of any other person on the ship. That is an example of the favour of God that comes with the anointing.

Humanity and Grace Combined

In earlier chapters, we spoke at some length of the grace and sovereign power of God at work in apostles. We must now recognise that our humanity remains, and is 'mixed in' with the grace of God at every point of the life of the church. This is entirely and properly biblical, since *"we have this treasure in jars of clay to show that this all-surpassing power is from God and not from us. We are hard pressed on every side, but not crushed; perplexed, but not in despair; persecuted, but not abandoned; struck down, but not destroyed. We always carry around in our body the death of Jesus, so that the life of Jesus may also be revealed in our body" (2 Corinthians 4:7-10).*

Here I have an important word for every believer. Accept that apostles are human, yet at the same time anointed by God to provide leadership, spiritual covering and government for the church. Accept that they do have the authority of Christ as His apostles. Accept these truths – and co-operate with Jesus to establish the leadership He wants, to build the wineskin He wants, for the church.

Though apostles are human, they are chosen to do a job for Christ, and therefore are given the authority to represent Him and serve their commission.

All the saints of the whole church need to accept this dynamic truth, and give to apostles acceptance, support, and honour.

Accept their authority — and allow them to make mistakes and be human — as long, of course, as they are what we expect every Christian to be, which is, open, honest, transparent, submitted in relationships, humble and penitent.

Support their purpose, helping them find the way ahead, the right way of Christ for the church. Offer much prayer on their behalf, give financially and with great generosity to establish their purpose, and yield the love of your heart to them. All these things we are exhorted to do for apostles by Holy Scripture.

Christ will bring them through, with or without you — but you should be part of the solution, not part of the problem — and you might as well share in an apostle's reward, rather than hinder your own.

And give honour (1 Corinthians 12:24). We have spoken elsewhere of the honour that should be given to leaders and spiritual fathers. Very often apostles are treated badly, but they need not be treated badly by you. You, who know the way of Christ, should now walk in the way of Christ.

False Apostles

We now come to an entirely different matter. The genuine apostle, in his humanity, must not be confused with the false apostle. The church must accept, honour and follow true apostles, yet at the same time be discerning, so as to guard against and reject the false apostle.

The early church, it seemed, knew they were supposed to test, or assess, the claims of apostles so as to guard against false ministry. It was common in the early church to receive travelling ministers, and communication was not what it is today. Jesus commended the Ephesian church for testing and rejecting false apostles (Revelation 2:2), and Paul remonstrated with the Corinthian church for failing to do so, after having been deceived by boastful men with false motivation (2 Corinthians 11:13).

At the same time, it would be a grave mistake to assume that false apostles are as prevalent as true and genuine apostles of Christ. This is simply not so, and the New Testament gives us a right and healthy perspective. Biblical references that honour apostles abound, whereas false apostles are referred to in only two places, (2 Corinthians 11:13, and Revelation 2:2) and neither of these passages are actually a warning against future false apostles. In the first, Paul's emotive appeal was bringing correction to a church after they had made serious mistakes, and in the second Jesus is commending another for having got it right.

In reality, the New Testament revelation is far more concerned about the danger of false prophets and false teacher/shepherds in the church, than with false apostles, although we should recognise that all these have similar characteristics. In a sense, the warning about one is a warning about all.

Jesus personally forewarned His apostles about false Christ's and false prophets (Matthew 7:15, 24:11, 24:24, Mark 13:22), but in the later teaching of the apostles themselves there are numerous references to false prophets (1 John 4:1, Revelation 2:20, Revelation 16:13), false teachers (1 Tim 1:3-7, 1 Tim 6:3-4, 2 Peter 2:1), false shepherds (Jude 12), false brothers (2 Corinthians 11:26, Galatians 2:4), false preachers (Philippians 1:15-18), and future teacher/ elders as 'savage wolves (Acts 20:29). This is why I made the earlier comment that there seems to be far less concern over false apostles, than over false prophets, teachers and shepherds, but we should not make too fine a point of that. The fact remains, the enemy will attempt to counterfeit every aspect of the life of the church, each ministry anointing, and the teaching of the truth itself.

Paul's Observations About False Apostles

"And I will keep on doing what I am doing in order to cut the ground from under those who want an opportunity to be considered equal with us in the things they boast about. For such men are false apostles, deceitful workmen, masquerading as apostles of Christ. And no wonder, for Satan himself masquerades as an angel of light. It is not surprising, then, if his servants masquerade as servants of righteousness. Their end will be what their actions deserve" (2 Corinthians 11:12-15).

In his second letter to the Corinthians, Paul has a lot to say about boasting. About half of all comments on boasting in the New Testament occur in this one epistle. There is a reason. Paul was countermanding the hollow, evil and arrogant boasting of false apostles, with a little boasting of his own. He felt it necessary to lay down a highly emotive appeal to the believers, to *"cut the ground from under"* the deceivers, and indeed he felt that the attitudes and foolishness of the believers had compelled his response. *"I have made a fool of myself, but you drove me to it. I ought to have been commended by you, for I am not in the least inferior to the "super-apostles," even though I am nothing" (2 Corinthians 12:11).*

He began his letter with *"Now this is our boast: Our conscience testifies that we have conducted ourselves in the world, and especially in our relations with you, in the holiness and sincerity that are from God. We have done so not according to worldly wisdom but according to God's grace" (2 Corinthians 1:12).* He is reminding them, early in the letter, of his qualification for apostolic ministry – holiness, sincerity, and the grace of God. This stands in stark comparison with what he will soon have to observe about others.

His direct observations about the false apostles are found in 2 Corinthians 10:12 — 11:20. They commend themselves, and boast beyond proper limits (2:12-13). They bring to the church the risk that the believers may be led astray from sincere and pure devotion to Christ (11: 3). They preach *another* Jesus, and a *different* gospel (11: 4). They create the impression that they are *"super-apostles"* (11: 5) and look for opportunity to be considered equal with the true apostles (11: 12), but they are false, deceitful, merely masquerading as apostles (11: 13). They are servants of Satan, and in the end will be judged (11: 15). They boast in a worldly, or fleshly way to impress the believers (11: 18), and the outcome is that the believers were enslaved, exploited, and taken advantage of (11:20). False apostles push themselves forward, even to the point of abuse and control (11:20).

The apostle reminded them, *"it is not the one who commends himself who is approved, but the one whom the Lord commends" (2 Corinthians 10:18).*

The Serious Warnings of Peter and Jude

It will be necessary for you to prayerfully read both 2 Peter 2:1-22, and Jude 3-23 to fully appreciate the seriousness and the extent of these warnings placed in Holy Scripture. These passages are not about false apostles, but about falsehood in leadership generally, and they reveal the serious condemnation and judgement to come that hangs over the heads of some who, outwardly, may look good in the church.

Following is a table outlining most of the ideas in these passages, although this hardly does justice to the power of the scripture itself. What is revealed is the amazing consistency of the biblical authors in their description of false shepherds/ prophets/teachers/apostles. Paul's words in 2 Corinthians 10 & 11, which we considered above, give us a remarkably similar picture of the behaviour and heart motivation of the false minister, as that below.

Comparative Analysis of False Shepherds/Teachers

Jude's Description (Jude 3-16)	Peter's Description (2 Peter 2)
Secretly slipped into the church	False teachers among you
Godless	Shameful, unrighteous
They change grace into license for immorality	Secretly introduce destructive heresies
Deny Jesus Christ our sovereign Lord	Denying the sovereign Lord
They will be later destroyed	Bringing swift destruction on themselves
Pollute their own bodies (Sexual immorality)	Carouse in broad daylight
Reject authority	Despise authority
Slander celestial beings	Not afraid to slander celestial beings
Speak abusively against things they do not understand	Blaspheme in matters they do not understand
What they understand by instinct, like unreasoning animals, will destroy them	They are like brute beasts, creatures of instinct, and like beasts they will perish
Follow the way of Cain, Balaam and Korah	Following the way of Balaam
Blemishes at your love feasts	Blots and blemishes, while they feast with you
Shepherds who feed only themselves	In their greed they exploit you, experts in greed
	Many will follow their shameful ways, and bring the way of truth into disrepute
Grumblers and faultfinders	Bold and arrogant
Boast about themselves	They mouth empty boastful words
	Seduce the unstable
Flatter others for their own advantage	
Follow their evil desires	Follow the corrupt desire of the sinful nature
	Eyes full of adultery, they never stop sinning
Follow mere natural instincts	
	Appealing to lusts, they entice people
Scoffers, who follow their own ungodly desires	
	They promise freedom, but are slaves of depravity
Cause division	
Do not have the Spirit	
Clouds without rain, blown along by the wind	Springs without water, Mists driven by a storm
Trees without fruit, and uprooted — twice dead	
Wild waves foaming up shame, Wandering stars	
Blackest darkness reserved forever	Blackest darkness is reserved for them

These descriptions are of church leaders who have insincere, evil motives, and they will suffer a terrible judgement. We must remember that outwardly they will often look benign. Indeed, many will look good, especially on first impressions. It is necessary to understand that whilst we are to know, recognise and honour those that lead us (1 Thessalonians 5:12), we are also instructed not to judge by appearances (John 7:24), and not to know them by natural means (2 Corinthians 5:16), but to know and discern all things by the Holy Spirit (1 Corinthians 2:10-16).

We must remember Jesus words. *"Watch out for false prophets. They come to you in sheep's clothing, but inwardly they are ferocious wolves. By their fruit you will recognize them. Do people pick grapes from thornbushes, or figs from thistles? Likewise every good tree bears good fruit, but a bad tree bears bad fruit. A good tree cannot bear bad fruit, and a bad tree cannot bear good fruit. Every tree that does not bear good fruit is cut down and thrown into the fire. Thus, by their fruit you will recognize them"* (Matthew 7:15-20).

Summarising the Characteristics of the False Leader

In summarising the characteristics of the false shepherd that have been given, we note certain common details that seem to be consistently part of the picture.

Firstly, at the root there is always a problem in the heart, from which springs a falseness (or error) in the motives, the morals and/or the message of the false minister. As the falseness or deception grows, it will often encompass all three of these areas. Corruption in the motives of the heart includes pride, greed and the need to control others, among other things. Paul mentioned envy, rivalry, selfish ambition, and insincerity in the hearts of some whose goal was to stir up trouble against Paul himself (Philippians 1:15-17) . Corruption in morality means they are still slaves to sin and their own fleshly desires, and this admits all kinds of secret sin. Error in the message can spring from any number of motives, including the above. This will result in the message of grace being perverted into either license or legalism, either of which by definition is *"another gospel" (Galatians 1:6-9, 2 Corinthians 11:4)*, and ultimately this is a denial of Jesus Christ, as Paul, Jude and Peter each have told us.

Secondly, false ministers are quick to claim leadership for themselves, but equally quick to find fault, and exclude and criticise others. They have been defined by Jude as grumblers and faultfinders, scoffers who cause division, and Peter said they were bold and arrogant.

Thirdly, they are motivated by self-interest rather than love of Christ and the

---

brethren, and this is *"the way of Balaam"*, whose heart craved the *"wages of wickedness"*. They use boasting and flattery to establish themselves and achieve their ends.

Fourthly, they despise authority, so they are likely to cynically oppose Christ's apostles, whom they seek to undermine.

Finally, another commonality is, they are under very serious judgement indeed. They will be repaid with *"harm"* for what they have done, *"their end will be what their actions deserve"*, *"their destruction has not been sleeping"*, and *"for whom blackest darkness has been reserved forever"*. *"Woe to them!"*

It is possible for a false apostle to function out of a false sense of calling. They may be genuinely mistaken, and therefore sincere. This will sometimes happen when someone has an old denominational mindset, and uses outward immediate success as a measure of their anointing. Others may think they are apostles, and yet be completely deceived, often by their own pride and selfish ambition. I have met people who claim to be building for Christ, but are only building for themselves. One of these was a young man who claimed to be an apostle, but had no understanding of the motives of his own heart. His biggest problem was these same items — uncontrolled pride, strong personal ambition, and the hidden motive of building for oneself. He looked good in the short-term, but has achieved nothing, and will not without a cleansing of the heart.

Another variation in the realm of falseness is that of the 'hireling'. Jesus said that the hired hand *"cares nothing for the sheep" (John 10:13)*. This kind of person is not motivated into the ministry by love for Christ and His people, but by love of self, and desire for the position, salary or other beneficial conditions. A friend told me a story coming from his own ministry. He visited a church to preach one weekend, and while there the Lord gave him a prophetic word for the pastor. In his heart, he decided not to give that minister the word he heard, which was an exhortation to repent of being a hireling. As he was leaving the church after the last meeting, the pastor approached him to say, "I know God has given you a prophetic word for me, and I would like you to tell me what it is." My friend explained that he did not want to share that word, but the pastor insisted. Therefore, my friend delivered to him a prophetic exhortation to repent of being in the ministry only for the pay and conditions, and change his heart toward the church. At this, the pastor lifted from his shirt pocket his paycheque, and said, "This is the only reason I'm here," and slipped the cheque back into his pocket.

All false leaders become pawns in the Devil's hands (2 Timothy 2:26), but some are more specific tools of Satan, actually planted by the enemy in the church. They are hidden representatives of the adversary. Others come into the church by believing the gospel, but have never had the evil motivations removed from their hearts by a full repentance and cleansing of the blood of Christ. An example of this is given in the stories of the early church. Simon, the sorcerer of Samaria, believed and was baptised, and followed the evangelist everywhere. When the power of the Spirit was given to the believers through the laying on of the apostle's hands, Simon offered Peter money to obtain the power. He had never repented of his hunger for power, and his personal need for the approval and control of others. He received one of the sternest rebukes in all of scripture when Peter answered him, *"May your money perish with you, because you thought you could buy the gift of God with money! You have no part or share in this ministry, because your heart is not right before God. Repent of this wickedness and pray to the Lord. Perhaps he will forgive you for having such a thought in your heart. For I see that you are full of bitterness and captive to sin" (Acts 8:20-23).*

The apostle Peter saw immediately that Simon was wrongly motivated — *"full of bitterness and captive to sin".* Even in response to the rebuke, he appeared more motivated to avoid consequences than to correct his heart. There is an appropriate, important and necessary place for the stern rebuke of wrong motives in the heart, and the church is poorer and more vulnerable when leaders avoid such conflict. Peter himself had tasted the seemingly harsh, but obviously needed and proper, rebuke of Jesus in the period of his own training for the ministry (Mathew 16:23).

False Shepherds at the End of the Age

At the end of the age there will be a satanic onslaught — Jesus said many false prophets will appear (Matthew 24:11) and deceive many people (but not necessarily believers). He added that false Christs and false prophets would perform great (false) signs and miracles in order to try and deceive the elect – but He adds, *"if that were possible" (Matthew 24:24).* It is not usual for the elect to be so easily deceived, but it all depends on their hearts.

I would make a number of points about the coming proliferation of false prophets and Christs, etc.

Firstly, this is no different to the initial apostolic age of the church, which had to struggle to sort out the false from the real in many matters. This is to be expected in a time when God is working to bring about great things in a new way, since the enemy seeks to control the gains of the Kingdom of Christ. The apostle John gave this report of such false activity in the days of the first apostles. *"Many deceivers... have gone out into the world. Any such person is the deceiver and the antichrist. Watch out that you do not lose what you have worked for, but that you may be rewarded fully" (2 John 7-8).*

Secondly, the number of *false* prophets or apostles will be *minimal* compared to the number of genuine apostles and prophets released into the church in the last days. This, as we observed earlier, is just as it was in the times of the New Testament authors.

Thirdly, they are a counterfeit. There can only be a counterfeit if there is also a genuine, otherwise the counterfeit is meaningless. Counterfeit money only has value if it is an attempt to copy real money. No criminal produces a $99 note, or a $110 note, because these do not exist. If at the end of the age there will be a resurgence of false apostles and prophets, it will be because the genuine article abounds. Satan will only be attempting to copy what God is doing. Furthermore, criminals counterfeit the more valuable notes, because this is worth more to them. This can only mean that apostles and prophets will be of great value to Christ and the church at the end of the age.

Avoiding the Counterfeit

We are most safely kept from being deceived by a counterfeit when we are completely familiar with the genuine. In a bank, the employees easily identify counterfeit banknotes simply because they are so familiar with the real, which they handle everyday. They know the feel of good money. In their hands and before their eyes, they can tell the difference easily. It is the people who do not handle money constantly that are fooled by the counterfeit.

Likewise, this principle is true in every spiritual matter. The way to guard against false prophecy is to be, by constant use, completely familiar with genuine prophecy. I have often advised that the way to protect the church from false intercessors is to train, not just the volunteer intercessors, but the whole church, in intercession, and the way to protect against false prophecy is to train, again, not a few but the whole church in prophecy. Then, if someone with false motives, claiming to be an intercessor or prophetically gifted, begins to fellowship with the saints, say in a cell or a prayer meeting, their falseness is readily apparent to the saints – it 'smells' to them . Potential problems are cut off early, and these wolves will not have power to draw sheep after themselves. Those churches and pastors who avoid these matters are far more likely to be deceived by the false.

Today, leaders and churches need to be fully informed and totally involved in the restoration of apostles and prophets to the church. In this way we can most safely guard our people against falsehood and deception.

Fallen Apostles

We come to possibly the saddest aspect of all. It is possible, and it has occurred, that a genuine apostle might fall from grace, into backsliding and sin, and become a false apostle. The principle also applies to prophets, teachers, elders, and to every believer.

The classic examples of this phenomena are those of Balaam the prophet in the Old Testament, and Judas the apostle of the Lamb in the New. There is no question but that both of these were genuinely called and anointed servants of Christ, who ministered in His name and with His anointings.

Every word recorded in the Bible as prophecy from the prophet Balaam is exceptional and holy prophecy. None of it constitutes a false word. Every word is of the Spirit of God, and Balaam's words are amongst the most beautiful and inspiring in all of scripture. For example, *"God is not a man, that he should lie, nor a son of man, that he should change his mind. Does he speak and then not act? Does he promise and not fulfill? I have received a command to bless; he has blessed, and I cannot change it" (Numbers 23:19-20).*

> Falsehood is not defined by the quality of the ministry, but by the heart of the minister

The witness of the Holy Spirit concerning the actual prophetic utterances of Balaam is this, *"The oracle of Balaam son of Beor, the oracle of one whose eye sees clearly, the oracle of one who hears the words of God, who has knowledge from the Most High, who sees a vision from the Almighty, who falls prostrate, and whose eyes are opened" (Numbers 24:15-16).* Nevertheless, he is considered the greatest, i.e. the worst and most evil, of the false prophets, such that he is the New Testament example of a false leader who loved the wages of wickedness.

Every word Balaam spoke was true, but the man became false. He caused Israel to sin, so that the curse that he was not able to pronounce by oracle (because his prophetic gift was so accurate and anointed of God), would come upon God's people.

We see then, that falsehood is not defined by the quality of the ministry, but by the heart of the minister. We also understand that where people present outwardly a good quality of ministry, this is not the proof of their righteousness or their walk with Christ.

Judas fell from what should have been a very secure position — next to Jesus Himself. Satan also fell from such a position, close to the throne of God. It will do us good to remember that we are kept secure by a humble dependent heart, not by position in the ministry. The closer we get to God by means of revelation, experience, ministry anointing and the like, the more we need to always remember that we are on God's Holy Mountain, and this is from where Satan fell.

Paul was conscious of the dangers of taking God for granted, and failing to press on in humble pursuit of our holy Saviour. *"I beat my body and make it my slave so that after I have preached to others, I myself will not be disqualified for the prize" (1 Corinthians 9:27).* The word here translated 'disqualified' literally means "reprobate, unapproved, rejected as worthless".

The Apostle John's Observation

The apostle John writes very revealingly of a church leader called Diotrephes, in his third epistle (3 John 9-10). John said Diotrephes *"loves to be first"*. This is a telling piece of information. Paul said in 1 Corinthians 12:28 that in the church it is to be *"first, apostles"*, and this can only mean that Diotrephes was claiming apostolic authority over the local church. John also said that he *"will have nothing to do with us"*. This makes Diotrephes, by definition, a false apostle. Possibly he was originally a genuine leader of God's people who had fallen, or was falling. He fails the test of the true apostle on both the following points.

Firstly, the true apostle is marked by humility, gentleness, considering others better than oneself, love and hospitality. Yet Diotrephes was *"gossiping maliciously"* about the apostles, he refused *"to welcome the brothers"*, he stopped others from offering hospitality to the brothers, and he *"puts them out of the church"*.

Secondly, he rejected the true apostle (John), and exercised malicious and manipulative control of the local church. We have here a classic example of the false apostle/prophet/shepherd. Further, John implied that Diotrephes was not of God when he made the comment found in 3 John 11.

On the other hand, John proceeds immediately to commend Demetrius, who stands in stark contrast to Diotrephes. He is well spoken of by the believers, and by the truth itself. As well, the apostle commends him, which is a faithful testimony.

A Pattern for Validating True Grace Gifts

This gives us the pattern for recognising the true apostle or prophet. God will provide two or three witnesses to establish every truth. This will come from the testimony of the believers who are around them, the testimony of just how their life compares to the Word of God, and the testimony of the apostles who are over them in the Lord.

In assessing the validity of leadership ministry, let the body of Christ take note of John's words in his second epistle, found at 2 John 7-11, and consider especially these instructions, *"If anyone comes to you and does not bring this teaching, do not take him into your house or welcome him. Anyone who welcomes him shares in his wicked work" (2 John 10-11).*

THE APOSTOLIC REVELATION

Chapter **11**

An Apostolic People

Foundational to the apostolic reformation is the idea that the whole church is to be an apostolic people. We are not just talking about the restoration of apostles to the church, but a restoration of the apostolic nature of the church itself!

I devoted the month of June, 1998, to prayer. Every weekday morning I would arrive at the church auditorium at 6 AM for 12 hours of prayer. Others would join me, coming and going as they were able, and together with them or alone I would worship, listen, intercede, and wait on God.

Early one morning the Spirit of God directed me to these words, *"I will instruct you and teach you in the way you should go; I will counsel you and watch over you. Do not be like the horse or the mule, which have no understanding but must be controlled by bit and bridle or they will not come to you" (Psalm 32:8-9).*

It was the word *'understanding'* over which the Spirit of God dwelt. Suddenly, it was alive with meaning as I entered into a revelation of the purposes of God.

A Vision for the Apostolic Company

This is the gist of the revelation. God is looking throughout the earth for a people upon whom He can pour out His Spirit in a particular way and for a particular purpose. He seeks a people who will allow Him to bring them into unity, enabling Him to give them a gift, the spirit of *'understanding'*. Then with *one heart* and *one mind* they will arise to do the work of God.

The size of the group is not important. It could be 200 people, or 50, but with deep unity and profound understanding given by the Spirit, there is no limit to what God can do through them. I sensed that God is looking now for such a people, and in the coming days there may be many such groups. But the key is *understanding*, supernaturally given as an anointing by the Lord to every person in the community, causing them to be of one heart and mind.

At first this idea seemed too idealistic, even though it was strongly impressed upon me. To my own mind it appeared highly improbable that groups of believers could have a unity so deeply pervasive that they would be of *one heart* and *one mind*. In the church all we have ever known is independence. So I turned to the Scriptures to find the biblical position.

I was amazed by what I discovered. God has done it before. What I had seen in prayer as God's plan for His people today, had been the immediate outcome of the day of Pentecost. It was church history. I read again these amazing words with new insight, *"All the believers were one in heart and mind"* (Acts 4:32), and I thought again about the amazing power of the believers of the early church.

I found also an earlier precedent in the history of Israel. *"Also in Judah the hand of God was on the people to give them unity of mind to carry out what the king and his officials had ordered, following the word of the LORD"* (2 Chronicles 30:12). So the Lord in faithfulness has placed two witnesses, one in the Old Testament and the other in the New, that show His power to transform communities by His Spirit, and reveal the purpose of God for His people. God always seeks to give His people 'understanding', and create community.

The 'Understanding' Principle

In many local churches there are few who have the spirit of understanding *as an anointing* which reveals the will of God for them as people.

Consider what happens in churches everywhere. Generally, the pastor will have understanding of the will of God in some measure, because it is part of the call and anointing to preach the word of God to God's people. Therefore, he will preach the need for everyone's prayer life to be effective. He will exhort and encourage every believer to be devoted to prayer, and walk with Christ daily. But usually the following week the people will be no more prayerful than they were the week before.

Another Sunday, he will preach holiness, exhorting the believers to live holy lives for Christ. But during the following week, very few will give any more thought to holiness than they did the week before.

The next Sunday, he will teach the need to win souls, for *"he who wins souls is wise" (Proverbs 11:30)*, and he will urge devotion to prayer for the lost, as well as boldness in witnessing. But during the following week, there will rarely be more witnessing or prayer for the lost in the lives of the believers.

The truth is, there are many congregations where lives are not moved greatly by the preaching of the word of God. There is a reason for this. Because the church lacks unity, the spirit of understanding is thinly distributed. It is upon the unity of the believers that the command to bless is given, and that commanded blessing is *"life" (Psalm 133:3)*.

I saw that God is looking for a people upon whom He can place the spirit of understanding, corporately and individually. Then each will have the same passion for the will of God to be done as the preacher, and together, with *one heart* and *one mind,* they will arise and do the will of God.

Understanding is a major key to spiritual advancement. The psalmist prayed, *"Give me understanding, and I will keep your law and obey it with all my heart" (Psalm 119:34)*. The Lord Himself had informed the prophet Isaiah, *"Therefore my people will go into exile for lack of understanding" (Isaiah 5:13)*.

Jesus' ministry was based on this principle. In response to the disciples' question, *"Why do you speak to the people in parables?" (Matthew 13:10)*, He gave a very definitive answer that reveals one of the primary principles of the kingdom of God. He said, *"The knowledge of the secrets of the kingdom of heaven has been given to you, but not to them. Whoever has will be given more, and he will have an abundance. Whoever does not have, even what he has will be taken from him. This is why I speak to them in parables" (Matthew 13:11-13)*.

Then He quoted Isaiah, *"You will be ever hearing but never understanding; you will be ever seeing but never perceiving. For this people's heart has become calloused; they hardly hear with their ears, and they have closed their eyes. Otherwise they might see with their eyes, hear with their ears, understand with their hearts and turn, and I would heal them" (Matthew 13:14-15)*.

The principle is this. God gives understanding to people who *want* understanding — to those who look to God and cry out for it. Then, to those who have understanding, He continues to give the gifts of God. But many of the people who came to Jesus were only looking for signs and wonders, for a miracle, or the miraculous food Jesus had been known to produce. They were not coming because they were hungry for God, therefore God did not reveal Himself or kingdom truth to them. This is the meaning behind the otherwise seemingly harsh, but actually profound revelation given by the same prophet, *"For this is a people without understanding; so their Maker has no compassion on them, and their Creator shows them no favor" (Isaiah 27:11).*

The Community Anointing in Pentecost

Waiting for the day of Pentecost, in Acts chapters 1 & 2, were a group of believers who met these two conditions. They had been brought into oneness by the ministry of Jesus, were faithful in the understanding they had been given, and therefore qualified for more. Upon these believers was poured out the Pentecost anointing. *"When the day of Pentecost came, they were all together in one place. Suddenly a sound like the blowing of a violent wind came from heaven and filled the whole house where they were sitting. They saw what seemed to be tongues of fire that separated and came to rest on each of them. All of them were filled with the Holy Spirit and began to speak in other tongues as the Spirit enabled them" (Acts 2:1-4).*

In our teaching about the day of Pentecost and the outpouring of the Holy Spirit, we have consistently shortchanged the truth of Pentecost. It has been taught repeatedly as an outpouring of the Holy Spirit that brought the baptism of the Spirit into the lives of the believers, and empowered them with gifts of the Holy Spirit to be witnesses for Jesus, and to take the gospel to the nations. All of this is true. But it is not the whole truth.

In Pentecost there are many anointings, and of special importance is the anointing for community. This is the anointing that brings *understanding* and the *spirit of unity*, and enables Christian *community* to be built. There is also here an anointing for leaders to understand how to build community, which is vastly different from building the church as an institution.

Acts chapter 2, which records the outpouring of the Spirit and the events of the day of Pentecost, closes with this climactic statement, *"They devoted themselves to the apostles' teaching and to the fellowship, to the breaking of bread and to prayer. Everyone was filled with awe, and many wonders and miraculous signs were done by the apostles. All the believers were together and had everything in common. Selling their possessions and goods, they gave to anyone as he had need. Every day they continued to meet together in the temple courts. They broke bread in their homes and ate together with glad and sincere hearts, praising God and enjoying the favor of all the people. And the Lord added to their number daily those who were being saved" (Acts 2:42-47).*

Here is a description of an amazing creation of community, which was the direct result of the Pentecost anointing being given to the believers. At the heart of this description is the statement, *"All the believers were together and had everything in common".* The direct result of the power of the Spirit resting on such a community of God's people was amazing power. In the chapters that follow we see example after example of what may be achieved, and what life may be like, when the power for community is given.

In Acts chapter 4, *"they raised their voices together in prayer to God" (Acts 4:24),* and the direct outcome was, *"After they prayed, the place where they were meeting was shaken. And they were all filled with the Holy Spirit and spoke the word of God boldly" (Acts 4:31).* The church today rarely sees this degree of the manifestation of God's power. I believe power manifestations of such magnitude require the church to be functioning in the community anointing.

The belief that the church was functioning in a *community anointing*, and that this is of strategic importance to the kingdom of God, is proven in the statement of Scripture which followed. *"All the believers were one in heart and mind. No one claimed that any of his possessions was his own, but they shared everything they had. With great power the apostles continued to testify to the resurrection of the Lord Jesus, and much grace was upon them all. There were no needy persons among them. For from time to time those who owned lands or houses sold them, brought the money from the sales and put it at the apostles' feet, and it was distributed to anyone as he had need" (Acts 4:32-35).*

The same power is evident in the story of Peter's miraculous escape from prison in Acts chapter 12. The church offered much prayer, and Peter's subsequent deliverance involved an angel, shining lights, chains falling off wrists, doors and the city gates opening by themselves, guards sleeping through all the commotion, and Peter 'coming to himself' after it was all over. Every day we hear of miracles the Lord is giving His people all over the world, but we rarely hear of miracles as great as this. I believe the church must be 'in community' for miracles of this nature to flow unhindered.

The 'community' anointing of Pentecost is foundational to such power in the church, not just the fact that the individuals were baptised with the power of the Spirit. Therefore, we must adjust our faith, our values, and our goals. We must change the way we pray, look for the release of all the anointings of Pentecost, and expect greater results from the work of the Spirit amongst us.

The church at Antioch was outstanding, even in its own day. This is another example of the church in community, and the resultant power. Many people came to Christ there, and when Barnabas arrived, having been sent by the apostles, he saw the *"evidence"* of the grace of God (Acts 11:21, 23). Great anointings were at work in this church, another example of what the power of the Spirit does with believing men and women, in community. And later, when they laid hands on the apostles they were sending out (Acts 13:1-3), great power went with them. Unity, with anointing, always translates into power.

Every apostolic company of saints is now to be looking to cooperate with the Spirit of Grace to bring about these results in these last days.

Furthermore, revival of the church and transformation of the community is to be found in this anointing. This is the power of spiritual awakening.

Example of The Moravian Brethren

In more recent church history, we have an exceptional example of an apostolic company that found this grace. The story of Count Zinzendorf and the Moravians is precisely a model for what God now wants to do with many apostolic companies throughout the earth. They were a group that had known disunity and division, even rebellion, but God heard prayer. Zinzendorf himself spent a whole night crying out to God for them, and an amazing change took place.

They experienced what has been called the Moravian Pentecost, and they commenced a prayer meeting which never ceased for well over 100 years. From their small company they sent missionaries to the darkest places, and those at home worked and lived sacrificially to support many that were sent out. They did more to evangelise the entire world in 20 years, than the whole church had done in 200 years. Their spirituality was exceptional, and they became a light to many people, including the great John Wesley. The story of the Moravian Brethren is a model, and an inspiration. To help pursue the grace of apostolic community, with its attendant power and fruit bearing, you should consider the story of God's grace at work amongst that people.

Authority to Every Believer

The early apostles exercised great authority, but so did the believers. The whole purpose of being in submission to apostles is that apostolic authority might flow to many. Every believer under apostolic leadership is meant to function in apostolic authority. Apostles commission believers to function in authority and power for Christ.

An apostolic company is clothed with Christ's authority. The church of the coming days will see manifestations of amazing power and authority, but not without the apostles in place in the body, who have been given authority over the church.

Authority flows to those in submission to authority, as we have discussed, but there are some other significant factors that will help every believer function in Christ's authority.

Obviously, faith is required, and this is established by the believer's knowledge of the word of God, and especially a revelation to his or her heart of the truth of our position in Christ as taught in Ephesians 1: 20-23, 2:5-6.

Having the fear of the Lord in the heart is another very significant factor. The exercise of authority must always be without arrogance, presumption or independence. There can be no taking God for granted. A right and holy fear of the Lord helps to safeguard our hearts, keeping us in humility and a right relationship with God and others. As a result, we can be trusted with greater authority. In the coming days authority will be given, and with it freedom also, but we must remember that in the end, Christ will judge.

A willingness to accept responsibility helps to establish authority. Jesus gave authority to the 12 and the 72, but this was because they were going out to preach, heal the sick and cast our demons. Jesus said we are to put our hand to the plough and not look back. Where the believer takes up responsibility in the kingdom of God, authority will become established.

> We will see many ordinary believers make great impact upon their communities through grace and authority

Furthermore, prayer is required for growth in grace. Christ's authority is a grace imparted to the believer, and as with every anointing, we obtain this through hunger for more of God. Constantly seeking after Christ, ordering the heart aright through prayer, and seeking to know His truth and walking in it, are important spiritual disciplines for growth in grace.

In the coming days of the restored apostolic church, we will see many ordinary believers make great impact upon their communities through the grace and authority of Jesus Christ that will rest on them.

The Spirit of Apostleship

If the believers are to be an apostolic people, and if the apostolic authority of Christ and the apostles is to rest on them, it will be because the *Spirit of apostleship* is in the believers.

The Spirit of apostleship is the Spirit of Christ, who said, *"As the Father has sent me, I am sending you" (John 20:21)*. It means that the believers will be of the same mind, the same spirit and the same purpose as the apostles. To put it another way, it will mean that the believers will have the same heart and the same vision as the apostles, will be one in spirit with them, will have the same passion in the heart, and the same devotion to the cause of Christ. They will be one people with the apostles in serving Christ, and be willing to make the same sacrifices and pay the same price. They will be an apostolic people.

It is not possible to be an apostolic people without having the *spirit* of apostleship.

There are a number of distinct features that are common to every apostolic figure in Scripture. This includes Abraham, Moses, David, Elijah, John the Baptist, Jesus, Peter, Paul and John.

Firstly, they were set apart by divine sovereign choice, to do the will of God, and *secondly*, to each one there was to be given revelation of the way ahead. To Abraham, God said, *"Leave ... and go ... I will show you" (Genesis 12:1)*. Of Paul, the Lord spoke to Ananias, *"This man is my chosen ... I will show him ..." (Acts 9:15-16)*.

Thirdly, the way chosen for them involved struggle, suffering, or great perseverance, with tests involving both patience and faith. The suffering of apostles is known to be of legendary proportions.

Fourthly, for these, Christ was everything. They had one heart, an undivided heart, and it was Christ's. John the Baptist had one focus, to point to Jesus. David was the man after God's own heart. Peter was the one who preached Christ alone. Paul considered every advantage in life as rubbish compared to Christ. John, the beloved, was exiled to Patmos because of his testimony of Jesus. A true apostle is always Christ's. Each has a Christ-centred heart, and a Christ-impassioned love.

These qualifications for the Spirit of apostleship should give every faithful believer who follows after Christ great hope and joy. Why? Because they are common to all God's called, chosen and faithful ones, not just to these few heroes of the faith. They are heroes of the faith so as to be examples, models for the rest of us, demonstrating how to walk with God, and what to expect and believe.

Every believer is called by the sovereign choice of God (Romans 8:28, Ephesians 1:18), and every believer has the promise of Jesus that revelation will be given to them by the Holy Spirit (John 16:12-15).

Every believer is called to a life of perseverance, sharing in the sufferings of Christ, and to mature under tests of patience and faith. John says he is our *"companion in the suffering and kingdom and patient endurance that are ours in Jesus ... because of the word of God and the testimony of Jesus" (Revelation 1:9).* Like Jesus and the apostles, the believer who walks in the spirit of apostleship is willing to suffer so that the Father's will may be done.

> Anything less, or anything else, is not the apostolic faith, but only religion.

Finally, every believer is called to surrender the whole heart to Christ, as did the apostles (Philippians 3:7-15), in unmixed and passionate love.

Apostolic christianity is an experience of walking with Christ, where for each believer these things are real, tangible and personal to their faith. Each believer experiences the dealings of God, as intimately and as personally as Abraham and Paul did. Anything less, or anything else, is not the apostolic faith, but only religion.

Dynamic Qualities of an Apostolic People

The word dynamic is used here purposefully. *Dynamic* refers to a motive force, something that is potent, and energetic.

These are values and ethics which are foundational to the nature of the apostolic church, and they are characteristic of an apostolic people. These are energising principles, and are clearly part of God's revelation for the life of His people. As we submit to Christ, and learn His way, the power of God flows through us.

One Heart, and One Mind - Unity in the Apostolic Church. An apostolic people is marked by a great desire for unity, although unity is not an end in itself. Its purpose is to obtain intimacy with God, and to bring the world to faith. Even so, the love and acceptance of one another is real. Apostles will bring unity to the church, both within each local fellowship, and between fellowships. The apostolic goal is a unity of the faith which is to be built upon the unity of the Spirit.

Humility, Teachableness, Submission. These values become life experience when we have the Spirit of Jesus. No one is able to change their own heart, but as we receive Jesus, we receive His Spirit, and we are enabled by the Holy Spirit to live and think and feel as Jesus would. There cannot be an apostolic people unless they are teachable and in submission to their leaders. Without these qualities there can be no unity, and there can be no visitation of the Spirit in power. Without teachableness there will be no growth in grace, and without submission there is no genuine authority in the believer. Without these graces in the heart, truth cannot be received. Humility precedes both of these qualities, and is essential for apostolic power.

Honouring Leaders. An apostolic people will learn to honour their leaders, not only because of the biblical command, but because this is a primary source of life and blessing which God has ordained. The ability to give honour is a mark of maturity, wisdom, and a pure heart. The impure always struggle to give honour, because it is against the nature of the flesh. In community, the mutual honouring of one another makes for a beautiful and peaceful experience of life. This is the wisdom that comes from heaven, mentioned in James 3:17-18, and which is the opposite of the striving of envy and selfish ambition that disturbs many Christian fellowships.

Covenant Relationship (faithfulness not convenience). In traditional churches, relationship is often based on convenience. The relationship continues while it is convenient, but when it no longer suits them, people walk away. Many Christians effectively live for themselves, and the result is that relationships are shallow. Apostolic Christianity calls us to discover meaningful relationships, based on faithfulness to one another. We are to become devoted to one another, as the apostle instructed. *"Be devoted to one another in brotherly love. Honor one another above yourselves" (Romans 12:10).* We are to be brothers and sisters, mothers and fathers to one another in the faith. We must overcome our cultural barriers, and discover what Christ wants for us in relationship with one another.

> We are to become devoted to one another, as the apostle instructed.

Accountability, Transparency, Openness, Honesty. Amongst an apostolic people, there is accountability through relationship. We are to live lives of transparency before one another. For this to be effective, we have to come to the place where we trust others. The Bible says that love always trusts, but of course this can only be the experience of those in community, where the issues that divide have been worked through, our hearts are at rest, and we accept one another. In community, and the apostolic faith, individuals do not pursue a private agenda. We live for the good of other people, and we are honest about ourselves, our purpose and our motives.

Love. The early apostolic church was recognised, by the believers and their enemies alike, as being a people of amazing love for one another. They were fulfilling the law of Christ. The church's enemies were chagrined by the love the believers had for one another, and this was foundational to their power. There is no other way to turn the world upside-down, and the apostolic church succeeded in doing this in one generation. This is the call of God upon today's church, to be an apostolic people for another generation, marked by the amazing, selfless, sacrificial love which is Christ in us.

Laying Down their Lives for the Brethren. Christ called us to love one another in the same way as He loved us. He loved us to the point of laying down His life for us, just as He remarked to His disciples, *"Greater love has no one than this, that he lay down his life for his friends" (John 15:13).* The apostle John later wrote this challenging appeal, *"This is how we know what love is: Jesus Christ laid down his life for us. And we ought to lay down our lives for our brothers" (1 John 3:16).* This describes the spirit of apostolic Christianity. Do not be surprised if, in the coming days, God calls some of His people to supreme sacrifice. In the meantime, know that the love of our hearts toward one another should be such that we would count the lives of other people worthy of sacrifice. This at least will call forth obedience to John's next statement, which was, *"If anyone has material possessions and sees his brother in need but has no pity on him, how can the love of God be in him? Dear children, let us not love with words or tongue but with actions and in truth" (1 John 3:17-18).* This is the spirit of an apostolic people.

Not democracy, but community. Democracy may be fine for nations, but it has never been God's plan for the church. Instead, the church is meant to rise above mere democracy, and find community. Democracy cannot produce community, as we discussed earlier. An apostolic company functions through relationship and by its people knowing and trusting each other deeply, not through the politics of who can get the votes. In community, it is not the opinion of the majority that counts — it is the Spirit of God bringing peace to the heart that guides and speaks. The voice of just one member can be used by God to bring either direction, or correction, and the believers whose hearts are right with one another sense an inner witness to the truth. In the end, the anointed leadership of the community carries the responsibility for understanding the heart of the people and the mind of the Spirit, no matter through whom it is being expressed.

Rights, but no rights. To be an apostolic people, we must give up our 'rights'. If we are not prepared to do this, we are not following the way of Christ, and therefore can never know His power. Christ was honoured by the Father and exalted to the highest place, specifically because He gave up His rights and trusted the Father instead. This is the message of Philippians chapter 2, where we are called to be like-minded and one in spirit and purpose with the believers, because we are united with Christ. We are called to look after the interests of others, as well as our own, and instructed to have the same values that Christ did when He made Himself nothing. Jesus did not count His equality with God as something to be held onto, but humbled Himself to become a servant to others. Likewise, the members of an apostolic people are not to demand their rights, but to trust the covering of God, and to be servants to their people. An apostolic people must be content to be 'nothing', and it is Christ who will exalt them in His way and time. This is the people who will inherit the apostolic promise, *"The God of peace will soon crush Satan under your feet" (Romans 16:20).*

The Call to Overcome

"To him who overcomes and does my will to the end, I will give authority over the nations ... just as I have received authority from my Father" (Revelation 2:26-27). The call to overcome is a universal call to every believer. The believer is to overcome sin, the world and the devil, and we have the grace of God and His commands to help us. His commands, when believed and obeyed, give life. Grace is the power of God that flows to every believer who steps out in faith to obey Him.

The word of God is very clear that the overcomer does God's will to the end, and it is these who have authority over the nations with Christ on the day of judgement. However, God sees the end from beginning, so in these days prior to Christ's coming, such overcomers may walk now in the authority of Christ over nations. In the coming days, the apostolic people of God will exercise great power in prayer over world events, and a great harvest of the nations will take place for the kingdom of God.

Inheritance also is linked to overcoming, for *"He who overcomes will inherit all this, and I will be his God and he will be my son" (Revelation 21:7).* The eternal inheritance described in Revelation 21 is not given to anyone – only to those who overcome by the power of God through faith, grace and obedience.

God has released into the world the apostolic and prophetic anointings of Christ. The call of God is for every believer to walk, with their leaders, in the grace of these anointings and be part of the victorious church of Jesus Christ in these final hours. The church of the last days, which sees the defeat of Babylon by the power of God, is addressed as *'saints and apostles and prophets'.* This is the overcoming church, instructed to rejoice with heaven over the fall of the great whore. *"Rejoice over her, O heaven! Rejoice, saints and apostles and prophets! God has judged her for the way she treated you" (Revelation 18:20).*

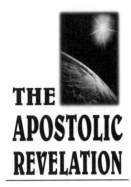

THE APOSTOLIC REVELATION

Chapter 12

Towards the New Apostolic Wineskin

It is the end of an era. The age of the institutional church is over, and large institutions are weakening before our very eyes, making way for the kingdom of God. This is not dissimilar to another change of era spoken of in Hebrews 8:13, *"By calling this covenant 'new,' he has made the first one obsolete; and what is obsolete and aging will soon disappear."*

Lost Ships, and the Change of an Era

There was a time when enormous ocean liners dominated the transport systems of the world. They were great ocean going vessels, carrying large numbers of people and serving many nations. They carried vast wealth, and young married couples, businessmen, family groups; all kinds of travellers took advantage of their services and enjoyed the age of steam.

Things changed and the world moved on. Better and more economical means of transport were discovered, and the great ships faded from the scene. Most of these ships were broken up for scrap, but some of them had very tragic ends.

The Titanic is the most famous of those ships with a tragic demise, but there are others. On May 7, 1915, the *Lusitania* was torpedoed by a German U-boat off the coast of Ireland. It sank in about 15 minutes with the great loss of 1,198 lives. Only 761 people survived. The strange thing was that the torpedo should not have been capable of sinking this ship. The U-boat was on its way home and had remaining only one small torpedo. The German captain knew that his torpedo could not sink the ship, but decided to fire it anyway. It transpired that after the small explosion occurred from the torpedo, a second more powerful explosion broke open the great ship. It has remained an unsolvable mystery as to what caused the secondary explosion, because no flammable materials, or explosive war materials, were on the ship. It is theorised that coal dust exploded, ignited by the blast of the torpedo.

Even more heart-wrenching is the tragedy of the *Empress of Ireland*, another great ocean liner which carried about 1500 passengers regularly on the transatlantic journey. On the occasion of its terrible demise, it was sailing down the St. Lawrence River, Canada, heading toward the open sea.

The passengers had embarked late in the day, and after the ship left the port of Quebec they were served dinner. The passengers retired to their cabins for the evening, for there would be time the next day to explore the ship in daylight. No rough water would be encountered until the ship reached the Atlantic, hundreds of miles downriver.

Sometime after midnight, during the small hours of the morning of May 29, 1914, they were 200 miles from port, when tragedy struck. The captain and the helmsman observed a ship coming in the opposite direction, which appeared to change course in front of them. The ship was a Norwegian collier (a coal tanker), the *Storstad*, and the helmsman on this vessel made a simple, but terrible, mistake. It appeared to him that the *Empress of Ireland* was approaching on the wrong side, so he changed course. Within minutes, a bank of fog rolled in across the river, obscuring all visibility. The staff on the *Empress* had no idea where the collier was, so they turned the vessel in what they thought was a safe direction, cut the engines, and began sounding the foghorn.

Suddenly, without warning, the collier, which had been built with an ice-breaking structure, appeared out of the fog at full speed, and rammed into the side of the ship. It struck the *Empress* in the worst possible place, amidships between the two engine rooms. Water instantly flooded the engine rooms, and cut all power to the ship. The entire ship was plunged into darkness, walls of water flooded through the many decks, and most of the passengers were trapped in darkness in the bowels of a ship they had not explored.

She sank in 14 minutes, with the loss of almost 1100 lives. The ship had 11 watertight compartments which could have saved the ship from sinking, but there was not time to close even one. There were 40 lifeboats, but in the dark there was only time to launch seven.

Many of the passengers were Christians. Canadian Salvationists were travelling to London for a Salvation Army Congress, and of the Salvation Army brass band aboard, there were only seven survivors.

The New Era — Relational Christianity

The story of the end of the era of passenger liners, and of these lost ships, has impressed itself strongly on my heart in recent days. I feel this is a picture that speaks to us about the institutional church, which also has come to the end of an era. In the same way that air transport has replaced the great ships, we will now see apostolic networks and relational Christianity replace these denominational institutions. This is not a bad thing, but a good thing, if we understand what God is doing.

Air transport, especially the invention of the jumbo jet, revolutionised the world. Now, huge numbers of people travel quickly, economically and frequently. The world has been opened up to many of the kind of people who could never travel before. Ship travel was more expensive and time-consuming, and the aeroplane represented great progress. Although an individual aircraft does not carry as many people as an ocean liner, there are now many more aircraft than there were ships. Many more people now fly than ever sailed.

Apostolic Christianity will bring this same liberty and freedom to the believers. Many more people will be involved in ministry and mission, far more will travel a better spiritual journey, following after Christ. It is a far more effective and economical wineskin, and through the renewed apostolic wineskin Christ's people will more effectively reach the nations, including our own Western nations.

Most of the great ships were eventually broken up for scrap. They were no longer economical to operate, and passenger numbers declined constantly, as more traveled by plane. I believe it will be like this for much of the institutional church, particularly where there is a refusal to embrace reform and apostolic principles. The component parts of value will be re-used, but in a different way. This does not represent a loss to the kingdom of God, as the real kingdom is in our hearts and in relationships, not in the outward form of the institutional church. The hearts and relationships continue, no matter what happens to official programs, buildings, committees and the like. The prayers of the saints continue, as does their witness, their family life, and their love for others. Real Christianity continues, and is actually made more effective without religious trappings and heavy institutional programming. We must trust God that He knows what He is doing in the hearts of His people, and for the good of His people.

God also has His eyes on the lost, His heart yearning for them. We know full well that traditional Christianity and the institutionalised church is having virtually no impact on the community around us. The large populations of our nations remain in darkness, totally unimpressed with the church as it is, and unable to hear our message.

The fact that the church has been, in our lifetimes, ineffective to reach our nations for Christ, should in itself be reason enough to make us want to change, rather than cling to our vested interests and the status quo. God is not interested in maintaining hollow facades, even if the real estate is worth millions of dollars. God's heart is for the truth of His love to reach the people. The only way for Him to do this is to take real people who love, and send them to the people at a grassroots level.

The institutional church has built great buildings in public places. It has a media presence, its leaders have fancy titles, and they sit on public committees and speak out on public issues. None of this impresses the unregenerate, or has any impact on the social fabric of the day. The institutional church was suitable and effective for a past era, but today the church must be a people with apostolic authority and power who no longer appear to represent an institution or a vested interest.

Therefore, much of the real church is going underground. By this I am referring to the *social* underground, the place where ordinary people meet and live and work. This is the church of the day, which Jesus will use with great power.

In the past, believers often related to a sacred building, such as a cathedral, or to an institution such as a denomination, for their spiritual identity. To feel the presence of God they went to a building that provided a religious atmosphere, or to feel they were right with God they had identity as a good Anglican, or Catholic, or Lutheran, or Pentecostal, or Baptist, or Salvationist, or Presbyterian (the list is interminable). Their identity and sense of salvation assurance was provided by praying in a religious building (cathedral Christianity), or by membership of a religious institution (institutional Christianity). But real Christianity is found where people relate to other believers, as family in Christ. They meet anywhere, pray everywhere, and it is their love for Christ and others that proves they are in the faith. This is apostolic Christianity.

Alas, just as some of these great ships came to a sudden end in tragedy and loss of life, it is possible that some of these great institutions will also have a tragic end. Like the torpedo that sank the Lusitania, enemy forces may fire at one, knowing very well that the weapon aimed cannot bring down that institution, but internal events and circumstances will be such that a secondary explosion will destroy the 'unsinkable'. Or alternatively, like the Empress of Ireland, human error combining with natural circumstances may bring about a terribly sorrowful, but unnecessary, outcome. When these things happen, good people get hurt.

May I say, this is not a prescription of what must happen, but an observation of what I believe is likely to happen. I have written concerning these things in the hope that through understanding the purposes of God, and clarifying the apostolic vision, we will avert unnecessary tragedy and 'loss of life'.

The Power of Tradition

Tradition and religion are very powerful forces, especially so because they are given strength from both human nature itself, and from the powers of darkness who have a vested interest to scheme against the gospel.

Mankind is by nature incorrigibly religious, for it is part of his fallen state. God's way is faith and grace, but man, because of his sinful nature, trusts in religion. Religion appeals to his flesh.

The tendency of every movement of the Christian church is to become bound by its traditions over time, so that what was of faith and grace becomes religious observance. Not only so, but Satan seeks to find ways for religious spirits to enter the church in the guise of orthodoxy, and begin to control and subvert. The letter of the law is enough to kill the spiritual life of the people, but often Satan finds opportunity for more. It is possible to turn tradition into idolatry, even while using the name of the triune God. Throughout the earth there is much religion that claims to be Christian, but is actually pagan and idolatrous.

Consider the following four statements that Jesus made in addressing the Pharisees and teachers of the law:

"They worship me in vain; their teachings are but rules taught by men."

"You have let go of the commands of God and are holding on to the traditions of men."

"You have a fine way of setting aside the commands of God in order to observe your own traditions!"

"Thus you nullify the word of God by your tradition that you have handed down. And you do many things like that" (Mark 7:7-9,13).

The same spiritual dangers that beset the religious leaders of Jesus' time continue to be present dangers for the church in every age. Followers of Christ must thoughtfully and prayerfully cleanse their hearts of the tendency toward religion and tradition and walk in obedient faith that leads to an experience of Jesus.

There are both spirits of religion and spirits of tradition. These seek to bind and control every church, every denomination, every leader and every believer. Unless we are walking in the Holy Spirit, with the heart humbly listening to His voice, we will have a tendency towards the spirit of religion, yet think we are Christian.

Jesus said that tradition nullifies the word of God. We have all seen this in churches everywhere. A preacher can pour his heart out declaring the word of God, but it will have little or no impact upon a congregation, because of their traditions. Is it not amazing that the word of God, which created all things, and can heal the sick and raise the dead, can be made of no effect by the power of tradition? When the church is bound by tradition, we simply do not hear His voice.

Traditions of Men Become False Doctrines

These traditions become strongholds, locking up the people of God. Each layer of tradition is like a set of security doors, one behind another. Traditions have often been initially established to protect the truth, but they end up protecting error, because error becomes enshrined and cannot be assailed.

This is done purposely by dark powers, because the tradition which protects error in turn protects the *powers of darkness* from being expelled from the life of the church. Thus the traditions of men become the doctrine of demons. Many institutions become infiltrated by evil spirits masquerading as principles of the church. This is to keep the people *in religion* rather than in Christ, or if they are in Christ, to keep them bound by the spirit of religion and devoid of the freedom of relationship and power in Christ.

For this reason the traditions of men become guarded (kept in place) by the powers of darkness. Many traditions surround such things as ordination, baptism, who may serve at the Lord's Table, etc. All of these traditions impose a limited view of the priesthood upon the church. The traditional church confuses *priesthood* with *leadership*. Both of these are forms of the ministry of Christ – but the priesthood is for every believer (1 Peter 2:4-5,9-10, Revelation 1:5-6), whereas the fivefold leadership ministry is for some (Ephesians 4:11-13).

Confusion over this results in *control* being exercised over the church, which is a religious spirit.

This is why there must be reform of the church, and why no minister of Christ, no faithful believer, can afford to cling to any denominational traditions that are contrary to the word of God and the mind of the Spirit for the church at this time.

The prophet Haggai speaks to this phenomena of everyone busy with their own vested interests, in our case building their own ecclesiastical houses, while the real house of God is disregarded and unloved.

> *'Then the word of the LORD came through the prophet Haggai: "Is it a time for you yourselves to be living in your paneled houses, while this house remains a ruin?"*

> *'Now this is what the LORD Almighty says: "Give careful thought to your ways. You have planted much, but have harvested little. You eat, but never have enough. You drink, but never have your fill. You put on clothes, but are not warm. You earn wages, only to put them in a purse with holes in it."*

> *'This is what the LORD Almighty says: "Give careful thought to your ways. ...You expected much, but see, it turned out to be little. What you brought home, I blew away. Why?" declares the LORD Almighty. "Because of my house, which remains a ruin, while each of you is busy with his own house' (Haggai 1:2-10).*

William Booth, the founder of The Salvation Army, understood very well the danger of tradition and vain religion possessing the people of God, and thereby making a movement useless. As the founder of that great Christian work which bore much fruit all over the earth, he gave this warning and set this example for leaders today:

> *"I do not want another ecclesiastical corpse cumbering the earth. When the Salvation Army ceases to be a militant body of red-hot men and women, whose supreme business is the saving of souls, I hope it will vanish utterly."*
>
> **General William Booth**

Uprooted Trees

For 17 years I have been driving the Bruce Highway between Rockhampton and Brisbane, a distance of about 640 km. I suppose I have made this journey in one direction or the other about a hundred times. Over the years, there have been constant improvements to the road, so that now we have a (mostly) excellent highway.

Last year on one of those trips, I experienced strong impressions of the mind of the Spirit. There were various places where new sections of road had been cut through the bush, and enormous Australian gum trees had been uprooted by bulldozers and pushed to one side. My attention was suddenly riveted upon these many dead and dying trees. There they were, giant eucalypts lying on their sides in death, their massive root systems exposed and broken. Even though I had seen them so often before, they were now heavy with meaning.

Repeatedly over several hours, I felt the Lord's impression that these big uprooted trees represented what was about to happen to many of the institutions of Christianity in the world. God is building a highway for the glory of the Lord to come into the nations. Anything that stands in the road of that highway will be removed.

What To Do Now

It is important for pastors, churches and denominational leaders to make a safe transition from tradition to the apostolic wineskin. There are certain practical things that will be fundamental to transitioning safely.

Firstly, you should look for apostles, and develop relationship with apostles, and prophets. This is not a step of commitment, but a step to familiarise yourself with the ministry, the vision and the giftedness of apostles. It will help greatly to have a personal understanding of the heart of apostles. To develop friendships will help to create trust and a 'feeling' for what God is doing and saying through the ministry of this grace gift. Relationship is the single most important dynamic in the apostolic church, and it is through trusting relationships that the gifts will flow and be a blessing.

Secondly, pray for God to provide an apostle to be a spiritual father to you and your people. Your ministry or your church does require apostolic covering. All leaders of ministries need an accountable relationship with a primary apostle. In answer to your prayer, God will bring about divine appointments.

Thirdly, pray for God to bring you and your church safely through transition. Do not take God for granted, but exercise faith for the best outcomes in the life of the church. At the same time, do not avoid discussion and confrontation. Speaking about the truth (with grace) is necessary for the progress and maturity of the church (Ephesians 4:15).

Fourthly, teach apostolic values and apostolic structure to your people.

Change the paradigms — it is important to instruct in right values before you change structures. By teaching and example, develop understanding and expectation in the hearts of your people.

Fifthly, develop the apostolic wineskin. Seek to transition from traditional structure to apostolic methods. This is primarily found in developing the relationships that will be important to your ministry or church, and the personal, covenant nature of those relationships. This does not necessarily mean rejecting a denomination, or its people, or its leaders. It means rejecting denominationalism as a mindset, but clinging to love and relationships, and seeking to work out the values of the apostolic church in a practical way.

To Apostles and Prophets, I would offer this encouragement. Do not take for granted that the power of these grace gifts will automatically flow through you in the coming days. You will need to seek God, so as to establish grace with God. The church in the coming days will need many apostles and prophets, but at the moment there are not many who can step into the breach at the level required. We need the outpouring of the greater anointing which God has promised for these gifts. To receive the coming anointing you will need to prepare your heart with humble seeking after God. Also, you must have established accountable relationships and apostolic covering.

For Prophets, remember that both the apostolic and prophetic ministries are foundational to the church of Jesus Christ, but prophets and apostles are two different things. Do not try to be an apostle, but seek to understand your own unique contribution to building the house of God. The apostle and the prophet both speak the word of God, but not in the same way. Both speak with authority and represent Christ, but the apostle does this as someone who has a governmental authority in the house. He does not need to say, "Thus saith the Lord," for he usually speaks as one having *"the mind controlled by the Spirit" (Romans 8:6)*. The apostle then, has a direct authority over the building of the house of God, but the prophet more of an indirect authority. Apostles are authority figures, and some people have psychological and spiritual problems with authority figures. The Lord also needs to be represented by, and speak through, anointed ministries that do not hold governmental responsibility over the church. Apostles and prophets should work together. Seek fruitful partnerships with apostles.

For House Churches and House Church Leaders I have this word. You are an important part of the body of Christ, and there is reason to believe that in the coming days there will be a multiplication of house churches. But God will not bless independence. Two principles are of paramount importance. Every house church must relate to an apostle, and every house church must seek to relate to the whole body of Christ in your locality. Failure to accept or honour these principles would disqualify a group from being a church. Independence is cultic. Experience has shown that where house churches keep to themselves, they stagnate, but where an apostle visits a house church to bless it, strengthen the foundations and declare it to be Christ's, they thrive.

A Special Word for Denominational Leaders. Yours may be the greatest challenge of all, to lead your people through days of great change, seeking to do the will of God while struggling with the pressure of everything that resists change. The problem is, the ground is shifting under our feet. If we do not move when God moves, we miss the grace of God. If we do not embrace reform, the old does not remain as it was for us anyway.

I felt especially blessed on my recent journey to India, where I was approached in one city by a denominational leader who wanted to discuss how he could transition his entire denomination into an apostolic wineskin. His was a pentecostal denomination, and he was responsible for providing leadership to hundreds of churches, and thousands of people. It was wonderful that he had the grace not to be defensive or feel threatened, but earnestly desired the best for his people, and sought to know the mind of the Lord.

There is an important message to be remembered in the story of King Saul and David. Saul was the anointed King of Israel, but God had anointed someone other than his son Jonathan to be the next king. The future kingdom of Israel was not to be led by the house of Saul, but by the house of David, just as the future church is not to be led by denominational officials, but by anointed apostles.

David's heart was to serve Saul with total loyalty and obedience. David only ever wanted to honour Saul, and would have fought his battles and strengthened his hands all his days, had Saul allowed him. But Saul was jealous of David, and the transition in the anointing made him fearful and suspicious, so that he despised the one who would have helped him the most.

Likewise, no true apostle will raise a hand against you, and the heart of every apostle will be to help you, strengthen you, and support you in battle. Your honour is safe with an apostle. Like David, a genuine apostle will not grasp for power, but will wait for only what God gives him.

It would be far better if every Christian institution and denominational leader sought to understand the apostolic anointing, and worked and prayed so as to cooperate with God in renewing and restoring the apostolic church. Wherever denominations embrace the apostolic message and the apostolic anointing, they will preserve their fruit, albeit in a different form. The wineskin must be made new.

However, if a denomination opposes the apostolic anointing, and resists the work of the Spirit in restoring apostles and the apostolic church, this will be counter-productive. Such opposition may result in their own loss, their wineskin ruined and their fruitfulness gone. This is a plea to be sensitive to the will of God.

Saul's son, Jonathan, is the right model for leaders facing change through the transferred anointing. Under normal circumstances, Jonathon would have been the next King of Israel. In his own heart he knew that David was to be King, and he loved David with all his heart. He devoted himself to covenant relationship with David, and sought to protect him. There are many Jonathans in the institutions of Christianity. These are those who would have been the future leaders of institutional Christianity. Their love is pure, and they would delight to see the rise and restoration of apostles to the church.

Every denominational leader will choose, either to love David and submit to him as Jonathan did, or be suspicious, jealous and controlling as Saul was concerning David. Through jealousy, Saul lost his blessing and his inheritance.

What To Do, When There is Nothing You Can Do

There have been those who have asked me the question, "What can we do even though we are not pastors, we have no influence, and can make no changes in the church?"

I went to bed one night with this question weighing upon me, and woke next morning with a fascinating answer from the Lord.

In reply to the question, He said that the believers were to accept the apostolic message to their hearts. They were to accept it, *in principle, in the heart*, and doing this in faith and in submission to Christ obtains God's blessing. Further, He said that doing this is the equivalent of what the people of Israel were doing when they submitted to John's baptism in the days before Jesus came.

The Spirit of God directed me to the Gospels, where I found these words. *"All the people, even the tax collectors, when they heard Jesus' words, acknowledged that God's way was right, because they had been baptized by John. But the Pharisees and experts in the law rejected God's purpose for themselves, because they had not been baptized by John" (Luke 7:29-30).*

Those who submitted to John's message and received his baptism received something else as well. They received an impartation of grace that gave understanding, blessing and spiritual sight. They were able to see and understand God's way, such that when they heard Jesus they knew the right way of God instinctively. This was a gift of grace.

The opposite was also true. Those who rejected John's message and would not submit to his baptism were blind and deaf to Jesus when He came. It so happened that those religious leaders who had not been baptised by John (as a result of believing his message) rejected God's purpose for themselves. They were unable to recognise and enter into the grace of God in Jesus, because they refused to recognise and enter into the grace of God in John.

So, if you can do nothing else, believe the apostolic message and take it to heart. Seek understanding, and by faith walk in this grace. It is a blessing to you, and it prepares you spiritually for what God is about to do. This message in itself carries an anointing which, if received, is a grace to prepare you for the coming days.

Now, give yourself to intercession for Christ to raise apostles, for the unity of the church, and for the building of the city eldership.

What Not To Do

Do not walk away from existing relationships, especially where these are healthy, and with good people in Christ.

Some well-meaning people, after reading of apostolic principles, might be tempted to walk away from participation in the local church. They might also be making a very big mistake. As frustrating as it might be to work with existing structures, remember that it is always easier to criticise what is, than to build what should be. Normally, one should not leave an existing church where you have meaningful relationships and friends. Stick with the people God has put you with as family. It is the whole church together that should deal with tradition and institutionalism. It is as a group under sound leadership that you should make a commitment to the life of the whole local church of the city, and the elders.

Do not leave the body where you have relationships, if it is in favour of independence. I recently heard of one couple who left a healthy congregation that had a very sound ministry. Their senior pastor is a mature, wise, godly man who seems to be emerging as an apostle, and in this church new people come to Christ constantly. The church is involved in social service, has an excellent prayer life, good worship, and a missionary emphasis. Sounds great! But this young couple left in the belief that they were to find a non-institutional Christianity, and started meeting with a handful of others in a house. Within a few weeks, this little group decided to hire a public venue and start a Sunday service — so much for their non-institutional Christianity. The fact is, all along God was leading their previous pastor and church into apostolic Christianity, one step at a time, and that's where they should have stayed — in committed relationships, and walking with the others to find the way of Christ.

Theirs is not the only story like that. At the same time, there will be others that Christ does lead to separate themselves from vain religion, or else to move on because He has another plan for their lives. Some believers then, will be stepping out in faith and obedience to the living God, while others may simply be mistaken, or deceived. In the coming days there will be people who make mistakes, but it has always been that way. The best safeguard is to have trusting, accountable relationships, keep submitted humble hearts, and listen to other people.

Institutionalism may be a form of bondage to tradition and its spirits, but independence is often deadly. Independence is bondage to the sinful nature, and is quite often a deception by lying spirits.

Remember the Destination – the City of God

The years 1996 to 1998 were a period where I was concerned about the attitudes of some of our people, and burdened for the life of our church, even though God was doing good things amongst us. The vision and spiritual life of the church was sound. We held great promises from the Lord about what He would do with us. But it was also a period in which storm clouds were gathering on the horizon, and I knew there would be a season of testing and trouble. In those days, God was about to test every heart in our church.

One afternoon I lay down to rest. Troubled with the problems and pressures of the church on my mind, I asked the Lord a question, "Lord, where is all this leading us?" There was an immediate answer. "To the City of God!" He said.

Later I was in Cambodia, when during intercession with a team one afternoon, I saw a vision. At first it was a still picture, but as I looked it became a movie. I was in a village which had one street and just a few houses on either side. Everything was barren. The houses were made of mud, and the street and the surrounding fields were just bare dirt. The street of the town continued into the distance, and in the movie I followed it. In the far distance was a beautiful sight

— a magnificent range of blue-black mountains, with an incredible rock rising out of the mountains and towering above all. Over those mountains and that rock stood a fabulous rainbow. But the path I was on led down into a valley. As I followed the path through the valley, suddenly I was overshadowed by a thick black cloud. There was no light, and no reflected light. I could not see the path, or even my hands or feet. There was, however, one thing that I could see – the rainbow! It occurred to me that if I walked in the direction of the rainbow, I would come out the other side of the black cloud. So I stepped forward tentatively, and after only one or two steps, I was suddenly out of the cloud. And there before me was a most incredible sight! A great city of gold was at the foot of those mountains, underneath the great rock and the rainbow.

The immediate message was obvious. On my path to the City of God there would come a time when things would be so black I would have nothing left but the promises of God (the rainbow). But if I would follow the promises, I would come to the City of God.

Soon after, I entered that season where things were black indeed, and it really did seem like I had nothing left but the vision provided by His promises. I held on, and the Lord Jesus has brought me to a far better place, and I now continue the journey. Nowadays, as I reconsider the vision He gave, I think it has a broader application, but that I will leave you to ponder.

The City of God is not only the eternal, ultimate expression of the New Jerusalem that we read about in Revelation 21. It is not just what we will be after the day of our redemption, and the coming of Christ.

In prophetic language, that City is also the people of God wherever they are on earth *("Our feet are standing in your gates, O Jerusalem", Psalm 122:2)*. The exhortations of the Book of Hebrews were written to saints in Christ, living in earthly circumstances, but the writer reminded them, *"you have come to Mount Zion, to the heavenly Jerusalem, the city of the living God" (Hebrews 12:22)*.

However, Jerusalem is *"built like a city that is closely compacted together" (Psalm 122:3)*. The believers are meant to be in such relationship that, in each locality where they dwell, they are an outward expression of, and enjoy an actual experience of, the City of God on earth. God is now building something in our generation that will be an amazing expression of the City of God in the earth. In my city and yours, God is building the City of God. I am fully expecting that in many places, wherever the church becomes one body in unity with one eldership, with apostolic/prophetic foundations, we will see a visible expression of the church as the dwelling place of God in the earth, a fulfillment of Ephesians 2:22.

The principal objectives for the apostolic reformation of the church should be clear goals upon which we focus the intercession of the saints, and key objectives for every anointed leader in the body of Christ. These are:

- Restoration of Apostles and Prophets
- Autonomous Churches
- The Church as One Body
- City Eldership
- Apostolic Covering
- Apostolic Companies
- The Church in Community
- Covenant Relationship
- Father & Son relationships in ministry

We, like Abraham, are looking for *"the city with foundations, whose architect and builder is God" (Hebrews 11:10).* The foundations of that City are apostles (Revelation 21:14, Ephesians 2:20-22).

The prophets spoke long ago concerning the reformation of the church as the city of God, and the restoration of apostles and prophets as foundations of that city,

They will rebuild the ancient ruins
and restore the places long devastated;
they will renew the ruined cities
that have been devastated for generations.

Isaiah 61:4

Your people will rebuild the ancient ruins
and will raise up the age-old foundations;
you will be called Repairer of Broken Walls,
Restorer of Streets with Dwellings.

Isaiah 58:12

"In that day I will restore David's fallen tent.
I will repair its broken places, restore its ruins,
and build it as it used to be,
so that they may possess the remnant of Edom
and all the nations that bear my name,"
declares the LORD, who will do these things.

Amos 9:11-12

These words are a promise and a prophecy for whoever would believe, and by faith walk with Christ for their fulfillment. _____ ◣

Prayer for Anointing

To receive the blessing of apostolic grace and the anointings of Christ, pray according to the following prayer.

"My Father in Heaven, I draw near to you in the name of Jesus.

"Thank you for your great love for me, and for the many ways in which your grace, your favour and your protection has blessed me and all your people.

"I ask for grace, a greater grace, and I ask that the Spirit of Christ would rest on me in power. I give myself to you for the service of Christ. I ask for the anointings of the Holy Spirit to equip me, to make me strong and wise and fruitful in the kingdom of God.

"Thank you for the apostolic anointings of Christ which are given to your people. I ask you to clothe me with the blessing of these anointings, and grant me grace to live according to the purposes of God for these last days. By faith in Jesus, I receive your Spirit, and I receive these grace and power anointings.

"I ask for the blessing and protection of the covering of Christ. Clothe me now with your presence, your power and your protection.

"Guide me by your Spirit, as you have promised, and make the way of God plain before me. Give me the Spirit of understanding that I may walk in a greater grace, and give me an undivided and pure heart, to follow Christ faithfully, and live in the holy fear of the Lord.

"I declare my love and devotion to you, and declare that you are a faithful and holy God. All that you do is just and right and true. My heart is yours, and I long for the day of Christ.

"I yield my heart and my will to you, to walk in submission to Christ, and in love with all your people, for the glory of Christ in the earth. Amen."

The Release of Anointing, and the Blessing of Peace

The following is my prayer for you:

"Father, in the name of Christ Jesus my Saviour, I seek your grace for every reader of this book who is hungry for God, whose heart is sincere, and who seeks to walk in apostolic grace under apostolic covering.

"I ask that the Spirit of the Lord would come upon them in power. I ask that you would multiply grace to them, to their hearts, families, homes, marriages, children and finances. I ask that you would grant apostolic grace to their churches, and apostolic power to their prayers and their witness.

"I pray for the release of the apostolic covering of Christ over the people of God, and ask that the leaders and all the believers would now walk in a greater authority, a greater protection, and a greater power. Make them fruitful in their service to Christ. In the name of Jesus, I release your anointings and the gifts of God to them.

"Open now the eyes of their hearts to see things previously hidden, and fill the church with the knowledge of the Lord.

"Grant now the release of the great anointings for apostles and prophets to rise and do the will of God throughout the earth. Release apostolic grace and favour to all the saints, and grant that the prayer of Jesus for us all to be one, would now be fulfilled.

"In the name of Jesus I release the blessing of peace to the hearts and lives of every person who reads this book.

"For the glory of God, and for the inheritance of the nations to come to Christ, I pray. Amen."

Peace International Apostolic Ministries

Peace Christian Community

PO Box 5137 CQMC
Rockhampton 4702 Australia

Email: mail@peace.org.au

Phone: 07 4926 2966
Fax: 07 4926 2656

Website: peace.org.au

PEACE INSTITUTE
OF APOSTOLIC MINISTRIES

The Apostolic Revelation

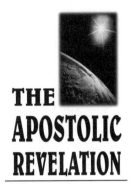

THE APOSTOLIC REVELATION

Appendix

Components of an Apostolic Constitution

For the sake of those who are considering church constitutions in the context of apostolic reform, this appendix contains a few sections from the Constitution of Peace International Christian Church. We set out to write an apostolic constitution in 1999, specifically because we felt the Lord was saying that we needed to make official structural changes in keeping with the values and beliefs we held. To hold the benefit of new wine, one must also have a new wineskin.

Please remember in reading this document that ideas have progressed and terminology has changed, even since 1999. The constitution now needs a revision. Nevertheless, it is useful here for the outline it gives of relationships and accountability between the Senior Minister, the Covering Apostle, and the Apostolic Council, and it defines their respective places and responsibilities.

If any reader would find a copy of the full text useful, you may send a request to the office of Peace International, and we will forward a copy. Alternatively, you may download any required information from our website.

1.5 Apostolic Covering
An apostolic covering shall be established and maintained over Peace International Christian Church and its associated ministries and auxiliaries.

If the Senior Minister of P.I.C.C. is himself an established apostle, then his apostolate and ministry shall be the apostolic covering of the church, and he shall be recognized as the apostle providing spiritual covering, fathering and mentoring for the church and its leaders. Such an apostle as Senior Minister must, however, have an accountable relationship with a senior apostle who will be a spiritual father to the Senior Minister, and also have accountable relationships with other apostles and establish an Apostolic Council as outlined in this constitution (Section 2.4).

Alternatively, should the Senior Minister of P.I.C.C. not be an apostle, then the Senior Minister shall identify the apostle who is to be his spiritual father. This apostle shall be the Chairman of the Apostolic Council and shall be the primary apostle in relational covering to the Leadership Team and P. I. C. C. as a church. Relationships between apostles, the Senior Minister and the church shall be made official and publicly advised to the body of P. I. C. C.

2. CHURCH GOVERNMENT:

2.1 Overview

We believe the church to be part of the kingdom of God, and that the government for the church is theocracy, in which Christ is sovereign and reigning head and that He generally builds, governs and sets His church in order through the leadership ministry of apostles. We therefore believe the church must have a covering of true apostles, and that the Senior Minister of the church should be the man of Christ's appointing as discerned by the leaders of the church. We believe that under the leadership of the Senior Minister, a team of leaders in covenant partnership for the gospel should be developed to help build, shepherd and teach the people of God, and carry forward, in partnership with all the people, the work of the gospel.

We set aside the notion that democracy is an appropriate form of government for the New Testament church as not supported by God's pattern shown in the Holy Scriptures, but we pursue community, which we believe to be the true pattern for the New Testament church.

2.2 Purpose

This church and its leadership shall be subject to Christ under apostolic government. The purpose is to build by the Spirit of the Lord, and in unity and love, a Christian community led by a Leadership Team in submission to an apostolic leader, who himself is subject to Christ and the covering of apostles in an accountable relationship.

2.3 The Senior Minister

The Senior Minister shall be that man appointed by Christ to be the apostolic (anointed) leader of the church. The Senior Minister is called and elected to lead, direct and govern with Christ's authority the life, ministry and affairs of the church. The ministry of the church becomes the ministry of the Senior Minister for the duration of his tenure. Should a vacancy occur, the choice of a Senior Minister shall be determined by the consensus or election of the Leadership Team in consultation with the Pastoral Team and the Apostolic Council. A Church Fellowship Meeting or Church Prayer Meeting may be called (Constitution 3.6).

The appointment of a Senior Minister to the position of Apostolic Leader of the church shall be made by the elders (Leadership Team) laying hands upon him in a public service of ordination to this ministry.

2.3.1 The Senior Minister's Role
The Senior Minister:

2.3.1.1 Is responsible through prayer and submission to Christ, for the vision, direction and life of the church.

2.3.1.2 Is responsible for the appointment of leaders, including the appointment of all pastors in the cell church structure, the nomination of

Elders and the appointment of department heads and deacons. All elders, pastors, department heads, deacons and other leaders are accountable to the Senior Minister for the conduct of their personal lives and ministries.

2.3.1.5   Shall endeavour to delegate effective authority and responsibility to other leaders and members of the apostolic cell church, so that many share the functions of ministry, whilst holding all office-bearers, leaders and members accountable for their ministry, Christian lifestyle and Christian home.

2.3.2   The Senior Minister's Accountability

2.3.2.1   The Senior Minister is to be transparent and accountable to his associate leaders and also to an apostolic council, which he will identify, establish and maintain for the good of his own life, ministry and the church. If the Senior Minister does not appoint or maintain an Apostolic Council, the Leadership Team may act to appoint an interim Apostolic Council.

2.3.2.2   Should a leadership crisis arise and there is a breakdown in relationship between the Senior Minister and the Leadership Team, or should it appear for good reason to the Leadership Team that the Senior Minister may no longer be fit for the leadership of the church, an ethical and transparent course of action is to be followed.

1. The elder who has a concern must share with the Senior Minister that concern in the first instance.

2. An elder may not canvas support or attempt to build a support base amongst the elders nor amongst the members, but must deal directly, honestly and transparently in all matters.

3. If the matter is not resolved between them, other elders may be involved and the Senior Minister has the prerogative of himself referring the matter to the leadership Team.

4. Any unresolved dispute amongst elders and the Senior Minister should be referred to the Apostolic Council for investigation and action, and the Senior Minister has the prerogative of involving the Apostolic Council.

5. If the Senior Minister will not himself act to involve the Apostolic Council in any matter requiring their attention or intervention then, providing he is informed of the action of the Leadership Team, and provided there is the support of a two-thirds majority, the Leadership Team has the power, through the Associate Senior Minister, to contact the Chairman of the Apostolic Council to investigate and address the matter, either in person or by sending other apostles who are members of the Apostolic Council.

6. Any complaint or concern about the Senior Minister may be overturned by a majority of elders.

7. The Apostolic Council shall endeavour to resolve harmoniously every matter, but shall have authority to act, either in accord with the Senior Minister or in accord with a majority of the Leadership Team, to resolve any matter and to correct, discipline or dismiss any person, whether a leader or a member of the church.

8. If the Chairman and the investigating members of the Apostolic Council agree with the majority of the Leadership Team, the Senior Minister may be rested, corrected or his appointment terminated and the position declared vacant. In the event of a termination of appointment, the Leadership Team may set about the task of calling a new Senior Minister. In lieu of notice, generous terms and conditions should be offered by the Leadership Team upon the retirement of the Senior Minister.

2.3.2.3   If the Senior Minister is considered guilty of any moral offence or sinful misconduct, the Leadership Team shall consult the Chairman of the Apostolic Council immediately. With the consent of the Chairman of the Apostolic Council, the ministry of the Senior Minister may be terminated immediately, or other appropriate disciplinary action taken, after the matter has been dealt with according to an ethical and biblical procedure. Any terms and conditions which may be offered will be at the discretion of the Leadership Team.

2.3.2.4   Under no circumstances will any accusation be entertained against the Senior Minister or any elder of the church except for a substantiated reason and with a minimum of two or three independent material witnesses.

2.3.2.5   If the Leadership Team calls upon the intervention of the Apostolic Council and it is found that the Apostolic Council for any reason is non-functioning, then the Senior Minister may be corrected, disciplined or removed by a unanimous vote of the remainder of the Leadership Team, or else the Leadership Team shall themselves call upon suitable apostles to fulfill the role of the Apostolic Council.

2.4   The Apostolic Council
An Apostolic Council will be developed by the Senior Minister. This will be comprised of international and other apostles who function in a voluntary capacity to provide accountability and covering for the Senior Minister and the church. The Apostolic Council shall be comprised of a Senior Apostle who will have the primary fathering and mentoring role toward the Senior Minister, and a group of other apostles with a minimum of two other apostles who through personal relationship with the Senior Minister will maintain an accountable watch over his life, ministry and the life of the church. The Apostolic Council shall have the specific function of being called upon by either the Senior Minister or a 2/3rds majority of the Leadership Team, should there be any breakdown of relationship within the leadership of the church or any other specific problem for which the intervention of the Apostolic Council is needed.

The church shall remain autonomous and self-governing, and the Apostolic

Council holds no power for intervention in the affairs of the church except when invited and acting in accord with either the Senior Minister or a 2/3rds majority of the Leadership Team.

2.6.2   The church is to recognize that the leaders of the church function spiritually under the anointing that is given to the primary leader by the Holy Spirit, and that God takes of the anointing that is on His anointed leader and places it upon the other leaders, especially the elders, so that in the house there is one spirit and one vision.

2.6.3   Leadership Team members are in co-operative partnership with the Senior Minister for the life, government and care of the church. They are appointed to support and strengthen the Senior Minister and Associate Senior Minister(s) and in unity of spirit to further the work of the ministry. They are advisers and counselors to the Senior Minister, and they are partners in the gospel who, in fulfilling the role of elders will watch over each other's lives and the whole flock of God. Each must be mindful they are not elected representatives of the people but appointed representatives of Christ and His apostles to help lead the people and bring the church to maturity.

2.6.4   The Leadership Team may not act independently of the Senior Minister excepting in matters pertaining to himself, and then as defined by this constitution in Section 2.3.2. Wherever this constitution states that the Leadership Team shall fulfill a particular function or exercise a certain authority, it is to be understood that such action or exercise of authority is with the Senior Minister's agreement and consent.

2.6.5   In all matters before the Leadership Team concerning the Senior Minister, and in the Senior Minister's absence, the Associate Senior Minister will be the leader of the Leadership Team. The Leadership Team will act through the Associate Senior Minister, unless for some reason he is unable to fulfill this duty.

2.9   Principles and Ethics of Leadership
All leaders of P.I.C.C. are required to walk in unity of spirit, to seek to be of one heart and mind in Christ and pursue the common goals and vision which Christ gives for the church. All leaders are to maintain voluntary accountability, submission and humility of heart in the Lord, and the ethics of Christian leadership are to be upheld at all times. Should any difficulty or issue of contention arise, the principle of going and speaking to the person alone in the first instance shall apply. General ethics of leadership and Christian community shall be formulated, established and taught within the church separately from this constitution.

To purchase additional copies of:

The
Apostolic
Revelation

please contact:

Selah Publishing Group, LLC

Toll free 800-917-2665

or visit our website at
www.selahbooks.com

RELEASING THE POWER OF INTERCESSION

A Distance-Education Study Course In Intercession and Spiritual Warfare

John Alley has taught extensively on the subject of intercession and spiritual warfare around the world. To bring the power of this teaching into your home, an in-depth, easy-to-understand, self-paced distance-education course has been prepared.

SOME OF THE SUBJECTS COVERED INCLUDE:
- The prayer ministry of every Christian
- Intercession in the local church
- Team ministry in intercession
- Worship and the Intercessor
- The Anointing of the Holy Spirit
- Listening and Inquiring of God
- Intercession for Leaders
- Dreams and their Interpretation
- Spiritual Warfare
- The Triumph of the Kingdom of God

There are fourteen units consisting of tapes and study notes.
The course comes in presentation binders for both tapes and notes.

PEACE INSTITUTE
OF APOSTOLIC MINISTRIES

TOTAL COST OF COURSE: $140AUD + $45AUD International or $20AUD Australian postage and handling.
Payment is accepted by VISA, Mastercard, AMEX or Bank Cheque in AUD.

To enrol, please contact:
PEACE INSTITUTE OF APOSTOLIC MINISTRIES
PO Box 5137, Central Queensland MC QLD 4702, Australia.
PHONE: (07) 4926-2966 ▪ International Phone: +61 7 4926-2966
FAX: (07) 4926-2656 ▪ International Fax: +61 7 4926-2656
EMAIL: mail@peace.org.au

For a prospectus, and further information, please visit: **www.peace.org.au**

AUDIO CASSETTE TEACHING ~ by John Alley

THE POWER OF ACCUSATION

This is a crucial message for every believer and every Christian leader. Accusation is a very destructive power. It is effectively the opposite of intercession. Left unconfronted, accusation can destroy lives and churches. Learn how to deal with the power of witchcraft that has been built against you, and your church or ministry, through accusation, and the simple steps in prayer to deal with accusation and bring you release and freedom. *– Single Cassette $5US*

DREAMS AND THEIR BIBLICAL INTERPRETATION

We all dream, and dreams are the indirect voice of God. The language of the Spirit is in pictures and symbols. Learn how your dreams are a symbolic message concerning your own inner life and walk with Christ. Learn to avoid the pitfalls of misinterpreting dreams and learn a successful and reliable approach to understanding and interpreting dreams. *– Single Cassette $5US*

HOW TO GET ANSWERS TO PRAYER

Learn six basic conditions for answered prayer. Overcome hindrances to your prayers, and discover a powerful faith for miracles that will help sustain your prayer life and see you believe for victory. *– Single Cassette $5US*

LISTENING PRAYER

Here are more detailed and extended insights on the subject of Listening Prayer, possibly one of the most important messages for our day. Listening prayer is the key to grace for this present age. Through listening we seek understanding and it is to the listening and understanding heart that God gives more grace. The wisdom, protection and favour of God comes to those who listen. Learn, in the three tape series, about the development of grace in your life through listening, learn how your prophetic sensitivity increases through silence before God. *– Single Cassette $5US*
– 3 Cassettes $15US

EXPOSING THE SPIRIT OF LAWLESSNESS

This is insightful and helpful teaching, based on recent revelation and experience, of just how lies, schemes of satan, and in particular the Jezebel spirit, can and does infiltrate believers and churches. Jesus said that *"Many will say to Me in that day, 'Lord, Lord, have we not prophesied in Your name, cast out demons in Your name, and done many wonders in Your name?' "And then I will declare to them, 'I never knew you; depart from Me, you who practice **lawlessness!**' "* (Matt 7:22-23 - NKJV). Understand, then, just what the spirit of lawlessness is, and keep your heart free.
– Single Cassette $5US

MAINTAINING THE GRACE OF REVIVAL

John Alley pondered the question *"How do you keep revival once it has been given?"* and came across some surprising answers. This message is an important contribution to help us keep what God is about to give us in the coming days. *– Single Cassette $5US*

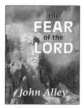